SURVEILLANCE
STATE

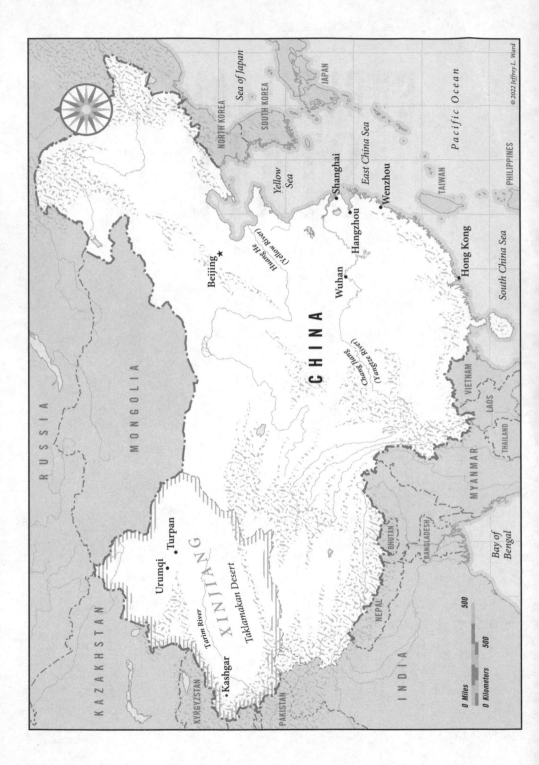

SURVEILLANCE
STATE

INSIDE CHINA'S QUEST TO LAUNCH A
NEW ERA OF SOCIAL CONTROL

Josh Chin and Liza Lin

ST. MARTIN'S PRESS
NEW YORK

First published in the United States by St. Martin's Press, an imprint of St. Martin's Publishing Group

Poem "My Habitat" by Tahir Hamut Izgil translated from the Uyghur by Darren Byler and Dilmurat Mutellip. Poems "Unity Road" and "Somewhere Else" by Tahir Hamut Izgil translated from the Uyghur by Joshua L. Freeman.

www.stmartins.com

Designed by Meryl Sussman Levavi
Map by Jeffrey L. Ward

Library of Congress Cataloging-in-Publication Data

Names: Chin, Josh, author. | Lin, Liza, author.
Title: Surveillance state : inside China's quest to launch a new era of social control / Josh Chin and Liza Lin.
Description: First edition. | New York : St. Martin's Press, 2022. | Includes bibliographical references and index.
Identifiers: LCCN 2022009004 | ISBN 9781250249296 (hardcover) | ISBN 9781250249302 (ebook)
Subjects: LCSH: Social control—China. | Electronic surveillance—China. | Artificial intelligence—Social aspects—China. | Internal security—Technological innovations—China. | China—Politics and government—2002-
Classification: LCC HN733.5 .C42888 2022 | DDC 303.3/30951—dc23/eng/20220509
LC record available at https://lccn.loc.gov/2022009004

First Edition: 2022

1   3   5   7   9   10   8   6   4   2

To our families, and to those in China and elsewhere
who helped us shed light while they were compelled
to stay in the shadows

CONTENTS

Part IV: The China Solution

AUTHORS' NOTE

This book is the product of five years of reporting in China, the United States, Africa, and other locations, much of it for *The Wall Street Journal*. Though we reported together, in the majority of cases we traveled and conducted interviews individually. The material from inside Xinjiang, for instance, is the result of reporting Josh did for the *Journal* in 2017 and 2018, while Liza handled most of the reporting from Hangzhou. Though much of the book benefits from our combined twenty-five years of experience living in and reporting on China, we've tried to keep ourselves out of the story as much as possible. On those rare occasions when we found it necessary to describe observations or interactions from our personal point of view, we have chosen to use the plural pronoun "we" to avoid the awkward distraction of referring to ourselves individually in the third person.

Throughout the book, we refer far more often to the Communist Party than we do to the Chinese government or China as a whole. Though its membership accounts for a little more than 5 percent of China's population, the Communist Party is the ultimate power in the country, standing above both the government and the legal system. It is also the driving force behind the conception, construction, and operation of the Chinese surveillance state.

On rare occasions we have changed names and biographical details to protect sources in China and elsewhere who face possible retribution for having spoken with us.

INTRODUCTION

DYSTOPIA ON THE DOORSTEP

They took Tahir Hamut's blood first. Next came his voice- and finger-prints. They saved his face for last.

The police officer gestured at a stool set up opposite the camera, and Tahir felt the weariness wash over him. He and his wife, Marhaba, had spent the entire afternoon in that windowless basement, wordlessly waiting their turn at each new station, not daring to ask why they were there. The officers gave away nothing. Each sat behind his or her computer like an irritable robot, issuing instructions in a flat tone tinged with half-hearted menace.

In other parts of China, police often functioned as little more than glorified security guards. Unarmed and undertrained, they could occasionally be found on the streets retreating in exasperation from gaggles of ornery retirees upset at being asked not to monopolize public space. It was different in Xinjiang. Here on the country's remote western edge, at the doorstep of Central Asia, the police were hard and well armed. Any interaction with them unfolded in an aura of peril and potential violence. The tension was tolerable in short bursts, but to confront it for hours was exhausting.

Tahir lowered himself onto the stool and watched as the officer fiddled with the camera. Instead of one large lens it had three mini-lenses mounted horizontally in a black casing roughly the length and thickness of a small billy club. He had worked as a filmmaker for more than fifteen years and had never seen anything like it.

The officer told Tahir to sit up straight, then adjusted the tripod until the lenses lined up perfectly with the center of his face. The camera was connected by a cable to a computer on the desk opposite him. A woman operating the computer issued instructions in a dull voice. Face the camera. Turn to the right, then all the way back to the left. Then turn back to face the camera. Then look up and down.

"Do it slowly," she said. "But not too slowly."

Tahir stared into the lens, his back straight and tense. He moved his head to the right, paused briefly, then began moving back to the left.

"Stop," the woman said. "Too fast. Do it over."

Tahir started again. The officer stopped him again. Too slow this time.

He got it right on the third try. As he moved, the lenses captured waves of light from a fluorescent bulb overhead as they bounced off his skin. The camera converted the waves into streams of ones and zeros that it fed into the computer, where a program transformed them into a mathematical likeness. The program assembled numbers to denote his high nose and dark complexion—traits that typically distinguished Uyghurs like him from China's dominant Han ethnic group. It registered his hooded eyes and thin-pressed lips, which he kept frozen in a mask of practiced impassivity. It also spun a series of integers to represent the swept-back salt-and-pepper hair that brushed his shoulders in a rakish mane—the type of cosmopolitan flourish that stood out in a hinterland outpost like Urumqi, almost 2,000 miles west of Beijing.

When he was done, the woman told him to open and close his mouth. Tahir stared into the lens and made an O with his lips, like a goldfish gulping water. After he closed his mouth the woman nodded.

"You can go."

Feeling dazed, he stood to the side as Marhaba had her turn. She struggled to maintain a consistent speed. With each failed attempt, her frustration grew. It took her six tries. When she was finished, the two climbed the stairs to the lobby of the police station and stepped out past a newly installed security gate into the early Urumqi evening.

In the distance, fading rays of May sunlight glinted off mountain peaks still wrapped in shawls of white snow. This was usually one of the nicest times of year in Xinjiang, a sliver of comfort sandwiched between the region's jagged winters and boiling summers. But the warming weather did little to melt away the chill that enveloped the region's Uyghur neighborhoods.

A rugged expanse of mountains, deserts, and steppe twice the size of Texas, Xinjiang has floated on the margins of the Chinese empire for millennia. It formally became a part of China in the late 1800s, when rulers of the last dynasty named it a province, but well more than a century later it still felt like another world. The differences were especially jarring in areas dominated by the Uyghurs, a Turkic Muslim group that traces its roots to the oasis towns dotting Xinjiang's southern deserts. Uyghur enclaves conjured an atmosphere closer to Istanbul than Beijing, with thrumming bazaars, shop signs in Arabic script, and calls to prayer echoing from minarets—expressions of a distinct identity that China's Communist Party wanted to erase.

Six months earlier, Party leaders had set in motion plans to impose an unprecedented level of control in Xinjiang. To aid the effort, local authorities had begun to weave a spider's web of digital sensors across the region that would make it easier for local authorities to monitor Uyghurs and the region's other Turkic minorities. Xinjiang had been crawling with surveillance for years, but the old systems required huge amounts of manual labor. Police could spend weeks scanning video footage or listening to audio recordings just to retrace the movements of a single target. The new systems used artificial intelligence to eliminate human inefficiencies. They could suck in feeds from hundreds of cameras and microphones simultaneously and sift through them to identify targets in a matter of minutes, sometimes even seconds—fast enough for security forces to scuttle out and wrap up their prey before it slipped away.

On their way home, Tahir and Marhaba drove past signs of the web's expansion: new clusters of pristine off-white surveillance cameras clinging like malevolent barnacles to lampposts and the sides of buildings; metal barriers wrapped in razor wire that funneled residents to entrance gates where their identities could be checked; police armed with handheld black smartphone scanners marching in and out of new outposts that had suddenly appeared at seemingly every intersection.

More and more the neighborhood felt like a war zone.

As he drove, Tahir felt a queasy blend of puzzlement and relief. The experience in the basement had been strange. He couldn't fathom what the police planned to do with everything they had recorded. Whatever it was would almost certainly not be to their benefit given the direction things were going in Xinjiang. More than anything, though, he was thankful the officers had allowed him and Marhaba to leave.

In recent days, the couple had heard tales from friends in southern Xinjiang about Uyghurs being snatched up by police and taken away to mysterious facilities. Police referred to the places as schools but wouldn't say what was being taught in them. As far as anyone knew, no one who had been sent to "study" had been allowed to return. Tahir figured it was just a matter of time before Uyghurs in Urumqi would start to be sent off as well.

Tahir also assumed his past made him a likely candidate to disappear. An artist known and respected among Xinjiang's intellectuals, he played an influential role in preserving and shaping the Uyghur culture that the Party saw as a source of resistance. He had a passport and a record of foreign travel, which meant he could have made connections with Xinjiang separatists abroad. And as a youth he had a track record for rebellion, including a leadership role in the 1989 Tiananmen Square protests, that at one point landed him in a labor camp. When he and Marhaba were called into the police station, he had assumed their time had come to be "educated." It was hard to believe they had been able to simply walk out.

Others were less fortunate. Over the next few weeks, Tahir and Marhaba watched as their neighborhood slowly emptied out. One day, Tahir wandered outside and realized the smell of the tandoor naan flatbread, a warm swirl of yeast and sesame that conjured a thousand memories, had suddenly disappeared. The young men who ran the ovens were nowhere to be found. Soon other young men—butchers, fruit vendors, drivers— began to vanish. Then middle-aged men and some women. Sidewalks that had previously swarmed with crowds on weekends became lonely expanses of concrete where scattered footsteps seemed to land with an echo.

It didn't take long for Uyghurs in Urumqi to draw connections between the spreading surveillance, the biometric data collection, and the disappearances. A proliferation of new security gates made it impossible for residents to move around the city without having their ID cards and faces scanned. Some Uyghurs' cards or faces set off alarms, which led to them being shuffled off to police stations, and from there to the shadowy schools. Reports began to circulate about a system the government had built to categorize Uyghurs according to how "safe" for society they were.

Over time, Tahir started to understand the implications of the visit to the police basement. The government now had a collection of his biometric markers, none of which he could change. With the scan of his face on file, the surveillance cameras could recognize him from any angle. If this new system decided he was a threat to the social order, he wouldn't have anywhere to hide.

Over the Communist Party's seven decades in power, Xinjiang has been China's most fractious region, riven by ethnic tensions between Uyghurs and Han Chinese migrants that have periodically exploded into deadly violence. Against the odds, the Party has brought the territory under total control using a combination of internment camps, brainwashing, and mass surveillance.

The Communist Party's offensive in Xinjiang ranks among the most unsettling political developments of the twenty-first century. Chinese leaders have revived totalitarian techniques of the past and blended them with futuristic technologies in an effort not to eradicate a religious minority but to reengineer it. The campaign is one part of a radical experiment to reinvent social control through technology that is forcing democracies around the world to confront the growing power of digital surveillance and to wrestle with new questions about the relationship between information, security, and individual liberty.

State surveillance has been with us as long as there have been states. As far back as 3800 BCE, Babylonian kings in what is now Iraq pioneered an embryonic form of mass data collection, using cuneiform and clay tablets to keep a constantly updated record of people and livestock. The ancient Egyptians, Romans, and Persians followed suit, conducting regular surveys of their populations that grew more detailed and sophisticated over time—efforts to render their societies "legible," in James C. Scott's memorable description. For any state, being able to read the populace—being able to see at a glance who lives where, how many people are in a given household, what they own, and how much they earn—is critical for basic acts of governing like levying taxes, conscripting soldiers, and doling out grain. Throughout history, social control has been inseparable from the harvesting of personal information.

The evolution of state surveillance has proceeded in lockstep with new leaps in technology. The arrival of photography in the 1840s revolutionized the identification of individuals. The invention of wiretapping a few decades later made it possible for police to eavesdrop undetected on private conversations. A century later, the popularization of the computer and the advent of the internet magnified the reach of virtually every existing surveillance tool and catalyzed the creation of innumerable new ones.

Since the end of the Cold War, the debate about state surveillance has focused largely on what limits should be placed around it. What is the balance between individual civil liberties, such as the right to privacy, and societal interests like public safety or the fair distribution of welfare? What is the minimum level of personal information a government needs to collect to do its job? Under Chinese leader Xi Jinping, the Communist Party has flipped the discussion on its head. The question

Xi now poses is: What public goals can a government accomplish when given maximum access to private data?

The volume of personal data theoretically available to the Party strains comprehension. By the start of 2020, close to 350 million cameras recorded the comings and goings in Chinese streets, in public squares, in subway stations, and around commercial buildings. More than 840 million smartphones bounced around in the purses and pockets of Chinese pedestrians, sending a steady stream of location data to telecom operators. Mobile payment systems logged millions of transactions a day in databases that offered searchable, ever-evolving portraits of human activity rendered in breathtaking detail.

As it continues to amass more data and develop new ways to process it, the Party dangles the promise of a perfectly engineered society: one in which the government has the power to track your every move with cameras that can recognize your face and the unique rhythms of your gait, microphones that can recognize your voice, and smartphone GPS systems that relay your location to within a few feet; in which government officials can scrutinize your private chat history, reading and viewing habits, internet purchases, and travel history and can crunch the data to judge how likely you are to help or harm public order; in which artificial intelligence companies work hand in glove with police to track down fugitives, find abducted children, and publicly shame jaywalkers; and in which public services, rewards for good deeds, and punishments for misbehavior are all delivered with mathematical precision and efficiency.

To be sure, much of this vision remains aspirational. Some of it the Party may only partly realize, and some of it might not materialize at all. But significant pieces of it are already taking shape in cities throughout China thanks to evolutionary leaps in artificial intelligence. Machines can now listen, see, and "think" on an entirely new level, making it possible to harvest personal data on a scale that a decade ago would have seemed impossible. The same machines can also help sift the data to dissect, and even predict, human behavior.

Many of these new surveillance tools were invented in Silicon Valley, where tech giants use them to compile behavioral portraits of their users to sell to advertisers. Where Google, Facebook, and Amazon exploit this technology for profit—part of the new trade in human futures that author Shoshana Zuboff has memorably dubbed "surveillance capitalism"—the Communist Party has adopted it as a means to maintain power.

Having just marked its centennial, the Party finds itself at an inflection point. Over roughly three decades following the death of founding leader Mao Zedong in 1976, it had retreated from people's lives, invested in infrastructure, and surfed a wave of historic economic growth that carried China from abject poverty to the upper end of middle-income status. Annual double-digit increases in GDP and rising standards of living guaranteed that Chinese people would fall in line. But over the past ten years, that growth has begun to slow. Exploding debt and demographic pressure threaten to weaken it further. Now, with the previous social contract starting to fray, the Party has turned to digital surveillance to help it write a new one.

Xi Jinping came of age in the waning years of Mao's rule, during the ideological fervor of the Cultural Revolution. He believes that only the Communist Party can restore China's historical might—what he calls "a great rejuvenation"—and insists that achieving that goal requires the Party to once again become the guiding force in the lives of Chinese people. Xi is a keen enough student of history to know that the utopian dreams of Mao and other twentieth-century totalitarians ended disastrously. He understands that the Cold War era's high priests of surveillance, East Germany's Stasi, failed to foresee their own demise in time despite compiling dossiers on suspicious citizens that would have stretched more than 111 miles laid end to end.

The difference for Xi lies in technology. What the Stasi did with close to 100,000 agents and more than 170,000 informants, China's own domestic spy agency has begun to automate using algorithms and its suffocatingly expansive network of digital sensors. Mass surveillance in China has become nearly instantaneous. Each change in an individual's behavior is now a digital brushstroke registered in real time and added to an ever-expanding portrait for the use, or abuse, of those who control the data.

This development has profound implications for the political direction of the world's most populous country. If Communist Party leaders envied democracies in the past, it was for their ability to deliver feedback. Democratic institutions like elections and the free press offer leaders in democracies a constant, reliable stream of information about how their policies are faring and mechanisms for correcting those that fail. Under Xi, the Party thinks it has the blueprint for the rival system it has long dreamed of building. By mining insight from surveillance data, it believes it can predict what people want without having to give them a vote or a voice. By solving social problems before they occur and quashing dissent before it spills out onto the streets, it believes it can strangle opposition in the crib.

Though there are echoes of George Orwell's *1984* in this vision, the best dystopian touchstone for the Communist Party's embrace of digital surveillance is an older novel (and one that inspired Orwell): *We*, by the Russian author and satirist Yevgeny Zamyatin. Completed in 1921 (coincidentally the same year the Party was founded), *We* tells the story of a cheerful, crime-free city-state hundreds of years in the future where citizens are known only by their alphanumeric code, live in buildings made of glass, and do everything according to a mathematical equation calculated by a ruler known as the Benefactor. The story's narrator, a happy cog in the machine of the state, likens the master equation to a railroad schedule, which he calls "that greatest of all ancient literary legacies." It ensures that society chugs along on time and along a predictable path. Meanwhile, teams of enforcers keep an eye out for those few who, like remainders, don't fit into the Benefactor's calculations and punish them accordingly.

As a real-world Benefactor, Xi does not confine his ambitions to China's borders. He hinted as much in a speech marking the ninety-fifth anniversary of the Party's founding in 2016, in which he took a shot at American political scientist Francis Fukuyama's hypothesis in *The End of History and the Last Man* that liberal democracy marked the end point of humankind's ideological evolution. "History never ended, nor can it ever end," he proclaimed. "The Chinese Communist Party and the Chinese people are full of confidence that they can provide a China Solution to humanity's search for better social systems."

From Africa to Europe, countries around the globe have shown an interest in what Xi is selling, in many cases literally purchasing Chinese-made surveillance systems designed to hone and strengthen state control. The list includes autocracies like Saudi Arabia and hybrid regimes like Uganda but also city governments in advanced democracies like France and Germany. The allure of the technology is offering inroads for the so-called China Solution in ways that have justifiably begun to cause alarm in democratic capitals.

This emerging global competition has sent political analysts rushing to dust off Cold War history books. The resurgence of a Communist power willing to challenge the United States makes that impulse understandable. But China is far more dynamic and interconnected with the global system than the Soviet Union ever was. As the place that gave birth to technologies the Party is using, Silicon Valley offers a perhaps more illuminating analogue: in rushing to exploit new surveillance tools before their flaws are fully understood and then selling their virtues to the rest of the world, Beijing is following a path eerily reminiscent of Mark Zuckerberg's motto, "Move fast and break things." The question is whether Western governments can be more effective in responding to Xi's disruptions than they have been with the Facebook founder's.

The Communist Party has remained steadfast in the face of push-back against its surveillance ambitions in Xinjiang and elsewhere—a defiance that has become even more resolute in the wake of the Covid-19 pandemic. In its initial stages, the spread of a deadly new coronavirus in the central Chinese city of Wuhan seemed like a grim indictment of the failures of Xi's China Solution. But as the Party muscled the virus under control with lockdowns and intensive tracking of virtually everyone in the country, and as death tolls elsewhere climbed to vertiginous heights, Covid-19 fortified the Party's confidence in its model of control and the indispensable value of pervasive state surveillance.

All of this comes at a time of profound weakness for democracy. Countries where democracy is deteriorating have outnumbered those where it's improving every year since 2006, according to ratings calculated by the Washington-based nonprofit Freedom House. In 2021, the discrepancy grew to record size, with seventy-three countries backsliding and only twenty-eight recording improvements. Nearly three-quarters of the world's population, including 330 million Americans, now live in countries where democracy is declining, the group found.

Set against this "democratic recession," the successes in restraining Covid-19 experienced by China and other countries that embraced digital tracking have intensified questions about the costs and benefits of state surveillance. The pandemic demonstrated the power of mass data collection to improve and save lives, not just derail them. If these technologies can revolutionize security, what do they mean for free will? Are we all headed for a world where the China Solution reigns supreme? Or is there a way to somehow reconcile machine-powered government audits of human behavior with the preservation of individual liberty?

This book is an effort to unpack the new era of state surveillance by exploring how and why China's Communist Party brought it into being, what it's like for those whose lives it has already altered, and what it means in a world suddenly unsure of the path forward. Given the gravity of what the Party hopes to accomplish, we believe it's critical to resist the temptation to hack the story of this country of 1.4 billion down to a narrative of simple oppression. With that in mind, we explore both the totalitarian darkness of Xinjiang and the breezy techno-utopias on the country's wealthy coast to show how the same algorithmic controls can terrorize or coddle depending on who and where you are. We also examine the unique motivations of Chinese tech companies and Chinese conceptions of privacy, both of which shape the surveillance state in unexpected ways.

Throughout these pages, we strive to be clear-eyed about the role democracies have played in midwifing the Chinese surveillance state, and their own susceptibility to the allure of social engineering. Many of the tools and concepts that the Communist Party is using to implement the China Solution were invented or first refined in Western countries. What makes the Party unique is its willingness and ability to apply them on a broad scale in real life. The results of this experiment will offer the rest of the world critical lessons about the benefits and the perils of marrying mass data collection and algorithmic machines to state power.

PART I

THE PLATFORM

1

"CRITICAL DATA"

On a brisk April day in 2017, a month before he and Marhaba were summoned to the police station basement, Tahir Hamut dropped into his friend's advertising agency in Urumqi for a visit. Walking through the door, he noticed a stack of white forms lying on a desk. His eyes brushed over them quickly, coming to a stop when they arrived at the title. Written in bold Chinese characters across the top was the phrase "Population Data Collection Form."

Tahir snatched a copy and held it up. "What's this?"

His friend wasn't sure. He said a local official had dropped them off earlier that day and demanded every staff member fill one out. Tahir looked closer. The form was a Tetris puzzle of paired boxes covering one side of a single page. One box in each pair contained a question and the other provided space for the answer. The information the boxes asked for at the top of the form was innocent enough: name, address, ID card number, marriage status, "cultural level" (a euphemism in China for education), and contact information.

Below that, however, they took on a more menacing feel.

Slightly down the page, one field titled "Religious Faith" offered respondents a list of options: *none, Muslim, Buddhist, Christian, other*, followed by a question: "Engage in Prayer?" (*yes/no*). From there, though, the fields grew more specific:

Number of times praying per day: *once, two to four times, five times*
Prayer venue: *home, mosque, other*
Participate in the Jummah [Friday prayer]: *yes/no*
Name of most frequented mosque: _____
Pilgrimage: *state-organized, private, waiting to go, no*
Religious teacher: *yes/no*
Religious education: *yes/no*
Place of instruction: _____
Name of instructor: _____

Every Uyghur in Urumqi was used to answering questions from police about their prayer habits, but these were more intrusive than usual. A subsequent section inquired about travel and international contacts, also with an emphasis on religion. Was the respondent a passport holder? Had they traveled abroad? How often and why? Had it been for pilgrimage? It also asked whether people had traveled or maintained personal contacts in one of "the twenty-six nations"—an informal list of countries, most of them majority-Muslim, that Xinjiang officials saw as problematic. The list included places known for extremist beliefs, like Saudi Arabia and Syria, but also Turkey (which had a large population of Uyghurs), Thailand (a popular stopover for Uyghurs fleeing persecution on their way to Turkey), and, for reasons that weren't entirely clear, Russia.

Some sections were intended for the authorities to fill out. One was titled "Stability-Related Circumstances." Its first field asked whether the respondent was a member of a "special population." Tahir took that as a reference to people the government suspected of separatism.

The Party was preoccupied with the separatist threat. Most Uyghurs Tahir knew entertained the dream—more of a fantasy, really—of a Xinjiang ruled by Uyghurs rather than the Communist Party. Twice in the past, in 1933 and 1944, the region's Turkic Muslims had succeeded in establishing their own state. The first East Turkestan Republic lasted only a year before it was crushed by a Chinese warlord. The second, bearing the same name, maintained fragile control over scattered parts of Xinjiang until 1949, when the entire region was absorbed into the newly formed People's Republic of China. Six decades later, Uyghurs would still sometimes greet foreign visitors with a whispered "Welcome to East Turkestan." But it was almost always just talk. A vanishingly small number had attacked police or set off bombs, almost always in response to a provocation by the authorities. Still, the Party was sensitive enough that any Uyghur unfortunate enough to be caught indulging the idea of an independent Xinjiang was liable to be labeled a potential separatist worthy of "special" attention.

Tahir's eyes continued down the page. The next field was less familiar. It asked for an "integrated comparison result." Tahir recalled reading news items referencing an "integrated joint-operations platform" that police in Xinjiang had recently begun to install, but the reports were vague on details. He guessed it might have something to do with that.

Several more fields asked for details about any relatives who had been put through something called "concentrated transformation through education." Tahir didn't know what that was either, though it brought to mind a strange encounter the previous month with the mother of one of his students. The woman was visiting from Kashgar, a former Silk Road oasis 900 miles east of Urumqi, where she worked in a famous hotel that Tahir and Marhaba had stayed in two years earlier. After arriving in Urumqi, she had told Tahir that Kashgar police were forcing Uyghurs to turn over their passports. Anyone whose passport showed evidence of travel to a Muslim country was taken away, no one knew exactly where, "for study." The woman left Urumqi a few days later, saying the hotel had ordered her back to Kashgar under pressure from local police. The police hadn't given a reason. She guessed it was because the owner of the hotel had taken the entire staff, including her, on a tour of Turkey the previous year. Tahir hadn't been able to reach her since.

Continuing to scan the form, Tahir's gaze drifted to the right-hand margin. There, under the label "critical data," was a series of checkboxes that also appeared to be reserved for the police to fill out:

- ☐ Uyghur
- ☐ Unemployed
- ☐ Passport holder
- ☐ Prays daily
- ☐ Has religious training
- ☐ Traveled to one of twenty-six nations
- ☐ Overstayed a visa while abroad
- ☐ Has contacts abroad
- ☐ Children out of school

And below that, at the bottom right-hand corner of the page, a final trio of choices:

- ☐ Safe
- ☐ Ordinary
- ☐ Unsafe

Safe. Ordinary. Unsafe. Which one was Tahir? It had been decades since he personally had felt anything like safe in Xinjiang, though he knew it wasn't his safety, or any Uyghur's, that the form's creators were referring to.

What worried him most, though, was the section on travel. For he and his family had been working on plans to escape.

Xinjiang occupies the entire far northwestern quarter of Chinese territory. It shares borders with eight countries (more than any other province or region in China), from Mongolia and Russia in the north to most of the Central Asian nations and India in the west. Tibet marks its southern border. The early twentieth-century American explorer Owen Lattimore described Xinjiang as "the pivot of Asia," marveling at how it connected some of the continent's greatest empires.

Starting in the second century BCE, traders on what would come to be known as the Silk Road trudged their way across Xinjiang's expanse, moving from oasis to oasis as they transmitted goods and ideas. Its importance to trade, and later its stores of oil and valuable minerals, made it coveted territory for Chinese rulers. But its remoteness and its dispersed population—Uyghurs, Kazakhs, Kyrgyz, and Mongols, who shared only distant cultural and linguistic connections, if any, to China—had always made it difficult to control.

The Party claims that Xinjiang has been a part of China "since ancient times," but no state based in China controlled the territory for a thousand years, between the retreat of the Tang Empire in 750 CE and reconquest by the Qing Dynasty's Manchu rulers in 1758. Qing emperors were at first content to rule from a distance as military overlords, putting local people in charge of affairs in their own areas. Only in 1884 did the Qing put Xinjiang under Chinese-style administration. In naming it Xinjiang, or "New Territory," the Manchus demonstrated just how novel an addition it was to the Chinese domain.

The Communist Party under Mao went further than any dynasty in imposing its will on the region. The founder of the People's Republic coveted Xinjiang not just for its resources but also for its position as a territorial buffer against the Soviet Union. To maintain control there, he established a vast paramilitary organization, the Xinjiang Production and Construction Corporation (more commonly known as the Bingtuan), made up of decommissioned Han Chinese soldiers. The Bingtuan's mission was threefold: enforce security, promote economic development through modern agriculture, and dilute the influence of minority populations by encouraging waves of Han migration. It was remarkably successful in meeting the last goal. The Han population in Xinjiang rose from 5 percent in 1949 to more than 40 percent in 1978.

Combined with Party assaults on Islam and other traditions that officials in Beijing considered "backward," the sudden influx of Han sowed anxiety among Uyghurs that over time morphed into a pervasive resentment of the Party and Han migrants. That in turn fed suspicion in Beijing that Uyghurs were not to be trusted.

In its search for a solution to Uyghur resistance, the Party's policies in Xinjiang pinballed between tolerance and oppression. In the early 1950s, it managed the region with a relatively light touch, adopting the Soviet belief that minority groups should be given a measure of self-determination and allowed to join the workers' revolution on their own terms. As Mao Zedong's politics grew more radical, the Party increasingly saw ethnicity as an "obstacle to progress" and moved aggressively to eradicate Uyghur traditions that interfered with assimilation, sparking protests big enough to require military intervention. After Mao's death in the late 1970s, the Party returned to the Soviet model, loosening religious controls and introducing affirmative-action-style policies, such as added points for Uyghurs on college entrance exams. But in the early 2010s, still unsatisfied with Uyghur loyalty, it started relying more on brute force to muscle them into submission.

Under Party rule, the Uyghurs' experiences mirrored the struggles of people living under occupation elsewhere in the world. In 2014, Xinjiang's Party chief introduced internal passports that restricted the movements of Uyghurs around Xinjiang and evoked the passbook system imposed on Black and Colored South Africans under apartheid. Like nonwhites in South Africa, Uyghurs had to carry their card whenever they left their home district. The card contained the names and contact information of officials in the bearer's hometown in case he or she needed to be bundled up and sent back. Han Chinese, like Afrikaners and other South African whites, could move about freely.

One noteworthy comparison came from the well-known Chinese writer Wang Lixiong. He was incarcerated in Xinjiang's Miquan prison in the late 1990s for photocopying a secret Bingtuan document and spent a year in a cell with a Uyghur prisoner, Mokhtar, who had been arrested for organizing a protest against racial discrimination. After his release, unsettled by what Mokhtar had told him about life in Xinjiang, Wang immersed himself in investigating the Uyghur plight. In 2007 he published a book summarizing his findings called *Your Western Regions, My East Turkestan*. It was a relatively open era, and Wang's book generated heated debate in intellectual circles for likening Uyghurs to Palestinians and warning that the region could descend into an "interminable ethnic war" of the kind that gripped Israel and the Palestinian territories.

In Xinjiang, as in Palestine, the conflict was rooted in complex, deeply felt, and ultimately unresolvable claims to contested land, Wang argued. Like the Israelis, Chinese authorities in Xinjiang often responded to challenges with disproportionate force. And as with the Palestinians, Uyghurs' pain at the loss of control over their homeland was exacerbated by cultural and ideological frictions with the potential to spark explosions of righteous anger.

One such explosion occurred in 2015, when Uyghurs armed with knives killed as many as fifty mostly Han workers and security guards in an attack on a coal mine in the city of Aksu. Security forces chased down and killed twenty-eight people they said were involved in the attack, which they blamed on an unnamed foreign terrorist organization. Authorities never explained why the mine was targeted.

The comparison with Palestine wasn't perfect. The Party controlled Xinjiang too tightly for Uyghurs to have the equivalent of the Palestine Liberation Organization to lead them or for Uyghurs to launch sustained mass uprisings like the Palestinians' intifadas. But as one Western scholar later noted, it was prophetic in one critical respect: a continuing cycle of conflict and crackdown over the coming years would eventually push Xinjiang to the same state of locked-in ethnic animosity, punctuated by outbursts of bloodshed, that dominates the West Bank and Gaza, though the unrest in Xinjiang would be far less frequent than it is in Palestine.

Views of Xinjiang among Han Chinese were complex. Years of preferential policies for ethnic minorities and investment in minority-dominated regions had bred resentment. State propaganda convinced many that the Party had dragged groups like the Tibetans and Uyghurs into the modern world. That they seemed to want independence from China struck many as ungrateful. A bloom of Islamophobia seeded by the post-9/11 War on Terror and fed by reports of Uyghur violence, which the government linked disingenuously to Islamic terror groups abroad, also encouraged a hard-line attitude toward Xinjiang. But public opinion was divided on how to solve the problems there. In an online survey conducted by a pair of Chinese scholars in the aftermath of one particularly serious attack by Uyghur terrorists in 2014, 40 percent "strongly disagreed" that force was an appropriate short-term response, and 70 percent disagreed that force was a good solution in the long term.

In late 2016, Party leaders frustrated with the status quo quietly ushered in an ambitious new phase in the campaign to eradicate Uyghur resistance. The plan marked the first time it would attempt to use cutting-edge tools being developed by Chinese surveillance companies to exert total control over an ethnic minority population.

◉

The authorities waited months before asking Tahir to fill out the data collection form. He couldn't explain the delay. One possibility is that he was already a known figure.

Tahir was a successful TV producer and commercial filmmaker. He also had a teaching position at the prestigious Xinjiang Arts Institute, where he was pursuing experiments in documentary film. But he derived more renown in Xinjiang from his poetry. Among the Turkic groups of Central Asia, poets are revered as heroes and seen as shapers of public life, on par with religious figures and political leaders. For more than two decades, Tahir had been known as a pioneer in modernist Uyghur poetry.

His writing carried an emotional depth and engagement with the sensory world that Joshua Freeman, a cultural historian at Princeton University, says helped redefine the scope of Uyghur literature. In 2017 he had recently started writing again after a long layoff. A poem he had composed the previous fall, titled "Unity Road" after a street name that appeared in every Xinjiang city like an authoritarian version of Martin Luther King Boulevard, captured the new sweep he had added to his style:

Night fell for the red-blooded,
for the black-blooded as well.
Dawn broke for the forgetful,
for the vengeful as well.

Hurrying back from the hot burial
he washed death from his face in the wind,
and then,
from faithful east to fickle west,
from mournful heights to joyous lows,
from familiar edges to the unknown center,
he set off with the step of a man who sinks in.

(Translated by Joshua L. Freeman)

Tahir was in his late forties but carried himself with the self-possession of someone decades older. At just under five feet six inches, he was shorter than average for a Uyghur. Despite that, he was an outsized presence, known for holding court at traditional cultural gatherings called *olturush*, or "sittings," where he spoke about Uyghur literature, film, food, and music with an intellect that left others both rapt and intimidated.

Tahir grew up during a period of relative calm in Xinjiang. The oldest of four brothers, he was born in 1969 on a farm run by the Bingtuan. Their settlement sat on the far northwestern edge of the Taklamakan Desert, an ocean of sand 600 miles long and made up of 200-foot shifting dunes that covers most of Xinjiang's southern half. His parents were peasants who had been lured to the farm by the promise of free housing and steady work. The family's two-room house didn't have electricity or running water, but it had an enormous sand dune out back that Tahir would scramble up and slide down on his feet, as if skiing. Other times, he and the other kids in the village would steal corn from the settlement storehouse and run out into the desert, where they'd heat the kernels with burning camel droppings and bury it in the sand to make popcorn.

In those years, the Communist Party promoted a Chinese identity that strived to be inclusive of minority groups. Despite barely speaking a word of Mandarin, Tahir identified as Chinese as a child. At the encouragement of their teachers, he and his friends tried to model themselves after Lei Feng, a People's Liberation Army soldier from northeast China whose (almost certainly fabricated) diary of daily good deeds the Party held up as a blueprint for selfless behavior that Chinese citizens should emulate. They also marveled at maps of China, tracing their fingers eastward from Xinjiang through the vastness of the country to Beijing—a journey that would have taken them a week by train had they been able to afford it.

By the time Tahir was a teenager, his family had scraped together enough money to afford electricity and a television set. Tahir developed obsessions with classic Chinese novels and television shows set in Beijing and Shanghai, and his desire to see the other China in real life pushed him to study hard for the college entrance exam. In 1987, at the age of seventeen, he tested into the Central Nationalities Institute, an elite school in the capital for training cadres to work in minority areas and educating talented minority students.

In Beijing, Tahir started down a path that would land him on the Communist Party's radar. He was shocked by the ignorance and disdain he encountered in the city's Han residents, who refused to believe him when he said he didn't ride camels to school back home and marveled out loud that he was literate. Still, he wandered the capital wide-eyed and full of wonder. The place was alive with a sense of experimentation and possibility that thrilled him.

When Beijing university students began marching to Tiananmen Square to protest for democratic reforms in the spring of 1989, Tahir became a leader in the movement and convinced his fellow Uyghur students to join. After authorities ordered troops to open fire on the protesters that June, he fled to Kashgar, a former Silk Road oasis in far western Xinjiang, but was soon ordered back to Beijing, where he was forced to write a confession that ran to 240 pages.

Despite, or maybe because of, his role during the protests, Tahir was groomed for leadership after his return. His senior year he was named chair of the students' association for his university department and deputy secretary of the department's Communist Youth League branch. University officials thought it looked odd for a non-Party member to represent the Youth League in meetings, but Tahir resisted joining. Finally, the officials filled out the application for him and called him in to sign it. He couldn't refuse.

As he approached graduation, Tahir was pulled further into the Party machinery. The Ministry of Public Security, which runs the country's police, tried to recruit him. Unwilling to become a cop, he turned down the ministry's offer in favor of a less compromising position as translator and instructor in minority issues at the Central Party School, the country's top training academy for Party cadres. Meanwhile, he started reading Chinese translations of American writers like Allen Ginsberg and Sylvia Plath and threw himself into writing poetry of his own.

After a few years living his double life in Beijing as an avant-garde apparatchik, Tahir grew restless. His position at the Party School had granted him access to otherwise forbidden historical materials, and he became intrigued reading about the two East Turkestan Republics. Rather than continue to waste time in Beijing, he resolved to travel to Turkey, where he could study the Uyghurs' history and cultural heritage free of censorship.

In the 1990s it was still difficult for Chinese citizens to secure permission from the government to travel abroad, so Tahir finagled a transfer to the Party School branch in Urumqi, where he paid a middleman $840 (a small fortune at the time, which he'd saved by living frugally in Beijing) to acquire a special passport given to Uyghurs doing business in Central Asia. He planned to cross the border into Kyrgyzstan and fly from there to Istanbul, but his bus got stuck in a snowstorm. While waiting for the storm to pass, Tahir was recognized by a customs agent with whom he'd gone to school in Beijing. The previous day, a group of Uyghurs had firebombed a police car in Urumqi, and border agents had been told to look out for Uyghurs trying to leave the country under suspicious circumstances. His former classmate had him detained.

After he was taken into custody, the police caught him trying to flush a notebook with the contact information of people involved in helping him get to Turkey. Later, they searched his apartment in Urumqi and found notes from a conversation he'd had about paramilitary troop numbers with an official in charge of frontier defense at the Central Party School. They accused him of trying to smuggle state secrets out of the country and locked him up in a detention center in Urumqi for eighteen months. When that was over, he was sentenced to another eighteen months of hard labor in Kashgar.

Kashgar nearly broke Tahir. Every day at 7:00 A.M., guards marched him and the other inmates into the desert, forcing them to chant Communist Party slogans. For the next twelve hours they worked in two-man teams collecting enough gravel to fill a bin the size of a refrigerator. Tahir cinched a cloth around his abdomen to keep his insides from bursting under the strain. One night, guards ordered him and the other prisoners to watch them punish a man who had failed to make his quota. They ordered the man to stand in a pool of water while they took turns electrifying it with shock batons. The man's high-pitched scream still haunted him decades later.

Released in 1998, Tahir reinvented himself in a way few others would have even attempted. With no prospects, he moved back to Urumqi and accepted a friend's invitation to try his hand at filmmaking. His first effort was *The Moon Is a Witness*, a ninety-nine-minute one-act drama about the life of a young Uyghur woman, based on a short story he and his friend both liked. Bucking Xinjiang's traditional conservatism, it depicted sexual themes and social taboos, including pregnancy out of wedlock, with almost scandalous frankness. It became an underground hit in Uyghur cities, passed around on cheap, low-res video compact discs. Encouraged, he made several more one-act films. In 2003 he parlayed that experience into a full-time job at a TV production company. A few years after that he was invited to teach film as an adjunct instructor at the Xinjiang Arts Institute.

Along the way, Tahir reconnected with Marhaba. He had met and befriended her shortly before he attempted to go to Turkey. After his release from the labor camp, he sought refuge in her kindness, and she helped him rebuild his life. They got married in the spring of 2001. Their first daughter, Aséna, was born two years later, and their second, Almila, five years after that. It was common for Uyghurs to be named after religious figures. For his daughters, Tahir had deliberately chosen names that didn't appear in the Koran to signal that Islam made up only a part of his family's identity. Aséna was the name of a she-wolf said to have given birth to the founder of an ancient Turkic clan in a cave near the oasis city of Turpan, south of Urumqi. Almila was Old Turkic for "red apple," a symbol of Turkic sovereignty.

As the summer of 2009 approached, Tahir's life appeared poised for another leap. That year, he, one of his brothers, and his brother-in-law set out to start a production company of their own. If they could pull it off, the move would give him more freedom, both creatively and financially. But an event in Shaoguan, a manufacturing city 2,400 miles away in the southern province of Guangdong, would overturn their plans.

That May, in a toy factory that had imported almost 800 Uyghur workers from a town near Kashgar, Han workers began to trade rumors of criminal activity among the Uyghurs, including one fabricated story that the Uyghurs had raped two Han women. One evening a young female trainee accidentally wandered into a dormitory occupied by Uyghur men and, perhaps on edge because of the rape rumors, ran screaming. No evidence suggests the men had done anything to justify the scream. Nevertheless, a Han mob gathered and swarmed the Uyghurs' dorm, killing at least two.

Xinjiang caught fire with the news. Uyghurs demanded the government punish the killers. On July 5, after weeks of inaction by officials, Uyghur college students in Urumqi organized a protest and were quickly joined by others. No one knew for certain when the protest turned violent (Uyghurs say it came after police started beating protesters), but it quickly grew savage. Groups of Uyghur men set fire to cars and attacked Han passersby with bricks and sticks. One foreign media report later quoted the owner of an Urumqi noodle shop saying he counted seventeen Han Chinese killed on one street alone. Security forces responded with live fire through the night and into the next morning. Police swept into Uyghur neighborhoods to make arrests. A day later, gangs of Han Chinese men armed with sticks and spiked clubs spilled into the streets, exacting revenge randomly on any Uyghurs they encountered. An official tally put the total number killed at nearly 200, though some Uyghur rights groups later estimated the number was at least twice that.

Tahir was in Kashgar at the time, helping prepare the opening ceremony for a cultural festival. Marhaba and his daughters were lucky enough to escape the riots and join him in Kashgar, but tensions between the Han and Uyghur residents still pulsed through Urumqi when they arrived home a month and a half later. One Friday night a couple of weeks after they returned, the violence flared up again following an explosion of rumors that Uyghur drug users were stabbing Han Chinese with HIV-tainted hypodermic needles. Han protesters returned to the streets looking for revenge. Tahir decided to pick up Marhaba from her job in downtown Urumqi to make sure she didn't walk home alone, but along the way he was spotted by a group of around a dozen Han, most of them young men, who chased him while chanting "Kill Uyghurs!" He tripped as he tried to escape, and they swarmed him on the ground, pummeling him with kicks and punches. He managed to escape by grabbing on to a railing, hurling himself over it, and sprinting into a nearby mosque where other Uyghurs had taken refuge. Bleeding profusely under his right eye, he waited until it seemed safe to leave and made his way to the hospital, where doctors told him the nerves in his face had been damaged. Immediately after the assault, his cheek would convulse every time he blinked. Physical therapy would help, but his face still occasionally twitched uncontrollably for years after.

The government later said that five people were killed and more than a dozen injured in the protests over the needles but didn't say whether the casualties were Uyghur or Han. The bloodshed would lead the authorities to crack down on Uyghurs more harshly than ever. To control the streets, Beijing deployed 14,000 paramilitary troops into Xinjiang from other provinces and bolstered the region's Special Police Units, recently created tactical units equipped with assault rifles and bulletproof vests. The security buildup continued over the following years as the Party sought to bring Xinjiang to heel with raw force. As Xi Jinping prepared to take power in 2012, police recruitment had increased by more than 50 percent since 2009, setting a new record.

In the midst of this ratcheting up of pressure, violence that had previously been contained within Xinjiang burst out of the region's borders for the first time. A Uyghur suicide attack in Beijing and a brutal assault with knives in a southwestern city sowed panic among Han Chinese. An even harsher crackdown followed. In 2014, the government passed a barrage of new rules limiting the practice of Islam and instituted the internal passport system, making it harder for Uyghurs to move around the region.

In a surprise move, the authorities also put a Uyghur economist named Ilham Tohti on trial for "inciting ethnic hatred." Tohti was China's most influential advocate for greater Uyghur autonomy inside China. Though sharp-tongued, he had never called for independence and was well connected in Beijing. When he was detained earlier in the year, Tahir and many others who knew him expected he would do a few years in prison at most. The court found him guilty and sentenced him to life.

Tohti's sentence hit Tahir hard. Over the previous few years, he had argued back and forth with himself about whether to try taking his family to the United States to claim political asylum. The notion of leaving Urumqi was painful. But the strain of worrying about his family's safety wasn't sustainable. The following year, as he wrestled with his decision, he wrote a poem that captured the exhaustion and exposure he felt living in the city. He called it "My Habitat."

This neighborhood with twenty-six buildings, is where my house is
  lofted
I, my wife, and my two girls
Floating like four balloons
Here
The meditating walls will never hear
The way the neighbor girl mimics a dog's barking
Here
Like indecent viewers countless windows
Gaze steadily at the naked mysteries inside
A door with three locks which I have to open every day
A pair of red eyes which I have to close everyday
A four-room house where I put on and take off my skin
every day

(Translated by Dilmurat Mutellip and Darren Byler)

Tahir and Marhaba started to notice the new police outposts in their neighborhood in southern Urumqi near the end of 2016. They popped up first at the major intersections: prefabricated boxes in gray or off-white, either one or two stories tall, with bars and wire mesh on the windows, a blue stripe running across the top, and the logo of the Public Security Bureau (PSB)—China's national five-star emblem floating atop the Great Wall—centered over a door. Most flew the Chinese flag from poles on their roofs. The bigger ones had red LED panels that flashed government slogans. Within a few months, they blanketed the entirety of Tianshan, the Uyghur-dominated district where their neighborhood was located, making it almost impossible to walk any distance without seeing at least one.

The government called them "convenience police stations." Posters near the doors advertised long lists of free products and services on offer inside: smartphone charging, legal education, reading glasses, newspapers and magazines, blood pressure meters, bike repair tools and tire pumps, cough drops, umbrellas, wheelchairs, bottled water, boiling water, oxygen bags, microwave ovens, and, for the bug-averse, mentholated mosquito repellent. But the stations' other features—riot gear, assault weapons, surveillance rooms concealed behind doors marked "No Unauthorized Entry"—offered a window into their true purpose. The beneficiaries of the "convenience" were Party leaders looking for a more efficient way to exert control over the Uyghur population.

Other changes soon followed. Metal fences were erected around gas stations, funneling drivers to security gates where they had to scan their faces to gain entrance. The same happened at bazaars and apartment complexes. Then came the cameras: Long "rifle-style" models with zoom lenses designed to shoot single locations in high-definition detail. Infrared versions for seeing at night. Spherical, wide-angle versions that hung from supports like dystopian grapefruit, some with rotating lower halves that would follow people as they walked down the street.

Like many Uyghurs, Tahir initially wrote off these developments as just the latest in a long series of "strike-hard" campaigns the Party had waged in Xinjiang. The data collection form had been the first real indication that something new was happening. The questions it asked, and the way it asked them, hinted at an assault more systematic than anything the Party had tried before. The next sign came when the authorities started collecting data of a more intimate kind.

A month after he first saw the data collection form in his friend's office, Tahir was feeling fidgety. His production company's main client, the state-run local TV station, had repeatedly delayed the renewal of its contract. Meanwhile, most of his employees had been called back to their hometowns, he assumed for "transformation through education." None had returned.

With little to do and eager for an escape, Tahir and Marhaba decided to take the girls out of school and drive south to Turpan, on the other side of the Tianshan Mountains, where they had a small house. The plan was to spend a long weekend taking refuge in the Turpan house's walled garden, which Tahir had planted with apricots, figs, jujubes, and, in a nod to the city's famous local vineyards, a few grapevines. As they rolled onto the highway in the family Buick, Tahir plugged his phone into the sound system and blasted the Uyghur dance music the girls preferred, driving toward the mountains. Then the music suddenly cut off, replaced with the sound of the phone ringing.

Everyone in the car fell silent as Tahir answered the call. On the other end was a woman from their local police station in Urumqi. She wanted Tahir and Marhaba to come into the station. "For fingerprint-ing," she said. The request didn't make sense. The police had already taken their fingerprints multiple times. But Tahir knew it was useless to argue. The best he could do was try to salvage the weekend. He explained that they were heading out of town and suggested they come in on Monday. The woman said that was fine. For the next two days, he and Marhaba sat in their garden in Turpan wondering if it was their turn to disappear.

The following Monday they left the girls at the apartment in Urumqi and drove the Buick to the police station. Inside, an officer motioned them to the basement. Tahir recalled a visit to the station the previous year to deal with paperwork for his passport, when he had been forced to wait for a Ministry of State Security agent who was busy interrogating a suspect below. He had sat there in the lobby for an hour, every few minutes catching the faint sound of human screams echoing up the staircase. As he looked at the staircase now, the sound of those screams came back to him. Whatever awaited them down there, it wasn't benign—but they had no choice. He looked at Marhaba, took a breath, and began the descent.

At the bottom of the steps, they found a low white corridor about sixty feet long. Fluorescent lights in the ceiling bathed the space in cold light. A series of offices lined the right side of the corridor with jail cells facing them on the left. A half dozen other Uyghurs were lined up in the corridor. They were all well dressed, educated-looking. A dozen more soon came in and lined up behind them.

Marhaba exchanged a few quiet words with the others, then turned to Tahir.

"Everyone here has a passport," she said. "Everyone recently traveled abroad."

In 2015, not long after Ilham Tohti was sentenced to life in prison, Tahir had applied for passports for the entire family and used them to take Marhaba on a two-week trip to Europe. He'd designed the trip as groundwork for a future in which he might have to escape permanently. Visa officers in the American embassy were notoriously suspicious, known to reject tourist applications at the slightest hint someone might be intending to stay in the United States permanently. Chinese officials were equally skeptical of outbound travel by Uyghurs. If he wanted to get his whole family out, he needed to avoid raising the suspicions of either Chinese or American officials. To do that, he had to persuade both sides he was a regular traveler.

Tahir had mapped out two "vacations" with his wife: one to Europe that they could use to reassure visa gatekeepers at the American embassy, and another to the United States to show Chinese officials they could be trusted to come back. The European trip had involved a brief stop in Turkey, one of the twenty-six Muslim countries referenced on the data collection form. Would those few days they'd spent in Istanbul be what got them dragged away?

As the line inched forward, Tahir glanced inside one of the cells on the left side of the corridor. Near the entrance he saw a "tiger chair," used to keep people immobile during interrogations. It had a platform attached to the armrests, like on a child's high chair, with two hoops of metal sliding through the surface into a pair of locks underneath and hinged rings jutting inward from each of the front legs. Past the chair, a metal ring with a chain attached stuck from the floor. Near the ring was a depression in the concrete stained the unmistakable color of blood. Tahir thought again of the screams and felt a wave of disgust rise up his throat.

Ahead of him, Tahir noticed a man was staring at the same scene, his eyes lingering on the depression, the rust-colored patch. A woman next to the man yanked repeatedly on his shirt. "Stop looking," the woman whispered. "Stop looking. Stop looking."

After fifteen minutes, Tahir and Marhaba arrived at the end of the line. A police officer sat inside an open door and asked for their names, then sent them further down the hall to a room where two people sat at a table piled with needles, cotton swabs, and rubber tubing. One of the people wore a blue police shirt but without a badge or ID number—an auxiliary officer, brought in to handle station grunt work. The other, a Uyghur woman in plain clothes, looked to Tahir like a local official of some sort. Next to the auxiliary officer sat a new-looking clear plastic box with half a dozen blood-filled vials sticking out of a foam-rubber insert. More of the plastic boxes were stacked behind him. The woman directed them to sit down, roll up their sleeves and extend their arms. Without explanation, the auxiliary cop grabbed one of Tahir's arms and reached for a section of tubing. Tahir glanced around, confused.

"You're taking blood? You don't have nurses to do this?" he asked, as lightly as he could manage.

"It's not a big deal," the auxiliary officer said. "It'll be over soon."

"What if I get infected?" Tahir responded, forcing a laugh.

Tahir looked to the side and saw a nearby police officer roll his eyes. He had wanted to ask what was going on, why they needed his blood, but decided not to push it further. Instead, he pulled back his sleeve and watched as the auxiliary officer fumbled awkwardly with the needle, then jabbed it into the crook of his arm, sending a gush of viscous vermilion liquid flowing into the attached vial.

After taking his blood, they sent Tahir back to the first room. Inside, he got a clear view of what he'd only glimpsed before. Half a dozen police manned three tables, each with computers attached to three different pieces of equipment: a microphone, a fingerprint machine, and a single-lens reflex camera attached to a bizarrely elongated rectangular lens. As he glanced around, one of the police officers pointed to a table covered in copies of the *Urumqi Evening News*. He told Tahir to choose a long article and start reading out loud into the microphone. Tahir picked an editorial about tensions between the United States and North Korea on the front of a Uyghur edition of the paper, sat down, and began reading.

Between lines, Tahir glanced up at the computer attached to the mic. A column of jagged lines was spreading horizontally across the screen—the patterns of his voice being rendered into waveforms. He'd seen the same patterns a thousand times while working on documentaries and TV shows, but whatever software they were using to record him, he didn't recognize it.

After two minutes, the police cut him off and gestured for him to move to the next station: fingerprinting, the ostensible reason for their visit. The police officer behind the computer told him to press and roll each finger onto a black box topped with a plate of smooth dark glass. Each time he rolled only part of the way or didn't press hard enough, the machine emitted a ragged screech. Finally he moved to the last station, where the camera with the strange lens waited.

After the camera had done its work, Tahir thought again about asking what it was all for, but again stopped himself. *Don't meet trouble halfway,* he told himself.

Outside, Tahir looked at the low sun bouncing its light off the mountains, then glanced down at his watch, which read 5:00 P.M. They'd been in the basement for three hours. They were both exhausted. The important thing, though, was that they had gotten out. They would get to go home to their daughters. For now at least, they were free.

Over the next few weeks, Tahir noticed buses parked near the convenience police stations in Tianshan District. Each one waited as police marched groups of Uyghurs, mostly young men, to the doors and barked at them to climb on board. Once each bus was full, it would drive off. At first it was only a few buses a few times a day, then a few more. After a while it was everywhere and around the clock. Every convenience police station seemed to fill up and send off at least one bus a day, every day, for weeks.

Over time, Tianshan began to feel deserted. Tahir tried doing the math in his head. At the time the district had more than thirty convenience police stations. A typical bus held around fifty people. Even if only half the stations sent buses each day, and even if the buses weren't full, they would have hauled away more than 10,000 people in the space of a month.

By force of habit, Tahir had stopped himself from thinking too much about what the police intended to do with the information they had collected about his body in the basement. Anyone who lived in China was accustomed to assaults on their privacy, Uyghurs more than others. It was foolish, even dangerous, to worry too much about something you couldn't control. But as the buses continued to fill and depart, the reality of the new surveillance began to set in. The authorities clearly had a list of some kind. If Tahir was on that list, the police could use any phone call, anything he touched, even strands of hair he left behind to identify him and round him up.

Most disturbing was what the police could do with his face. Facial recognition technology turned faces into the equivalent of fingerprints, but with one critical difference: unlike the whorls at the tip of a finger, the unique features of a face could be scanned from a distance. The underlying technology had been around for years, but new algorithms made it faster and more accurate. Now it was possible to automatically and simultaneously compare face prints from thousands of camera feeds and security checkpoints against a blacklist with tens of thousands of names in just a few seconds—swift enough to track people in real time as they moved across the city. In China, the technology could be linked to the country's national ID database to create what was in effect a digital lineup of more than a billion people. New advances also made the systems better at identifying people under imperfect conditions, especially when, as was the case with Tahir, they had a 3D model of the target's face.

Over the following months, their peril began to come into sharper focus.

The first warning came toward the end of June, when Tahir and Marhaba realized it had been a week since they'd heard from Kamil, one of their closest friends. Kamil had gone to America with his wife and daughter in 2016 to take up a position as a visiting scholar at a university in the Midwest. With government pressure on Uyghurs increasing in Xinjiang, he wavered about whether to seek asylum. Friends and colleagues in the United States had urged him to stay, but two of his fellow scholars in Urumqi had vouched for him and would face punishment if he didn't go back. He and his wife landed in Urumqi in February, just as the new security regime was ramping up.

The two families had been in almost daily contact since then, either by text message or via the popular Chinese messaging app WeChat, so the silence was noteworthy. Marhaba sent a voice message over WeChat to Kamil's wife, Munire, asking how things were and whether Kamil was at home. Munire wrote back to say he wasn't there. Then she stopped replying.

Concerned, Tahir and Marhaba decided to pay them a visit. Once in the apartment they asked about Kamil. Munire put a finger to her lips, pointed to the ceiling, and gestured with her eyes around the apartment to indicate someone might be listening, then took them down to the apartment complex's main courtyard.

Once outside, she burst into tears. Between sobs, she related how police had come to Kamil's office several days earlier and taken him away without warning or explanation. He had reappeared at the apartment two days later in the company of three agents from the Ministry of State Security, who proceeded to ransack the house before leaving with Kamil and armfuls of documents. The next day, Kamil texted to inform her the state security agents were taking him to Kashgar and asked her to bring him some clothes. Taking the clothes from her at the gate of the state security compound, Kamil struggled to speak through his tears. The agents told her to trust them and not to contact them about Kamil's case. She hadn't heard anything since.

Tahir felt a rush of panic. He recalled that when he had been sent to the labor camp, police rounded up two of his closest friends and interrogated them for days. He had to assume they would do the same to Kamil's friends now—though with the environment the way it was, Tahir was as likely to be taken to a camp or prison as to a police station's interrogation room.

Returning home, he and Marhaba talked through the night about what might happen. He dug out the deeds for the car and the apartment and handed them to her along with all of the family bank cards and passwords. They agreed that if the police came for him, she would sell the car and their home, buy a cheaper apartment, and use the rest of the money to support herself and the girls. "Don't contact anyone, and don't come looking for me," he told her. "Just do what you need to do." If he survived, he would find them. If he didn't, she would be powerless to do anything about it anyway.

Recently he had heard stories from other Uyghurs of police knocking in the night and grabbing people in their doorways. Some people reportedly had been taken away wearing only their underwear. He started sleeping with a set of warm clothes stacked next to his bed so he would have something to throw on in the event a nighttime raid led to him spending the winter in a cell somewhere.

Days later, Tahir got a call from the neighborhood committee official. His heart jumped up to his throat, but it quickly settled back down after he learned what the call was about. The official wanted Tahir to let him into the TV production company's office to scan its QR code. A two-dimensional version of a bar code, the now ubiquitous QR code was adopted early in China and used by people everywhere to add each other on social media or transfer money back and forth through mobile payment systems. In Xinjiang, the authorities required all Uyghur homes and businesses to post one inside the door that police could scan to bring up a list of registered residents and employees. The authorities came by daily to scan the code and check that everyone they saw was on the list.

Tahir drove to the office and opened the door for the official, who scanned the code and left. Moments after Tahir sat down, his phone rang again. This time it was the police, and this time the order caused Tahir's heart to sink: he had to go to the station the next day to hand over his family's passports.

When he returned home with the news, his oldest daughter, Aséna, fifteen at the time, burst into tears. Later she would tell him it felt like she'd been pushed off a building. She had been troubled by the convenience police stations and the feeling of constant scrutiny, and by paper police seals that had started appearing on the apartment doors of disappeared neighbors. Her parents had recently secured tourist visas for the whole family to travel to the United States. Imagining what it would be like to escape the suffocation had armored her with hope. It was the only thing that made her days bearable. Now she watched it receding into the distance.

Tahir had prepared himself for the possibility their plan would fail. Marhaba had been hesitant about the escape idea all along, afraid to leave Xinjiang and her relatives behind. Both had been through so much in the past, and they felt confident they could survive in Urumqi even under this new regime. But seeing their eldest daughter sink into darkness, her usual joy snatched away with such violence, Tahir resolved to find a way to get the passports back.

He worked through the night, searching online for a story they could sell to the authorities. By the time the sun rose the next morning, he had what he thought was a solution, but it was a long shot. And they would have to try to pull it off as the Party continued to tighten its grip.

2

ENGINEERS OF THE SOUL

On a clear day in February 2017, four months before Tahir and his family handed over their passports, a motorcade carrying local officials cut through Tianshan District and rolled to a stop on a quiet stretch of Dawan North Road, less than a ten-minute walk from where the Hamut family lived. A baritone voice in the back of one of the vehicles boomed an order to call the police.

The officers of Urumqi Convenience Police Station TS-081 were the first to respond, swarming out into the freezing air in SWAT-style black uniforms, strapped with pistols and shotguns. A minute later teams from two more stations, TS-064 and TS-066, charged in to join them. The motorcade had stopped in front of Western Region International Trade City, a wholesale market plastered with ads hawking home appliances, auto parts, and fur coats in a jumble of Chinese, Uyghur, and Russian. Nothing looked amiss there. The other side of the street, where a liquor store sat sandwiched between an onion pancake shop and a Muslim noodle soup restaurant, was also quiet. The police seemed to have been called for no reason.

A trim older man emerged from one of the vehicles. He sported a head of unnaturally black hair, parted uncompromisingly on the left side, and wore a police-issue padded jacket with fake fur collar, stripped of the usual police patches. In both respects, he was indistinguishable from hundreds of other senior Communist Party officials, a noteworthy number of whom shared an affinity for hair dye and man-of-the-people polyester outerwear. But if he looked like a typical official, the assembled police officers knew the man to be anything but. His face—marked by haughty cheekbones and heavy eye bags that together gave an impression of extreme impatience—had flashed across television screens and stared out from the front pages of newspapers for weeks. Just days earlier, he had appeared in front of 10,000 fully armed police, militia, and paramilitary troops at an exhibition center in the northern part of the city, where he ordered them to "destroy root and branch" of Uyghur separatism and bury Uyghur "terrorists" in "a People's War of tsunami-like proportions."

This was Chen Quanguo, Xinjiang's new Communist Party boss.

Chen arrived in Urumqi with a fierce reputation. In both his work and his personal affect, he seemed driven by an uncompromising disdain for wasted effort. Video of his public appearances invariably showed him standing motionless, left hand holding the right in front of his waist, whether he was speaking or watching a dance performance. In the presence of children, he managed to smile with an almost grandfatherly warmth, but the expression in his eyes never rose past freezing.

Chen's demeanor reflected a decades-long scramble up a rubble-strewn path. Unlike Xi Jinping and many others in the upper echelons of Chinese politics who were the children of the Communist Party's revolutionary royalty, Chen had built his career up from nothing. His parents were peasants from Pingyu, a mountainous county in the central province of Henan. He was born in 1955, just as the country was experiencing the ravages of Mao Zedong's catastrophic Great Leap Forward. He left home at eighteen to join the People's Liberation Army as an artilleryman and became a member of the Communist Party in 1976 at age twenty-two, just as the Cultural Revolution was ending. When the government reopened universities two years later, he tested into the economics department at Zhengzhou University and returned to Pingyu to take up a Party post overseeing a local commune. From there, he shot up the ranks, earning his first post as Communist Party secretary, in nearby Suiping County, at thirty-three. The appointment made him the youngest county Party boss in Henan in the post-Mao era.

When he moved to Urumqi, he was fresh off a tour as Party secretary in Tibet, where between 2011 and 2016 he helped suffocate a revival of protests against Beijing's heavy-handed rule that was spearheaded by desperate Buddhist monks. Part of his success in Tibet had come from radically improving the time it took police to respond to protests. Arriving in Urumqi, he wasted no time in rolling out similar measures in Xinjiang. Soon he started conducting spot checks by measuring the time it took for police to respond to an emergency call. The results that February day on Dawan North Road suggested the new systems he'd put in place were already working well.

In bank heist movies, police have a way of showing up just as the robbers are rushing into the getaway car. In reality, they're much slower. Comparing 2015 and 2016 data from fifty-seven cities around the United States, one Stanford University researcher found the average police response time for top-priority emergency calls was almost twenty-five minutes. Police in Houston, Texas, a city roughly the same size as Urumqi, are among the fastest in the United States, according to a 2019 study by home security website ASecureLife.com, arriving at the scene of an emergency call in close to six minutes on average. Urumqi's police were in a different league: according to Chen's watch, the two slower units had responded to the call in under two minutes. The officers of TS-081, meanwhile, had responded in a Hollywood-worthy fifty-four seconds.

Still, Chen thought they could have been faster. "With every second shaved off the arrival of decisive force, public safety improves another notch," the *Xinjiang Daily*, a Party-controlled newspaper, quoted him as saying. The question of exactly which "public" Chen was referring to went unsaid, though few Uyghurs reading the story would have assumed their safety was at the front of his mind.

How could Xinjiang's security machinery possibly get more efficient?

Chen and his team of antiterror experts had a simple answer that drew on the Party's growing obsession with the predictive power of data: it needed to neutralize threats before they arose.

◉

At the time of Chen's police response test, the Communist Party believed it faced a crisis in Xinjiang. The cause, in the Party's eyes, was a volatile mingling of ethnonationalist feeling, particularly among the Uyghurs, and extremist religious ideas imported from abroad. It was the sort of combination, Beijing believed, that could explode at any moment.

Radical Islam's influence in Xinjiang was something of a self-fulfilling prophecy. Prior to 2001, Chinese leaders had seen the problems in Xinjiang as primarily the product of ethnic tensions—an understanding at least somewhat shared by Uyghur rights advocates. That began to change in the aftermath of the 9/11 attacks. Seizing on the US-led Global War on Terror, the Party rebranded its struggle with the Uyghurs as a battle against terrorism and religious extremism. While it continued to manage Xinjiang in more or less the same way as it had before, with crackdowns focused largely on Uyghurs' political aspirations, outwardly it blamed religious extremism for any strife that became public.

Uyghur aspirations for autonomy originally had scant connection with radical Islam. The Muslim tradition that prevailed in Xinjiang throughout most of its modern history bore little resemblance to Wahhabism and other fundamentalist strains that feed terrorist groups in the Middle East and Central Asia. Uyghurs tended to shun pork but enthusiastically ignored prohibitions on alcohol. Even in dark times, Uyghur gatherings exuded a joy that wanted little to do with anything so restrained as religious fundamentalism. Chinese state media were happy to exploit that exuberance when it suited them, broadcasting footage of Uyghurs dancing as proof that the Party's policies imbued minority groups with a sense of satisfaction.

As the authorities in Xinjiang continued to hang the terrorism label on violent expressions of Uyghur frustration, including the 2009 Urumqi riots, younger Uyghurs rebelled by seeking out identities divorced from China and the Party. Many used social media to explore different branches of Islam, with some following foreign imams online. Continued government crackdowns helped push more and more Uyghurs to seek solace in Islam, including some extreme Salafist teachings that previously had enjoyed little appeal in the region. By the time Xi Jinping came to power in 2012, religious fervor had come to play a more prominent role in Uyghur resistance, though Beijing was arguably just as responsible for that development as any of the foreign terrorist organizations it blamed, if not more so.

The interweaving of religious and ethnic resistance in Xinjiang wasn't just an ideological problem for the Party. It was also practical. Despite being remote, Xinjiang was central to Xi's most cherished foreign policy idea: a trillion-dollar global infrastructure plan called the Belt and Road Initiative that would resurrect old Silk Road–era trading systems and reorient international commerce around the Chinese economy. One aim of the plan was to funnel Chinese goods through Central Asia to the Middle East and Europe through railway networks that would travel, just like the Silk Road caravans, through the mountain passes of Xinjiang. An uprising among Uyghurs could scuttle those plans, eviscerating billions of dollars in investment. It would also make the Party look weak, both abroad and, worse, at home.

The Party got a glimpse of its nightmare scenario almost immediately. Xi announced the Belt and Road Initiative during a visit to Kazakhstan, just across the border from Xinjiang, in September 2013. The next month, an SUV hopped a curb in central Beijing, mowed through a crowd of civilians, then crashed and burst into flames in front of Mao Zedong's portrait on Tiananmen, the Gate of Heavenly Peace. The sight of a black column of smoke shooting skyward in front of Tiananmen Square, in the center of one of the most heavily guarded areas of the country, left people stunned. Police later identified the occupants of the SUV as a family from Xinjiang and ruled the incident a suicide attack. The following March, a group of eight Uyghurs armed with long knives slashed their way through dense crowds of travelers outside the main train station in the southwestern city of Kunming, killing 29 civilians and injuring 143 more. Other attacks followed inside Xinjiang.

In April 2014, Xi went on a four-day visit to the region. State media showed him visiting police stations and looking with approval at racks of riot-control weapons. According to secret transcripts later leaked to *The New York Times*, he ordered local officials and police to "show absolutely no mercy" in dealing with separatists. On the last day he met with officials in Urumqi and warned them about the danger of extremist religious ideas. Hours later, two Uyghur separatists launched a suicide bomb attack outside an Urumqi train station, killing one and injuring dozens more.

The attacks quickly became a Rorschach test. To the Party leadership and large numbers of Han Chinese, they were yet more evidence of the corrupting influence of extremist Islam on Uyghurs. Shortly after the Beijing SUV attack, the Turkestan Islamic Party, a Uyghur jihadist group scattered across Central Asia and the Middle East, praised it in a video published online. Police reported finding gasoline, two knives, and steel sticks inside the SUV, "as well as a flag with extremist religious content."

Western scholars of Xinjiang, Uyghurs in exile, and journalists who traveled in the region tended to see the attacks instead as the crystallization of decades of accumulated anger and frustration at the Party's policies in Xinjiang. A lack of transparency and routine harassment of reporters in Xinjiang made it difficult to discern the truth, but the available evidence suggested it was the Party that bore ultimate responsibility for the violence.

Prior to the attacks, independent research suggested that no more than a tiny fraction of Uyghurs ever conceived of their struggle in Xinjiang in terms of jihad. There were plenty of instances, however, of Uyghurs chafing against heavy-handed policing, restrictions on normal religious practice, government policies that favored Han business interests, the extraction of natural resources, and the steady drip of Han racism they suffered in the course of daily life.

Beyond that, skeptics of the government's view observed, the Turkestan Islamic Party never actually claimed responsibility for organizing the Beijing SUV attack. Moreover, the perpetrators—a husband, wife, and mother—didn't fit the description of a typical terrorist cell. The Beijing attack and others like it appeared less the product of an organized campaign, as anthropologist Sean Roberts writes, and more a reflection "of how widespread the frustration and rage had become within the Uyghur population."

Some Communist Party elites had in the past warned that a hard-line approach in Xinjiang would backfire and argued instead for policies focused more on economic development. Among them was Xi's late father. In 1985, after decades spent managing religious and ethnic issues, including in Xinjiang, Xi Zhongxun, by then a member of the Party's ruling Politburo, made a strong statement in favor of more openness. "Looking back upon history, countless facts prove that, with regards to dealing with religious issues, the more that our policies are tight and inflexible, the more that in practical terms religion is suppressed, things run counter to one's wishes, the exact opposite result occurs," the elder Xi said. "It's not only impossible to guide activities in the area allowed by policy and law, but in fact makes activities leave the normal track, or even allows people with ulterior motives to use the situation."

Whether because he disagreed or thought the time had passed, the younger Xi took a harder path. Returning to Beijing from Urumqi, he likened religious extremism to taking drugs and warned that failure to solve the problem would have ripple effects throughout the country. At a high-level meeting on Xinjiang policy, he ordered a new "People's War" on terrorism that cast the Uyghur mind as a battlefield and radical Islam as a well-armed enemy that would yield only to force. "The weapons of the people's democratic dictatorship must be wielded without any hesitation or wavering," he said.

Somewhat surprisingly in retrospect, Xi warned against suggestions that Islam as a whole should be swept aside or restricted in Xinjiang, a notion that he called "biased, even wrong." Here he may have been thinking of his father, or been seeking to limit collateral damage. The attacks had set off a wave of Islamophobia among Han Chinese that threatened to engulf Hui Muslims, who were culturally closer to the Han and more accepting of Party rule. Or he may have been paying lip service to the government's official policy of religious tolerance, which Chinese officials cited whenever confronted by journalists or diplomats with evidence of religious persecution.

Whatever the case, the distinction appeared lost on the officials tasked with carrying out the new war. In 2014, authorities in Xinjiang launched a "de-radicalization" campaign that targeted not extremist activity but normal Islamic customs. A few years earlier, authorities had launched a campaign, known as "Project Beauty," that encouraged Uyghur women to "let their hair down and show their pretty faces" by shunning head-scarves and veils. A similar campaign had targeted young men with long beards. Both were now coded into law. At the same time, security officials drafted a new counterterrorism law (later rubber-stamped by lawmakers) that broadened the definition of terrorist activity to include "thought, speech or behavior" that sought to split the state.

A year later, the number of attacks—at least those that were publicly reported—had fallen sharply. But officials complained that thousands of Uyghurs were fleeing through an underground railroad system to join terrorist groups. Large numbers of Uyghurs had indeed been flee-ing Xinjiang since 2009, mostly through Southeast Asia. Some were picked up in Thailand and sent back to China, while others made it to Turkey. The Associated Press later confirmed that a few thousand Uy-ghurs had found their way to Syria to train with the Turkestan Islamic Party and fight with al-Qaeda against Syrian president Bashar al-Assad. Interviews conducted by the AP suggested that most of the Uyghurs fighting in Syria had been recruited in Turkey and weren't interested in global jihad, or even the outcome of the Syrian civil war. Their focus was on the Party. "We didn't care how the fighting went or who Assad was," one former Uyghur fighter, who'd fled Xinjiang after the 2009 crackdown, told the wire service. "We just wanted to learn how to use the weapons and then go back to China."

Party leaders felt the time had come for a new approach. For a few years, the government in Xinjiang had quietly experimented with send-ing small groups of resistant Uyghurs to dedicated facilities where they were subjected to psychological techniques previously used to reha-bilitate drug addicts and members of fringe religious movements. Re-searchers and officials there said the early results had been promising. Meanwhile, technology companies in Beijing were developing tools that made it possible to automatically track large numbers of people, including by their faces, and crunch data to predict which individuals were most likely to cause trouble. Authorities began to consider combining these two developments in an ambitious effort to reengineer Uyghur society so that it was more compliant with the Party's agenda. In Chen Quanguo, they had an ideal candidate to lead it.

◉

Chen Quanguo rose into the upper echelons of Party power by becoming one of its most effective exterminators of ideological threats. He'd begun to carve out that role nearly twenty years earlier in Henan.

A hot, landlocked province straddling the Yellow River, Henan occupies part of what is traditionally considered the cradle of Chinese civilization. For two centuries, beginning in 25 CE, it was the seat of power for the Han Dynasty. By Chen's time, however, the province's star had dimmed. It was known around China as a poor place and a hotbed of religious ferment. During Chen's tenure, it became a prolific source of adherents for the Falun Gong, a popular religious movement that combined slow-moving *qigong* exercises with Buddhist and Taoist beliefs about the cultivation of virtue and reincarnation. Chinese leaders had been caught off guard in 1999 when more than 10,000 members of the group surrounded the central government compound in Beijing, demanding state recognition. The Party's response was a nationwide crackdown.

A senior official by then, Chen was tasked with helping crush the movement. He presided over the burning of Falun Gong books and CDs. Later he helped purge or forcibly reeducate wayward local Party members. During that time, Henan became one of the country's most enthusiastic builders of so-called Reeducation Through Labor camps, where Falun Gong members, minor criminals, political dissidents, and others the Party deemed undesirable could be sent without trial for up to four years. Falun Gong followers were subjected to a new process called "transformation through education"—the same phrase Tahir Hamut would later encounter on the data collection form in Urumqi—in which they were forced to sing patriotic songs, watch propaganda videos, and renounce their beliefs under threat of torture.

In 2011, Chen was promoted to the top Party post in Tibet. In Lhasa, his experience wrangling with religious dissenters proved invaluable. No figure had done more to sully the Party's image internationally than the Dalai Lama, Tibetan Buddhism's leader-in-exile whose rock-star popularity had made Tibetan independence a cause célèbre around the world. Years earlier, the Dalai Lama had abandoned calls for independence in favor of greater autonomy, but recently the nonviolent resistance movement he inspired had taken on a troubling new form.

In protest against government constraints on their religion, language, and way of life, at least a dozen Tibetans inside China, most of them young monks and nuns, had lit themselves on fire in 2010, the year before Chen arrived. Images of their smoldering bodies ricocheted around the world, casting China in an ugly light. The Party seemed powerless to respond. Tibet is vast, with people scattered in cities and villages often connected by serpentine roads that can take hours, if not days, to traverse. By the time authorities arrived at the site of a self-immolation, it was usually too late: the fire had been lit, and smartphone video was making its way to the internet.

Chen immediately set about instituting changes. Rather than have police gathered in big, centralized stations, Chen built smaller stations and sprinkled them throughout the region—precursors of the convenience police stations that would later pop up in Tahir's neighborhood. The stations used "grid-style management," a technique that divides communities into small zones for easier monitoring. Connected to networks of surveillance cameras, the stations allowed police to track Tibetans who might try to self-immolate and respond quickly with fire extinguishers if they did. They could then interrogate survivors for the names of other Tibetans who might harbor similar plans.

The year Chen arrived, more than eighty Tibetans burned themselves alive. The next year the number fell below thirty. The following year it was eleven, then seven, and after that it stayed in the single digits. Touring Lhasa in 2012 in the company of reporters from state-run media, a triumphant Chen touted the value of his initiative to a local shopkeeper. "Convenience police stations are the people's guardian angels," he said. Chen was shamelessly conflating the interests of regular citizens with the Party's, but it didn't matter. His audience was in Beijing, and they'd soon get the message.

In August 2016, with Tibet now firmly under control, the Party leadership tapped Chen to run Xinjiang. The appointment marked a milestone: never in the Communist Party's nearly seven decades in power had an official been assigned the top spot in both of China's far western territories. In a speech outlining his policy approach not long after arriving in Urumqi, Chen promised to "place the work of maintaining stability ahead of everything else." That would involve "detaining [suspects] early, quickly and thoroughly." He also called for more sophisticated controls that would allow authorities to "make good forcing moves on the chess board."

Chen wasted little time. Over his first four months in charge, he built 4,900 convenience police stations—giving Xinjiang twenty times as many police stations per capita as Chicago—the vast majority in neighborhoods dominated by Uyghurs. He would order construction of at least 2,800 more over the following year and a half. Each police station was connected to a network of surveillance cameras and to a series of plastic alarm buttons installed in nearby businesses that owners could push to alert authorities of suspicious behavior. Soon, local police patrols started notching unheard-of response times.

Meanwhile, Chen had already started work on the data collection that would, in theory at least, make response times moot.

History is littered with examples of how data gathered even under neutral or positive auspices can later be exploited for regrettable, and sometimes terrifying, ends. Censuses conducted in Europe in the early twentieth century that asked people to note their religious affiliation later helped the SS identify the largest pockets of Jews in each country they occupied during World War II. The US census of 1940, the country's most ambitious and wide-ranging to that point, would be used two years later to help Washington identify blocks of Japanese Americans and ship them off to World War II internment camps.

The survey effort Chen Quanguo launched in Xinjiang in 2017 reflected an evolution in the understanding of data's power to deliver social control. Censuses conducted by the United States and European governments in the first half of the previous century had been broad, designed for a wide range of uses. Chen's was targeted with precision at a single goal: predicting which individuals were most likely to pose a threat to the Party's interests.

In the cities, Chen started by distributing data collection forms like the one police handed to Tahir. The more difficult and more urgent effort came in the countryside, where resistance to the Party was strongest. In Tibet, Chen had ordered groups of Party members from the cities to live temporarily in villages, where they delivered government dictates and conducted "gratitude education" to teach locals how to appreciate life under Party rule. Xinjiang had already begun copying the practice before Chen took over there. Now he modified it, tasking the visitors with collecting intelligence on their hosts. He sent more than a million people (most carrying gifts like electric kettles or cooking oil, and most, though not all, Han Chinese) to rural areas scattered around the region, where they invited themselves into Uyghur and Kazakh homes and portrayed themselves as "big brothers" or "big sisters."

In the course of investigating the "family" visit program, Darren Byler, an anthropologist at the University of Washington, discovered a handbook for "relatives" conducting visits in the Kashgar area. It started with a set of basic, mostly self-evident instructions on how to initiate a visit, the inclusion of which spoke to the disdain Han officials typically displayed in their interactions with Uyghur families:

1. Knock before entering.
2. Greet people when you see them.
3. Be polite when stepping through the door.
4. Behave in a decent manner.
5. Hug the children.
6. Be respectful to the elderly.
7. Accept objects with two hands.

8. Say thanks after being served.

9. Avoid imposing on them.

10. Say goodbye when leaving.

The officials were tasked with collecting the same information as the form Tahir received, but they were also encouraged to look for signs of separatist sentiment. The manual told them not to jump straight into interrogations but rather to find a natural place in the conversation to slip in pertinent questions and to expect to conduct two or more visits before a family would start to reveal what they really thought. It encouraged the big brothers and sisters to look out for hints of potential problems: family members who seemed flustered or evasive, a vehicle that didn't belong to the family parked outside, items in the house "obviously not in keeping" with their income and social status, a lot of knives or axes, a lack of interest in regular TV programs, and religious decorations. It recommended using playtime to put questions to the children because "children don't lie."

Some of the methods visiting officials used weren't included in the handbook. If they thought they were dealing with a particularly deceitful family, participants later told Byler, they might try to trick its members into revealing their true feelings. They would offer the husband a cigarette or beer, extend a hand in greeting to a family member of the opposite sex (a taboo), or bring ground meat over and suggest everyone make dumplings together. If the family didn't accept the beer, or recoiled from the offered hand, or inquired whether the meat was halal, then it was a sign of an unhealthy, excessively traditional mindset. "All of this was valuable evidence," Byler wrote. "Everything that could be detected would be recorded."

Once the intelligence was gathered, the police needed a way to weaponize it. For that, Chen turned to the integrated joint-operations platform.

The platform made a brief appearance in the public eye in 2015, when the chief engineer of China Electronics Technology Group Corporation, or CETC, one of the country's biggest state-owned military contractors, told Bloomberg News about a "united information environment" the company was building to draw portraits of terrorist suspects and flag unusual behavior to police. Years later, the human rights organization Human Rights Watch used government and company records to show that the data-management platform being used in Xinjiang had been furnished to local police by a subsidiary of CETC and was more or less the same terrorist-predicting system described to Bloomberg.

China borrowed the idea of "integrated joint operations" from the US military. Switching their attention from the Cold War to the War on Terror in the early 2000s, American military commanders developed new methods for coordinating operations among the various branches in order to confront the more nimble, unpredictable enemies it faced in Iraq and Afghanistan. In discussing modern warfare, US and Chinese military experts both refer to the same impenetrable acronym, C4ISR, which stands for "command, control, communications, computers, intelligence, surveillance, and reconnaissance." It refers to a system-of-systems that ties together human decision-makers ("command and control" in military speak) with communications equipment, high-powered computers, intelligence gathering, and digital surveillance and reconnaissance into a single, efficient counterinsurgency apparatus. CETC's platform in Xinjiang drew from the same idea: a mishmash of surveillance data and human intelligence gathered from around the region would flow into a centralized database, where police and officials could access and use it to identify potential threats.

Government procurement notices show police in Xinjiang began installing the platform in August 2016, the same month Chen Quanguo arrived. A smartphone app that police used to interact with it, reverse-engineered by Human Rights Watch, showed that the data came from a web of sources that extended beyond surveillance cameras and human intelligence gathering. Information from security checkpoints, visitor management centers at residential compounds, and Wi-Fi "sniffers" that detect the unique ID numbers of smartphones and computers all flowed into the platform, along with information about mail deliveries, electricity use, and gas station visits. The app also encouraged police to collect information by hand from people they encountered, including car license plate numbers, bank accounts, names and IDs of family members, and social media accounts, and to note the presence of "suspicious" software on smartphones. All of this was linked to biometric markers like those the Urumqi police collected from Tahir and Marhaba during their visit to the basement.

How the platform processed this ocean of data was a black box, but one of its most important results was a ranking of people according to the level of threat they posed to social order. In 2019, the International Consortium of Investigative Journalists obtained an internal Xinjiang police notice that showed that the platform generated a roster of more than 24,000 "suspicious persons" over the course of one week in the summer two years earlier. Some potential causes of suspicion seemed justifiable in the context of counterterrorism, at least on the surface. Included in that category were using a mismatched ID, spreading Wahhabism, and knowing how to make explosives. Others spanned a range from unfair to capricious. Among those: collecting money for mosques "with enthusiasm," moving into a locale, moving out of a locale, returning home after being away a long time, returning from abroad, being connected to someone abroad, and "for no apparent reason, being unwilling to enjoy policies that benefit the people or failing to participate in activities organized by the government or the Party."

When someone on the suspicious-person list passed a checkpoint, the platform sent a color-coded alert through the app to nearby police. For those on the lower rungs of suspicion—for instance, the relatives of someone who had been detained—the app issued a yellow alert that prompted police to stop the person and gather more information or keep them for interrogation. People on the higher rungs, such as those who had been jailed for participating in the 2009 Urumqi riots, elicited a red alert and were to be immediately taken into custody.

If the Party's sole aim had been to prevent terrorism, all this effort would have been a waste. Research by data scientists shows that predicting terrorist attacks with reasonable accuracy is, if not impossible, then very close to it. That's because even in regions where extremist ideas are popular, only a tiny proportion of the population—a fraction of 1 percent—cross the line into outright terrorism. Any predictive algorithm fed on such a minuscule amount of data is bound to fail. Data about activities adjacent to terrorism—the kind the Xinjiang platform was designed to collect—doesn't solve the problem, no matter how plentiful it might be. "You need yeast to make bread," one expert in counterterrorism told Bloomberg in response to CETC's prediction claims. "You can't make up for a lack of yeast by adding more flour."

It would soon become clear, however, that Chen had something more sweeping in mind than forecasting terror attacks.

◉

To understand what Chen Quanguo had planned, we first have to take a brief trip back to 2015, when local officials in Xinjiang launched a pilot program to apply to resistant Uyghurs the tactics developed to reprogram Falun Gong members.

Rather than send radicalized Uyghurs to prison, the officials instead enlisted state-sanctioned religious leaders to meet with them face-to-face. Using a mix of religious instruction and psychological counseling, the officials said, the religious leaders were able to inculcate their targets with a correct understanding of Islam, the law, and patriotism. At the end, they said, the reformed individual would swear on the Chinese constitution to put the nation before their religious community.

The experiment was such a success that Beijing-based news organization Phoenix New Media featured it in a multipart series on Xinjiang. The story, illustrated with stock photos of Uyghurs smiling and dancing, quoted an official marveling at what just twenty days of meetings could accomplish. Educated about the violence of recent attacks, he said, "some people burst in tears on the spot, realizing that extremist ideas had brought them to this point."

Officials in Xinjiang began building dedicated "transformation through education" centers to reform Muslims they saw as especially fervent. By the time Chen arrived in late 2016, a handful of the facilities had already been built. Chen oversaw plans to expand construction. By the following spring, cities and villages across Xinjiang were building new centers at a frenzied pace. Government bid tenders and budget documents show the renovation and construction bill for the camps in the first year ran in excess of $100 million.

Government documents would later show a clear link between the surveillance platform and the construction boom. Among the 24,000 people that the ICIJ police notice said were flagged as suspicious during that one week in the summer of 2017, two-thirds were detained by police. A few hundred were formally arrested and sent to prison. The other 15,000 were shipped off to one of Chen's new facilities.

Some of the projects involved retrofitting vocational schools with new security fences and camera systems. Other facilities were built from scratch, seeming to pop up overnight in rural fields and on the outskirts of cities. The facilities were listed in bid documents as "training and education centers," but it wasn't education bureaus building them. Instead, the procurement notices came from police and judicial bureaus—the agencies in charge of the country's security apparatus.

Word of the facilities began to circulate outside China in the latter half of 2017 as Uyghurs living abroad relayed stories they'd heard about relatives being taken away. Chinese officials initially denied the buildings' existence. Later, as reports proliferated of more Uyghurs disappearing, the government described them as vocational boarding schools where people who had been "incited, coerced or induced into participating in terrorist or extremist activities" and those who "posed a real danger but did not cause actual harm" were being invited to improve their lives by studying Mandarin and learning new skills. Officials said attendance was voluntary.

One facility we discovered toward the end of 2017 suggested otherwise. Located down a dirt road squeezed by dense clusters of trees on the outskirts of Kashgar, it had been described in plans submitted to contractors earlier that year as a "legal education center." It looked unlike any school we'd ever seen. Guard towers marked out the corners, connected by twenty-foot walls painted white and topped with razor wire. The walls enclosed three rows of identical white buildings, each four stories tall with barred windows. A small police station with flashing red, white, and blue lights sat to the left of the central entrance, which was large enough to fit a bus. Officers armed with shotguns milled about outside, eyeing groups of Uyghurs who had gathered on the other side of the road to inquire about family members inside.

On the wall to the right of the entrance, a slogan proclaimed in thick red characters: "All ethnic groups should gather in a tight embrace, like the seeds of the pomegranate." Pomegranates, the ruby-colored fruit with deep red juice cloistered inside bundled clusters of seeds, had been adopted by the Communist Party as a cheerful symbol of (hoped for) social harmony in Xinjiang. In this instance, the fruit felt like a darker metaphor, one that evoked detainees crammed together in a cell.

Driving past the slogan in a taxi, we spotted a group of men wearing office attire and badges standing not far from the police station. We got out of the car and asked what sort of school required such high levels of security. "It's not safe for you to be asking such questions," one of the men said. "You should leave now." Not wanting to cause trouble for our driver, a local Uyghur, we decided to take the advice and go.

After our visit, satellite images showed that the facility continued to grow in size and severity. The original plans had called for "teaching buildings" totaling 250,000 square feet, the equivalent of five American football fields. Over the next few months, construction crews would add an immense parking lot, dorms, more walls and guard towers, and 135,000 square feet of detention and custody buildings.

The camps looked like enlarged versions of the Reeducation Through Labor camps that Falun Gong practitioners had been sent to in Henan and that Tahir Hamut had endured in his youth. A cache of procurement documents collected by the French newswire Agence France-Press offered a hint to what they were like inside. The documents, copied by an AFP reporter just before government censors began mass-deleting them, requested haunting lists of equipment. One camp in Hotan, in southern Xinjiang, asked for 2,768 police batons, 550 electric cattle prods, 1,367 pairs of handcuffs, and 2,792 cans of pepper spray. Others sought suppliers for infrared monitoring systems, razor wire, phone surveillance systems, riot shields, helmets, tear gas, net guns, stun guns, spears, billy clubs, spiked clubs called "wolf's teeth," and tiger chairs like the one Tahir had seen in the police station basement. In Urumqi, officials issued an emergency request to provide staff members at one facility with Tasers. They argued that nonlethal weapons would lower the possibility of serious injury "in some situations where it is not necessary to use standard firearms."

As the year wore on, it started to become apparent what sort of education Chen was delivering. After quiet lobbying from the government of Kazakhstan, a small number of ethnic Kazakhs held in the camps were allowed to escape across the border and began recounting their experiences. One former detainee described being bound to a chair for up to nine hours at a time and interrogated about links to religious groups abroad. Afterward, he and other inmates would be roused at 5:00 A.M. and forced to go on forty-five-minute runs, shouting, "The Communist Party is good!" Breakfast was bread and barely flavored soup. The rest of the day was taken up by political study, which involved reading Communist Party documents, watching videos of Xi Jinping, and singing patriotic songs. They were told to not pray or fast during Ramadan.

A Kazakh woman named Sayragul Sauytbay said she'd been forced to work in camps training their "political educators." She described the facility to the Canadian newspaper *The Globe and Mail* as "a prison in the mountains" where every activity, even using the toilet, was monitored. "People didn't dare to speak even a single word out loud. Everyone was silent, endlessly mute, because we were all afraid of accidentally saying something wrong." Some former detainees said they were tortured or forced to eat pork. Those claims were impossible to prove, but others released later from different camps recalled similar treatment. Several who went into the camps with health problems, in particular the elderly, died while inside, their bodies returned to their families with little or no explanation.

Across Xinjiang, Uyghur towns and Uyghur-dominated neighborhoods in cities took on a ghostly aspect. With each passing week, more men disappeared into the camps. Stores and restaurants began to close, and bazaars that once thrummed with the clamor of haggling shoppers quieted to a murmur. Uyghurs living abroad swapped news they'd heard through WeChat of relatives being taken away, until eventually people back home cut off communication, afraid to say anything on the app that might trigger the platform.

When Chen launched the sweep of "suspicious" people in early 2017, he had ordered police and paramilitary troops to "round up everyone who should be rounded up." With the government refusing to say how many people the camps held, Adrian Zenz, a German researcher with experience digging through Chinese government websites, set about calculating an independent estimate. Based partly on a document leaked to a Japanese news organization, he offered a "speculative" range of between several hundred thousand and just over a million—close to a tenth of Xinjiang's Muslim population. As more information seeped out of the region in the following years, he would revise it higher.

◉

As speculation about Chen's camps continued to grow, grave questions arose around what the Party hoped to accomplish. "This is a horrendous situation that makes a mockery of the Party's claim that it is pursuing the 'rule of law,'" wrote Jerome Cohen, a venerable scholar of Chinese law at New York University. "It invites comparisons with the early years of Hitler's attack on the Jews." Privately, some overseas Uyghurs worried that Beijing might be about to unleash a second Holocaust. Listening to the Party talk about Xinjiang, it was easy to understand their anxiety.

Echoing Third Reich rhetoric, authorities in Xinjiang had begun to use the language of disease to portray Uyghurs they saw as recalcitrant. The Xinjiang branch of the Communist Youth League described people sent to the camps as having been "infected" with extremist ideas and in need of treatment. Officials in the southern Xinjiang city of Hotan issued a document instructing officials to send anyone they found afflicted with "an ideological 'virus'" with haste into the "residential care" of a reeducation facility.

As ominous as this language was, and as shocking as the camps were, a repeat of the Holocaust seemed unlikely. China's government was savvy enough to know it couldn't get away with mass murder of a religious minority in the twenty-first century. The stain of such a crime would destroy Beijing's ambitions to build China into a respected global power. Nor would killing off the Uyghurs fit with the Party's decades of propaganda touting its concern for the welfare of ethnic minorities. Indeed, a deeper look into the country's debate about ethnic policy suggested that Chinese leaders had a different type of solution in mind.

Though officially the Party still adhered to the Soviet model for managing ethnic minority populations, it had quietly started to change its thinking. The shift began in the early 2010s when a group of Party intellectuals began to attack the Soviet model as a threat to social unity. They argued that special treatment given to minorities had engendered resentment among Han Chinese, which appeared to have intensified after the Urumqi riots in 2009 and similar unrest in Lhasa the year before. In 2011, two members of the group wrote a paper calling for a "second-generation" ethnic policy loosely inspired by the American "melting pot" ideal, which, they argued, had helped the United States "maintain national unity and develop vitality and social order." The paper encouraged the Party to eliminate special treatment for minorities as a way to "strengthen the sense of being Chinese while weakening the ethnic identities that separate Han from the minorities."

One of the architects of this new vision was a counterterrorism expert named Hu Lianhe. Around the same time Chen Quanguo moved from Lhasa to Urumqi, Hu was also sent to Xinjiang to help lead an agency tasked with managing ethnic affairs—a signal of Xi Jinping's support for his ideas. Hu stayed out of the spotlight, making it difficult to know what he was doing in his new role. Nevertheless, a 2010 essay he wrote for the official newspaper of the Beijing city government hinted at his approach. The Party needed to see its quest for a stable society as "a comprehensive systems engineering project," he wrote, referencing a field of study that had enormous influence on the Party's approach to surveillance (covered more in Chapter 3). Stability could best be achieved, he continued, by "standardizing people's behavior and liberating them in order to establish a beneficial order." For Hu, an avowed nationalist, it went without saying that the behavioral standard would be set by the majority Han Chinese. And in the case of Xinjiang's Muslims, the liberation would be from the constraints of their own culture.

The notion of standardizing behavior reflected a core conviction within the Party that conditioning was more expedient than persuasion. John Garnaut, an advisor to Australian prime minister Malcolm Turnbull who had previously worked for years as a foreign correspondent in Beijing, noted in an internal presentation to Australian government officials in 2017 that Party leaders had long believed they could break people down through the imposition of total control and thereby "condition the human mind in the same way that Pavlov had learned to condition dogs in a Moscow laboratory." In his time, Mao cast writers and artists in the role of the dog trainers, enamored of their collective power to cultivate beliefs and behaviors on a mass scale. In that, Garnaut noted, the Chinese leader shared a conviction with Joseph Stalin, who in an address in 1932 praised writers as "engineers of the human soul."

But literary and artistic propaganda was just one of the tools the Party used to break down opposition. They also used more direct methods. This first became evident to the outside world during the Korean War, when reports circulated of American prisoners of war confessing to horrendous crimes while being held in Chinese prison camps. The confessions came after the POWs had been subjected to sleep deprivation, solitary confinement, and round-the-clock propaganda. Chinese officials referred to the process as *xinao*, or "washing the brain." Over time, it gave birth to the English term "brainwashing."

In Xinjiang, Chen and Hu favored the latter approach. As the campaign unfolded, local officials openly described the camps as "washing clean the brains" of detainees. By breaking Uyghurs down and rebuilding their sense of self, the Party was trying to eliminate that part of their souls that compelled them to resist. Rather than eradicate Uyghurs, it was attempting to reprogram them.

◉

Much of this remained unknown to Tahir Hamut in the summer of 2017, but he knew enough to realize his daughters risked losing their futures if they stayed in Xinjiang.

Upon learning that they would have to turn in the family's passports, Tahir and Marhaba settled on the only plan that seemed likely to extricate them from Chen's tightening grip: to fake a medical condition for Aséna that required treatment in the United States. Two years earlier, in order to prepare Aséna to study abroad, they had invented an ear condition that got her out of school for a year so she could spend more time improving her English. This time it would be much harder to pull off, but it was the best solution they could come up with.

Searching online, Tahir had found stories of Chinese children going to the United States to get treatment for epilepsy. It was an invisible condition, which meant they would only need medical records attesting that Aséna had it. The next day, as he went to hand in the passports at the police station, Tahir told the officer that his daughter had displayed symptoms of epilepsy and said the American visas in their passports were there because they had intended to seek care for her in the United States.

The officer said he still had to take the passports, but they could apply to get them back in July. That gave them two weeks to gather the documents.

Inventing a medical condition was not easy, but it was possible with enough money and the right connections. Carting gifts and cash, Tahir started calling in a lifetime of favors. He wrangled a fake electroencephalogram, then found someone at a local hospital to put an official stamp on fake medical records that would show Aséna had made regular visits. In the end, it cost him close to $10,000. It was a significant sum of money in Xinjiang—money they had planned to help get themselves settled in the United States—but there was no other choice. On July 10, he handed the documents over to the police.

A week later the police told them new orders had come down: no family that had traveled abroad would get their passports back. Tahir called a contact with the Ministry of State Security (MSS) to see if there was anything they could do. After all that effort, there must be someone who could be persuaded to help them for the right price. The MSS official said he couldn't help. The decision had been made.

Tahir slipped into a despondent limbo. With his staff having disappeared and most of his contracts canceled, he shut down his TV production company. The local police still needed to periodically scan the company's QR code, so he gave them the key to the office and told them to let themselves in. To occupy his time and work off anxiety, he took to running laps around a nearby basketball court—twenty or thirty each day. Otherwise, he read books and watched movies. Sometimes he walked around the neighborhood, talking briefly with people he recognized, but conversations soon grew cruelly monotonous. All anyone talked about was who had disappeared.

By July, the surveillance state Chen had built now hovered over Uyghurs like an apparition. At any moment it could materialize out of the dark and drag people away into the unknown. Police had set up desks on sidewalks where they would order pedestrians to hand over their smartphones, then plug them into scanning devices called "Anti-Terrorism Swords" that searched for more than 53,000 identifiers of Islamic or political activity. Anyone whose phone had a copy of the Koran, encrypted chat apps like WhatsApp, or a virtual private network for getting around the country's internet filters would be taken in for interrogation. Even photos of Turkish film characters were enough to get someone dragged into a police station.

Homes weren't much safer. Police had started making daily visits to some families to scan their QR codes and search for unapproved guests. Sometimes they ran through the rooms, examining bookshelves and rummaging through cupboards in a search for religious material. People gave away or hid their Korans to avoid trouble. Marhaba grew paranoid that the QR code had a hidden listening device. Tahir couldn't persuade her otherwise, even though it was printed on paper. And even if he was right, he couldn't say for sure there wasn't a microphone lurking somewhere else.

The psychological strain started to take its toll on Marhaba. Her patience worn thin by incessant ID checks and tightening restrictions, she began challenging police who stopped her on the street, asking them to justify their crushing scrutiny of Uyghurs. Tahir and his daughters both worried that one day she would go too far and get taken away.

Tahir had to contend with another worry. After spending so much money on travel, and on creating Aséna's "epilepsy," the family's savings were dwindling. Without any work, Tahir worried they'd soon run out of money. They sold the house and rented a smaller place. The QR code came with them. In the new place, Tahir stopped shaving and walked around most of the day in shorts and slippers, even outside. The rest of the family grew concerned. They'd been hearing stories from the neighborhood of previously healthy people developing depression, even heart problems, as a result of the pressure. If Tahir's mood continued its downward spiral, they worried, his body might eventually follow.

Then came a new flicker of hope. In early August, Tahir called the police to ask about retrieving Aséna's medical documents.

"There's a new situation," the officer said. A window had opened for people with special circumstances to apply to get their passports back. "But it's already mid-August; summer vacation is almost over. Will you have enough time to go and come back before school starts again?"

Springing to life, Tahir told the officer they'd make it work.

The family reapplied to retrieve their passports, then started the waiting game again. When no news had arrived after ten days, Marhaba, convinced they would be denied again, went to visit her family in Ili, in northern Xinjiang. Tahir stayed back with the girls.

The next morning, Tahir and the girls were sleeping on the couch when the phone rang. It was Marhaba calling to say she'd gotten another call from the police—this time telling her their passports were ready to pick up.

Tahir laughed loudly enough to wake his daughters. The three of them danced together briefly in front of the couch, then Tahir rushed downstairs to the Buick. Aséna warned her father not to get pulled over. "Dad, be careful. We've won," she said. "Don't rush."

Arriving at a new government building where several departments had been centralized, Tahir rushed into the lobby and scanned a row of service windows until he saw the one marked "Public Security Bureau." He walked to the window and handed over his ID card. When the policewoman came back, she was only carrying two passports, his and Marhaba's. When he'd turned in the family's passports, the police had told him to keep Almila's at home but asked to be given Aséna's. Tahir told the police officer there should be three.

"All I found under your name are these two," she said.

Tahir felt a rush of panic. "We're going to the United States to get treatment for my daughter. How is it possible that her passport is not there?"

She insisted there was only the pair.

Tahir stayed as calm and polite as possible. "Can you please check one more time?"

The police officer looked at a document lying on the desk in front of her. It was a list of people whose passports were approved for return. As she scanned it, Tahir saw it had been stamped by six departments: the local police station, the local Ministry of State Security office, the Tianshan District PSB, the Urumqi Municipal PSB, the PSB Foreign Affairs Office, and the Xinjiang regional Public Security Office. It was surprising that anyone's application could make it through that gauntlet of approvals.

"Oh, you're right," the police officer said. "It *is* three."

She fished out Aséna's passport, handed it to Tahir, and had him sign a form to confirm receipt.

Tahir wanted to get the passports out of that building as quickly as possible, but he couldn't resist sneaking another look at the names on the passport-return list before he left. There were fifty or sixty altogether, most of them Kazakh. Only a few were Uyghur. He turned and walked out as quickly as he could without running.

Outside, Tahir called Marhaba and told her to get back to Urumqi as soon as possible. They called their travel agent and bought new tickets for a flight that would leave two days later. The next day they started packing. By sheer luck, the money from their apartment sale had just arrived in their bank account. They could take only what they could carry on the plane, and would need to leave behind anything sensitive that might get them stopped leaving China. That meant nearly all of their books and years of video footage. To be safe, they also decided to abandon most of the family's pictures, including those from Tahir's days as a student leader in 1989.

When the taxi came, Tahir and Marhaba warned their daughters not to cry. If the driver turned out to be Han and saw them with tears in their eyes, he might get suspicious and tell the police.

At the airport, they unloaded their bags from the taxi and made their way to the security checkpoint. A guard motioned Tahir into a special lane for extra screening equipped with a full-body scanner. Marhaba took the girls and most of the luggage and went through a normal entrance. Seeing them with their bags, a police officer walked up to Aséna and Almila. "So much luggage. Where are you going?" he asked. Even after whittling down their possessions to almost nothing, had they still brought too much? Everyone had rehearsed what they would say if they got stopped. The girls knew they couldn't say anything about going abroad.

"We're going to Beijing for vacation," Aséna said.

Marhaba picked up the script. Eid al-Fitr, the celebration of the end of Ramadan, was coming up, she noted. "The girls like to eat and they don't have the right food in Beijing, so we're bringing it with us," she said. "Almost all of it is food."

The police officer looked at the girls, nodded, and waved them on. An hour later, their plane was taxiing to the runway for the four-hour flight to Beijing. As the plane picked up speed and lifted off, they watched Urumqi and the jagged peaks of the Tianshan Mountains fall away beneath them. Tahir allowed himself a sigh of relief, but only for a moment. They still had more security checks to pass.

The family stayed overnight in Beijing, then woke early for their flight to the United States. Standing in line at the border control area at Beijing Capital International Airport, Tahir was tense. With the word "Uyghur" stamped in their passports, they knew to expect a second look, and maybe a third or fourth, from the woman in the blue police uniform on the other side of the plexiglass. Others might be watching through the cameras mounted on the divider behind her.

When it was his turn, Tahir handed his passport through a cutout in the plexiglass as Marhaba and the girls waited in line behind him. The woman swiped the passport through the scanner, leaned in close to look at her computer screen, then picked up the phone. Moments later, a man in a suit walked over and exchanged a few words with the woman, too softly to hear.

Tahir felt anxiety start to gather in his chest when the man in the suit suddenly laughed, and the two leaned in close to look at the woman's computer screen. The man said a few more words to the woman, then walked away, never having once looked at Tahir. With two thuds, the woman stamped Tahir's passport and boarding pass, then handed them back. Marhaba and the girls passed through after him without so much as a question.

Disembarking for a layover in Boston, the family experienced a new level of wonder. The first things they noticed were the smells: perfume from the duty-free shop, freshly baked bread, Starbucks coffee—beckoning aromas that conjured wealth and well-being. Impatient to immerse themselves, Aséna and Almila sprinted over to the Starbucks. Some of Aséna's better-traveled friends had posted pictures on WeChat of themselves smiling with cups bearing the famous green mermaid logo held close to their faces. It seemed amazing, almost mythical, and now here one was, right in front of them. The girls asked Tahir to buy them croissants. As they sat eating the buttery pastries, they marveled at the parade of travelers strolling past: Black, white, Brown, yellow, some fat and some skinny, some buttoned up and others scantily clad. It was like something out of a movie.

As the family got settled in the United States, it gradually dawned on Tahir that he was one of the last prominent Uyghur intellectuals to get out of Xinjiang before Chen slammed the doors shut. Every week seemed to bring news of another scholar or musician or poet gone missing. Most of them, like Tahir, had worked at least partly within the establishment, but that provided them with no protection. Tahir realized he had been smart, or lucky, or some combination of both to have started making plans to escape early on in the crackdown, before Chen's surveillance machine was fully up and running. Soon, though, he would also realize that no Uyghurs could fully escape it, even those who made it out of China.

PART II

BACK TO THE FUTURE

3

MAN AND MACHINE

Almost four decades before Tahir fled to the United States to try to escape the Chinese surveillance state, one of its progenitors found himself at the Port of Los Angeles surrounded by a pack of reporters as he prepared to travel in the opposite direction.

Qian Xuesen (or Tsien Hsueh-shen, as the newspapers Romanized it at the time) was a professor of jet propulsion at the California Institute of Technology and a protégé of the legendary mathematician Theodore von Kármán. He was also, along with Kármán, one of the architects of the American military's long-range missile program. Since 1951, he had been out of the public eye, forbidden by federal authorities from leaving the boundaries of Los Angeles County. This was his first time talking to the American press in years. It would also be his last.

A scattering of clouds floated overhead as Qian and his family faced the gaggle on a dock dividing the harbor's western and eastern basins. With cameras flashing, the engineer stood straight-backed near the gangway in a crisp dark suit and tightly knotted tie, his wife and two children by his side. His facial expression, like his clothing, was impeccably arranged, eyes calm and mouth slightly upturned in a half-smile that projected a guarded confidence. The SS *President Cleveland,* a 600-foot steamship built to carry troops during World War II and since repurposed to carry civilian passengers, sat waiting to carry them first to Yokohama and then to Hong Kong. From there, Qian planned to cross the border into the People's Republic of China, established barely more than half a decade earlier following a bitter civil war.

The reporters had flocked to the port to document what they believed to be the end of a long, confusing episode in the United States' fight to rid itself of Communist influences—one that had left Kármán and several other prominent figures in the booming field of American aerospace feeling bruised and frustrated. In fact, they were there to witness the start of a new era in Chinese engineering that would not only equip the young Communist state with its own missile and space programs but also pave a pathway for Xi Jinping's China Solution.

The role Qian would eventually play in propelling China into a technological and ideological clash with the United States seems almost fated in retrospect. Born in Hangzhou in 1911, the year China's last dynasty crumbled, he had traveled to the United States on a scholarship to study aeronautics and quickly impressed professors with his precision and imagination. The US military granted him clearance to work on classified projects during World War II, despite his not being an American citizen, after Kármán recommended him to the Army Air Forces as an "undisputed genius." At age thirty-seven, he was named founding director of a new jet propulsion center at the California Institute of Technology funded by the Guggenheim family.

Not long after, his career plummeted back to earth. With Wisconsin senator Joseph McCarthy deep into his campaign to bleach any vestige of Communism out of American politics, federal agents visited Qian at his Caltech office in June 1950 saying they had seen his name on a list of Communist Party members dating to his days as a grad student. Despite Qian's denials, the military revoked his security clearance. When the engineer, humiliated and unable to continue his classified work, tried to travel back to China with his family, customs officials seized his luggage and accused him of trying to smuggle classified documents to Beijing. Qian spent two weeks in a cell, then the next several years under federal surveillance.

With the FBI tracking his activities, Qian spent much of his time huddled in his home in Los Angeles, immersing himself in a new area of study built around revolutionary insights into the relationship between information and control. Known as cybernetics, the field was, as scholar Thomas Rid would later describe it, "a veritable ideology of machines." It would have profound (if now largely forgotten) impacts on computing, telecommunications, neuroscience, military strategy, artificial intelligence, and dozens of other disciplines of critical importance in the twenty-first century. Qian saw in it a way to reimagine how engineers approached complex problems, which he described in a book that he published in 1954, and which itself would prove influential.

The year after the book's launch, Beijing learned that Qian had grown disillusioned with the United States. The Chinese quietly negotiated with Washington for his release, reportedly in exchange for eleven American airmen captured during the Korean War. Undersecretary of the Navy Dan Kimball would later call Qian's persecution and expulsion "the stupidest thing this country ever did," saying the scientist's value to the American military was "worth five divisions anywhere."

Watching as Qian prepared to depart, one of the reporters asked if he ever planned to return to the United States. "I have no reason to come back," Qian said. His voice, high-pitched, still carried a trace of an accent despite two decades spent in California and Massachusetts. "I have thought about it for a long time. I plan to do my best to help the Chinese people build up the nation to where they can live with dignity and happiness." Perhaps hoping to hammer home to American readers what they were losing, Qian also said he wanted to correct popular perceptions that he was merely a rocket expert. "I am what is known as an applied scientist who helps engineers solve their problems," he explained. "The science of rocketry is just a small part of this field."

Shortly after arriving in Beijing, Qian set about building China's ballistic missile program almost from scratch. But, true to his word, he also applied his ideas far beyond rocketry. As his career progressed, he would use the principles of cybernetics as the launchpad for an elaborate system that blended human with machine to solve what he saw as the greatest of engineering problems: human society. The idea was audacious, as well as shot through with hubris and utopian folly. It also fired the imaginations of Communist Party leaders, who would later adopt it as the beating heart of their surveillance state. In the end, the missile scientist would indeed help bring some measure of dignity and happiness to his homeland, but plenty of infamy and misery as well.

◉

When Mao Zedong and the Communist Party came to power in 1949, they inherited a challenge that had sooner or later defeated every one of China's preceding dynasties: how to sustain rule over a large population spread over a vast territory. If conquering the empire was difficult, managing it was orders of magnitude more so.

Chinese dynasties stumbled down a wide variety of paths to collapse, but in many instances they first lost their way as a result of the same problem: breakdowns in the flow of information. The oldest complete census still in existence dates to 2 CE, when the court of the Han Dynasty—from which the country's dominant Han Chinese take their name—dispatched officials to compile a written record of all 57.7 million people then living in what is now considered the Chinese heartland. Historical records suggest Chinese emperors ordered regular censuses over the centuries that followed. But between surveys, they were typically cloistered in palaces, dependent on vast bureaucracies to tell them what was going on outside. Corrupt or incompetent officials often distorted the picture rulers received, which in turn led to paranoia and bad decisions, and sometimes to collapse.

A student of history who reportedly slept in a bed more than half covered in books, Mao was steeped in tales of emperors who had been dethroned after losing touch with what was happening outside their palaces. When he came to power, he made certain the Party had eyes everywhere. Armies of journalists for Party-run newspapers filed confidential "internal reference" reports to top leaders from every province. A 300,000-strong Ministry of Public Security (MPS) scoured the country for spies and other internal threats. Party cells in communes and urban work units tracked every aspect of residents' lives, from meals and medical care to education and entertainment.

Nevertheless, it didn't take the Party long to stumble into a catastrophic failure of its own. Less than a decade after establishing the People's Republic, Mao insisted on implementing the Great Leap Forward, a series of delusional industrial policies that led directly to the Great Chinese Famine. Still euphemistically referred to inside China as the "three years of difficulty," the famine took hold as rural communes, some mired in drought, sent most of their grain to Beijing to satisfy impossible production quotas. Author Yang Jisheng, in a chilling history of the disaster, quotes a journalist who rode a bus through rural Henan province as the dying began: "Looking out the window, I could see one corpse after another in the ditches along the roadway, but no one on the bus dared to talk about the starvation." Yang found twenty recorded cases of cannibalism just in Henan, and rumors of many more. The final death toll is estimated at around 30 million people.

As the famine began to take hold, leaders in Beijing should have known what was unfolding. But rather than reflect the truth, the Party's informers, like their predecessors over the course of history, told Mao what they thought he wanted to hear. Local officials suppressed reports of starvation, and newspapers staged photos of grain crops so dense that children could stand on top of them. Networks of domestic agents run by the MPS, meanwhile, were hobbled by bureaucratic infighting, inexperience, and incompetence, which on occasion led to them spying on each other without knowing it.

The economist Amartya Sen famously observed that a famine has never occurred in a country with a functioning democratic system. A free press and the prospect of election defeat, he argued, are enough to scare leaders in democracies into taking action to head off mass starvation before it happens. In China, though, censorship and propaganda made it impossible for regular people and officials to grasp the nationwide nature of the disaster. "While the famine was going on, there was also a starving of information," Sen said in a 2001 interview. The censorship "had the effect of hoodwinking not only the public but ultimately hoodwinking the state."

The Party's Central Committee didn't officially accept the existence of food shortages until the summer of 1959, several months into the crisis. Even then, leaders refused to believe production numbers had been faked. "The peculiar feature of this year is the big increase in output combined with a big food shortage," remarked one top Party official. Mao's elaborate intelligence-gathering machinery had been short-circuited by flaws in the very political system it was meant to serve.

Remarkably, the Communist Party held on to power even as Mao ushered in another crisis with the Cultural Revolution. For a decade beginning in 1966, Mao defended himself against internal critics of his earlier failures by creating a cult of personality and riding a wave of adulation from gangs of Red Guards, whom he sent on a hallucinatory, murderous mission to rid the country of malign political influences. After Mao's death in 1976, in the wake of another 2 to 3 million people lost through killings and suicide, the Party would look for new, less destructive ways to answer their late leader's famous exhortation to "serve the people."

Qian Xuesen was a fraught figure in this new age of reform. Some in the country's scientific community held him partly responsible for the great famine. Despite having zero formal training in agriculture, Qian had published an article in 1958 that claimed China could increase crop yields twentyfold with sufficient additions of manure and labor. Many Chinese intellectuals believed that Qian's paper had bolstered Mao's conviction to carry through with the Great Leap Forward.

But Qian had also built the country's missile program. In 1966 he presided with one of the Party's top military leaders over its first nuclear missile test, and four years later he helped launch its first satellite. Soon he would begin to argue that the ideas he had applied in shepherding these advances could enable the Party to do the same with Chinese society. His was hardly the only voice vying to be heard in the atmosphere of openness that unfolded following Mao's exit, but his achievements ensured it would get heard at the highest levels in Beijing.

◉

Many of Qian's ideas traced back to one particular book that captured his attention as he had sat cloistered in his Los Angeles study during his days under FBI watch: *Cybernetics: Or Control and Communication in the Animal and the Machine*, by the American mathematician and former child prodigy Norbert Wiener. Published in 1948, the book examined the remarkably similar ways in which complex systems, both mechanical and biological, used information to exert control.

The ideas Wiener introduced in *Cybernetics* had emerged from work he had done to improve anti-aircraft targeting systems used against German fighter planes during World War II. He theorized that it was possible to build models that could project the future path of an aircraft based on a mathematical analysis of its past behavior. Since pilots determined the aircrafts' movements, the project helped convince Wiener that it was possible to use math to predict human behavior.

The question at the center of Wiener's work was how people navigate a world prone to chaos. He found his answer in feedback loops. As they interact with their environment, he observed, all animals use a constant stream of information, or feedback, about what has happened around them to build a model in their minds for what is likely to happen next. With each new piece of information they adjust the model, hopefully in ways that better predict the future, whether over the next month or the next millisecond.

Take as an example a basketball player trying to catch a pass from a teammate. Though it may not seem so to experienced players, the mechanics of snatching a ball out of the air are complex. A hundred factors can influence the ball's movement: speed, angle, spin, a path-altering brush with a defender's fingertips. The swirl of unknowns is impossible to account for with much certainty. Instead, the player relies on feedback loops to model its path in her mind. As the ball lofts through space, her eyes send continuously updated signals about its position, speed, and trajectory to her brain, which translates that data into a series of muscle twitches that adjust the position of her arms. Meanwhile, the skin on her hands sends signals about the sensation of movement through space back to the brain so it can judge whether the muscles are contracting with the right force. These bolts of data fire back and forth dozens of times with every passing moment, each loop leading to tiny adjustments in the player's perception of the ball's path and the positioning of her body until the pass hits her hands. A novice experiences the complexity of this process viscerally with each missed pass. For the veteran player, it's automatic.

Similar dynamics apply to a cat landing after a long fall and a hunter attempting to shoot a duck. They also describe the operation of certain mechanical systems. One of Wiener's favorite examples of the latter was the steering engine, a contraption developed in the late nineteenth century to ensure that the rudders on large steam-powered ships mirrored the position of the captain's wheel regardless of the weight of the vessel or the temperament of the water. To do this, the engines used an arrangement of hydraulic valves that were sensitive to friction, which automatically adjusted the position of the rudder based on the pressure of passing water. The term "cybernetics" came from the Greek word *cybernétēs*, or "steersman."

Wiener's core insight—that grasping the flow of information is critical to understanding how the world works—was revolutionary at the time. Cybernetics' analogy between self-regulation in animals and purposeful machines inspired new work in fields as diverse as anthropology and prosthetics manufacturing, and would help usher in the information age. Starting in the 1950s, cybernetics became a pop-culture phenomenon, capturing the imaginations of artists and science fiction writers (and introducing words like "cyborg" and "cyberspace" to the English language). It also had a profound effect on systems engineering, a fast-growing field concerned with the design and management of complex systems that had also grown out of weapons development efforts during World War II.

Qian Xuesen played a vital part in introducing ideas from cybernetics to systems engineering. In Qian's eyes, most engineers, overly focused on their own narrow areas of expertise, lacked the imagination to do breakthrough work. He thought cybernetics would help them evolve by giving them a framework to step back and see how changes to one part of a complex system ripple through to the others. "Looking at things in broad outline and in an organized way often leads to fruitful new avenues of approach to old problems," he wrote in the introduction to his own book, *Engineering Cybernetics*, which would come to be regarded in engineering circles as a landmark text. The book explored how to use Wiener's ideas to develop technologies for automation and build reliable systems from unreliable parts.

Pages from the first draft of *Engineering Cybernetics*, written in tiny, excruciatingly uniform handwriting, hang in a plexiglass case inside the Qian Xuesen Museum on the campus of Shanghai Jiaotong University, where Qian studied as an undergraduate. Displays above and below celebrate the results he achieved in China using the ideas he developed in his book. The centerpiece, rising up from the basement, is a full-sized three-story replica of the Dongfeng ballistic missile he built in 1965, cementing China's status as a nuclear power.

On the second floor of the museum, one of the lesser-visited exhibits displays a schematic diagram for a system Qian envisioned that aimed to solve complex economic and social problems such as persistent inflation and political corruption by integrating human knowledge with computer modeling. He called it meta-synthetic engineering.

Wiener had been wary of extending his theory to these uses. He turned down repeated requests from legendary anthropologists Margaret Mead and Gregory Bateson to apply his ideas to the solving of social problems, arguing that there wasn't sufficient good-quality data for cybernetics to have "an appreciable therapeutic effect on the present diseases of society."

Developments in the United States over the next couple of decades seemed to confirm Wiener's apprehensions. In the 1960s, the state of California invited bids from local aerospace companies to use systems engineering to inject scientific efficiency into its management of areas like transportation, criminal justice, and social welfare. The hope, Governor Pat Brown said, was to use "know-how that will get a man to the moon to get Dad to work on time." Nearly all of the efforts failed to produce improvements. Conducting a review of how they went wrong, University of California sociologist Ida R. Hoos argued the projects proved that the effectiveness of social systems is measured in values that can't be reduced to math. Hiring a systems engineer to solve malfunctioning social systems, she wrote, was like calling "a hydraulic engineer to cure an ailing heart because his specialty is pumping systems."

Word of California's ill-fated experiments appears not to have reached Qian. Or if it did, he dismissed it. In 1981, he worked with his protégé, a scientist named Song Jian, on an update to his book, which made an explicit case for applying systems engineering to social problems. "Under the conditions of socialism, a new science will eventually be born: That is social cybernetics," the pair wrote in the new preface, describing Wiener's earlier skepticism as "too conservative." It was true, they wrote, that social cybernetics wouldn't work in capitalistic societies, which in Friedrich Engels's terms were too vulnerable to the "anarchy" of market-based production. Socialistic societies were different, however. They could be designed in such a way as to be automatically self-correcting. Qian and Song, the rocket scientists, were proposing a guidance system for society based on the same cybernetic feedback concepts that missiles used to automatically home in on their targets.

Their timing was impeccable. Qian and Song completed work on the updated book just as the Communist Party was entering its most experimental phase. A brief struggle for control of the Party ended in victory for Deng Xiaoping, a pragmatist famous for repeating a saying from his home province of Sichuan that any cat, no matter its color, was good as long as it could catch mice. The wealth and power of the West convinced Party leaders to introduce market reforms and even flirt with political liberalization. At the same time, they tested out Qian's ideas for a new, more systematic model of top-down control.

The biggest test was already underway. In 1978, Song Jian had traveled to Helsinki for a conference on systems science. There he learned about the Club of Rome, a group of scientists alarmed by the growing human population, which they feared would deplete the earth's re-sources to the point of undermining economic progress. The group had developed an elaborate mathematical model that produced scenarios for managing the population and distributing resources in what it be-lieved was a scientifically optimal manner. The approach was criticized in the West for treating populations of human beings as if they were cohorts of fruit flies in a lab. Song found it an easy sell back in Beijing, where leaders had already begun to worry that the country's population was growing out of control.

While accounts differ over precisely how much of China's one-child policy is attributable to Song, Qian's protégé indisputably helped drive its design. Song and his team submitted projections to Party leaders showing that without intervention, China's population would swell to more than 4 billion—a size they predicted would result in the eviscera-tion of resources and the environment—within the next century. They calculated the country's ideal population at around 700 million and found that getting there by 2080 would require bringing the fertility rate for women down close to a single child as quickly as possible. The family-planning regime the Party imposed nationwide in 1980 allowed some couples, including ethnic minorities and farmers, to have multi-ple children, but for most the limit was applied with brutal force.

The side effects of the new policy were grim: an explosion of forced abortions and sterilizations, and, in a society that preferred male chil-dren, the abandonment or murder of untold numbers of female babies. Equally as disastrous, the planners' calculations turned out to have been wrong. Not only were the costs of a large population not as severe as Song had assumed, but the policy exacerbated a falling birth rate that would have occurred naturally as China developed, leaving the country with too few working-age adults to support a now rapidly aging society. But the discovery of that mistake wouldn't happen for decades. In the meantime, Chinese leaders regarded Song's ideas as brilliant.

Capitalizing on his momentum, Song argued for an even broader approach in an influential report to top Party officials delivered in 1984. The widespread application of systems engineering was not just important but necessary, he wrote, if Chinese society wanted to achieve its best possible future. And doing so meant embracing new advances in information technology. "Only if we fully grasp [the concepts of] information, data, systems analysis, and decision modeling, can we truly possess 'foresight and sagacity,' and generate the courage and a bold vision consistent with the flow of history." In order to control the sprawling, complex system that was Chinese society, the Party needed to build good predictive models. Building those models required collecting massive amounts of data, and emerging technologies such as the computer promised to make that easier. Channeling insights from his mentor, Song had begun to make the case for mass digital surveillance.

In the meantime, the Party's experiments with liberalization were producing mixed results. The loosening of controls had invigorated the economy, but by the late 1980s inflation was out of control, at one point pushing 30 percent. Newly exposed to the commercial and cultural products of advanced democracies, intellectuals and students were staging protests and calling for political reforms. On April 15, 1989, the death by heart attack of popular reformist leader Hu Yaobang, who had been ousted as general secretary by conservative rivals two years before, set off what would become the Tiananmen Square pro-democracy movement. Thousands of students poured into the square and refused to leave. They erected a plaster homage to the Statue of Liberty and named her the Goddess of Democracy. Other pro-democracy protests would flare up in more than 300 other cities. Deng Xiaoping imposed martial law in Beijing, but residents gathered en masse to prevent People's Liberation Army troops from entering the city.

Having loosened the reins on Chinese society, the Party began to worry it might be bucked out of the saddle. On the evening of June 3, leaders in Beijing ordered troops back into the city, authorizing them to "use any means" to clear the square. China's government has never accounted for how many people were killed by the volleys of bullets the soldiers unleashed. Estimates by survivors range from a few hundred to several thousand. Regardless of the death toll, the protests and the violence that ended them carved a wound in the Party's psyche that forced a change in its calculus. From that point on, it would continue with market reforms but end any serious experiments with political liberalization.

Qian stood ready to capitalize. On the same day as Hu Yaobang's death, he published an essay in a journal run by the Chinese Academy of Social Sciences that would later seem eerily prophetic. In it, he described Chinese society as an immense supersystem made up of economic, political, and ideological subsystems. It was folly to expect changes in one not to have ripple effects in the others, he warned. "If the development of these three facets of civilization isn't harmonized"— Party-speak for made to work smoothly without conflict—"from the point of view of systems science, it will push the entire social system from order to disorder, chaos, and collapse," he wrote. Shortly after the tanks left Beijing in June, with the Party believing it had rescued its rule from the brink of collapse, he publicly denounced the pro-democracy movement and referred to a prominent astrophysicist who had encouraged the students as the "scum of the nation."

The following year, Qian took his ideas for managing society a step further. In an article for the *Chinese Journal of Nature*, he described human societies as an example of an "open complex giant system," a category that also includes the human nervous system and galaxies like the Milky Way. These massive systems are made up of millions of subsystems that interact both with each other and with the outside world. Compared to smaller closed systems, like those used to control rockets and satellites, they are vastly more difficult to predict and control with math alone. "Not even a supercomputer is up to the task," Qian wrote, "and there won't be enough computing power in the future to do this work either." He argued that the solution was to add people (of a certain kind) to the mix. Sociologists, economists, political scientists, geologists, psychologists—experts in all fields—should be trained in systems science, armed with data, and enlisted in the building of models sophisticated enough to predict and optimize the complexities of societal change, Qian said. This "meta-synthetic" approach to social engineering, he predicted, would unite the natural and social sciences into a new discipline that would usher in the socialist dream.

As China limped into a post-Tiananmen world, accolades for Qian continued to flow. In 1991 he was given the First-Level Model Hero Prize, China's highest honor for a scientist. Around the same time, propaganda officials launched a "Learn from Qian Xuesen" movement. His ideas began to be taught at the Central Party School, the country's top training academy for political leaders in Beijing, and were credited by scholars with influencing the political theories of then-president Jiang Zemin. Later, he had an asteroid named after him.

The Party had good reason to celebrate Qian. The suddenness of the crisis the Party faced in 1989 had put many in China in mind of an old saying: "A single spark can set the prairie ablaze." Most knew the line because Mao had used it in a famous letter intended to raise morale after a massacre of communists in Shanghai had led some in the Party to doubt the prospects for revolution. Once inspirational, the metaphor had now morphed into a warning. The Party had just barely escaped being engulfed by a fire sparked by the death of one of its own leaders. Top officials realized that another spark might come from anywhere: inside or outside the Party, from home or abroad. The ideas Qian had brought to China about how to manage society offered a way not just to fight fires but possibly to prevent them from breaking out in the first place.

Signs of Qian's influence in this sphere started to become apparent in the early 2000s, when the Party instituted early versions of a "grid management" system to help police keep tighter control over urban neighborhoods. The system, which divided neighborhoods along a grid, was built to encourage a smooth flow of information and enable quick action to head off problems. Each square on the grid was assigned a manager, whose job it was to report goings-on to the police, take photos and video where necessary, and intervene when trouble appeared to be brewing. A series of efforts to build up digital infrastructure, collectively known as the "Golden Projects," brought grid management into the digital age. They also reflected Qian and Song's emphasis on the importance of collecting data in order to grasp the nature of systemic problems.

The most impactful of the projects, the Golden Shield project, focused on exploiting information to neutralize security threats. One critical component, built using cutting-edge firewall technology from the United States and Canada, was a fine-tuned system for filtering out unwanted internet content. The other key element was the construction of a computer network connecting the Ministry of Public Security with local police bureaus around the country, combined with a national online database containing the ID numbers and personal information of every adult in the country. On that foundation the Party hoped to build a surveillance system that would incorporate tracking of internet use at the individual level, closed-circuit cameras, and smart ID cards. Plans also called for the eventual incorporation of speech and facial recognition—a full fifteen years before they would be put to use in the crackdown on the Uyghurs.

In 2008, a year before his death, Qian received a home visit from the Party's then-leader, Hu Jintao. Hu was riding high at the time. Beijing was about to host its first Olympics, and Shanghai was gearing up to hold a World Expo. China's economy was pumping out growth numbers that left economists dumbfounded. The country's scientists had recently launched Chang'e 1, an uncrewed spacecraft that marked the start of a new lunar exploration program. Hu attributed much of China's success to the Party's new emphasis on "scientific development" and social stability, themes Qian had highlighted in the essay he published on the eve of the Tiananmen Square crisis.

Bowing over a frail but smiling Qian, Hu took the scientist's hand and offered him due credit. "Mr. Qian, you've made so many contributions in your scientific career. After studying them, I deeply felt their wisdom," the Chinese leader said. He recalled studying Qian's work on systems engineering at the Central Party School in the 1980s, in particular the scientist's exhortation to approach complex problems from the point of view of an entire system rather than fixating on any one issue in isolation. "That was a very original idea," Hu said.

After Qian's death, the insights he and his students had shared with the Party helped it continue to maintain control, and thrive, in ways that have surprised the world. While most Chinese people have come to realize Mao Zedong was merely human, one Chinese scientist told *Science* magazine in 2018, "To a circle of scientists in China, Qian Xuesen is now, in their mind, the new god." If Qian seemed prophetic after Tiananmen Square, however, putting his commandments into practice could be a challenge. In the Hu Jintao era, both grid management and the Golden Shield had short-circuited on several occasions, sometimes to a degree that made leaders in Beijing nervous. The Party's effort to reboot its approach to control wouldn't begin in earnest until after November 4, 2012, the day that it anointed a powerful new general secretary.

4

THE CHINA DREAM

When he strode onto the stage in the Great Hall of People to an explosion of camera flashes to deliver his first speech as the Communist Party's new leader, Xi Jinping was still a mystery to many in China. The paunchy fifty-nine-year-old with an impassive smile had been chosen by Party elders to rise to the top post and the country's presidency five years earlier but gave few clues about what he planned to do once he got there. He had caused a brief ripple during a 2009 visit to Mexico City, where he lashed out in an unexpectedly pugnacious speech at "bored foreigners with full bellies and nothing to do" who he said unfairly criticized China. Otherwise, he had hovered at the edge of the limelight, biding his time until this moment.

Over the weeks leading up to Xi's speech, the atmosphere in Beijing had grown thick with speculation about how he would handle the challenges facing the Party. Ballooning corruption under Xi's predecessors had badly damaged the Party's credibility. Meanwhile, tectonic trends in China's economy and society were altering the political landscape in ways that observers in and outside the country warned could throw the Party off balance. Almost every economist predicted that economic growth would soon slip below 6 percent—well below the 8 percent threshold many believed the Party needed to maintain to keep society in line. The Party was also struggling to contend with a strange new phenomenon online that was spreading like wildfire and demonstrated a frightening power to amplify discontent: social media.

Fifteen months earlier, anonymous messages had started circulating on Twitter calling for simultaneous protests in a dozen Chinese cities aimed at launching a "Jasmine Revolution" modeled on the Arab Spring. Word of the protests found their way onto Weibo, a Twitter-like social media platform that had accumulated 140 million users in just two years and become a sort of virtual town square for the country's educated urbanites. The few hundred protesters who showed up in Beijing and Shanghai were vastly outnumbered by police.

A more severe crisis arrived a few months later, in the summer of 2011, when two high-speed trains collided during a lightning storm outside the coastal city of Wenzhou. The accident killed 40 and left 170 injured. Images of officials directing construction crews to break up and bury some of the destroyed cars went hypersonic on Weibo. Censors struggled to keep up as users accused the government of a literal cover-up. "China today is a train traveling through a lightning storm. None of us are spectators; all of us are passengers," one anonymous Weibo user wrote in a comment that ricocheted around the Chinese internet.

The Communist Party had long been haunted by the specter of "color revolutions" like those that took down Communist governments in the former Soviet Union. Leaders in Beijing had watched with alarm through 2010 as Facebook and other Western social media platforms fueled the Arab Spring protests that engulfed autocratic regimes in much of the rest of North Africa and the Middle East. The government had already blocked Facebook and Twitter, only to be menaced by its own homegrown social media platforms.

For decades, Chinese leaders had gotten by using what foreign reporters and Western China scholars came to describe as the "muddle through" approach, cobbling together policy ideas and political messages just coherent enough to keep the engine of state capitalism humming. With the new pressures the Party was facing, few believed muddling through would be feasible for much longer. What's more, the Party faced a daunting historical reality: it was nearing the end of life expectancy for a one-party regime. Xi would wrap up the second of his two customary terms in 2022, by which time the People's Republic would have been in place for seventy-three years. Only the Soviet Union, which held together for seventy-four years before Mikhail Gorbachev's reforms led to its dissolution in 1991, had lasted longer.

In November 2012, as the audience gathered for Xi's coronation, it was clear the next generation of Chinese leaders would have to take the country in a more deliberate direction, but the Party, ever secretive, had been tight-lipped about its plans. The hope was strong among politicians, businesspeople, and China scholars in the West that the pressure and uncertainties the country was facing would nudge Xi to embrace more of the liberalism the Party had flirted with in the 1980s, before it deployed troops to crush pro-democracy demonstrations around Tiananmen Square. The Party was too lumbering and corrupt to manage further change, the reasoning went, and could only solve the country's current problems by loosening its grip.

A few close observers of Chinese politics had warned about a nationalistic bent they detected in Xi, pointing to the Mexico outburst as evidence. But many others clung to the idea that he would follow in his late father's footsteps: Xi Zhongxun had been a respected Party leader who helped Deng Xiaoping introduce market reforms in the 1980s—reason enough in some minds to expect that his son would also turn out to be a liberalizer.

When Xi walked across the vermilion carpet inside the Great Hall of the People, anticipation had morphed into intrigue. He and the other six members of the Party's new ruling Politburo Standing Committee had been scheduled to appear a full hour earlier. The delay was unusual for an event so relentlessly stage-managed, sparking speculation of a last-minute crisis. Xi stepped forward, bent his head to the microphone, and used his first words as leader of the world's largest country to cut the tension. "Sorry to keep you waiting," he said with a breezy humility that elicited surprised laughter from the audience.

In the speech that followed, Xi judged the country's present and future with an unusual candor. "In this new situation, our party faces many severe challenges, and there are many pressing problems within the Party that need to be resolved," he said, concluding with an appeal to his "friends from the press" to help China learn more about the world and vice versa. To optimistic minds scouring the event for clues about China's future, the tone of his comments felt like the preamble to a more open and humane era to come.

That impression would turn out to be mistaken. Days later, in a tone unsettlingly reminiscent of Mexico City, Xi began to lay out a nationalistic vision that placed the Party at the center of a final push to reclaim China's lost glory. He gave what would come to be known as his "China Dream" speech inside the National Museum, on the opposite side of Tiananmen Square from the Great Hall of the People, in front of an exhibit of relics from the First Opium War.

He had chosen the backdrop carefully. The three-year conflict with England over the British narcotics trade had ended in 1842 with a crushing defeat for the Qing rulers and launched a period of decline known inside China as the Century of Humiliation. "Looking back at the past, every comrade in the entire Party must keep this firmly in mind: if we are backward, we will take a beating," Xi said. But now, he continued, the Party needed to help Chinese people look forward. "We believe that realizing the great rejuvenation of the Chinese nation is the greatest Chinese dream of the Chinese nation in modern times."

Three years before Donald Trump started stitching "Make America Great Again" on red baseball caps, Xi had delivered the Chinese equivalent. Then, in the summer of 2013, a secret Communist Party communiqué smuggled out into the open offered an unfiltered view of the ideology that powered his vision.

The communiqué was the ninth issued that year. Its official title was "A Communiqué on the Current State of the Ideological Sphere." Most chose to refer to it as Document No. 9. Disseminated widely among senior Party members, it spelled out a list of ideological threats to the China Dream. Among them were Western constitutional democracy, universal values, civil society, neoliberalism, freedom of the press, and criticism of the Party's version of history. "The concept of constitutional democracy originated a long time ago, and recently the idea has been hyped ever more frequently," the document intoned, warning of those who criticized the Party's leaders for placing themselves above the country's constitution. "Their goal is to use Western constitutional democracy to undermine the Party's leadership, abolish the People's Democracy . . . and bring about a change of allegiance by bringing Western political systems to China." Officials needed to be on guard against these influences, the document said, and take every opportunity to extinguish them.

The communiqué offered just a taste of what was to come. Over the next few years, Xi would outline an ideology that wasn't merely anti-Western but a throwback to a troubled earlier era of Chinese politics. He cast the China Dream as the latest evolutionary phase of a grand historical project that began with Mao Zedong's revolution, one that gave the Communist Party a reason to reassert its primacy in all aspects of life in the country. Total surveillance would serve as the backbone of that vision, enabling the Party to anticipate the needs of the people while rooting out threats to its power from forces like those outlined in Document No. 9.

In the reform years, China had distanced itself from Mao as a political figure, transforming him into an object of kitsch. Though his portrait still hung above the Gate of Heavenly Peace, it was more common to see his visage framed in small squares of gold-colored plastic and dangling from the rearview mirrors of Beijing taxis as a charm against traffic accidents. More than just attempting to rehabilitate Mao, Xi began in some ways to emulate him. He became the "Chairman of Everything," sitting at the head of every important committee. Over time, senior officials and state media began referring to him as the "national helmsman," a nod to "Great Helmsman," the moniker Mao had taken up as he launched the Cultural Revolution.

In important respects, however, Xi was different from Mao. He was more methodical, less bombastic, and had a markedly distinct view of China's future. As sinologist Jude Blanchette writes, "Xi's vision of a tightly disciplined political order was about as far away from Mao's millenarian radicalism as could be." Xi also had access to technologies that the Party's original helmsman likely never dreamed of, and that made it possible for him to imagine a far more precise politics.

Xi seemed to grasp the importance of that advantage early on. In one of his first major speeches as president in 2013, he declared it a priority to turn China into a tech power. "An important reason that Western countries were able to hold sway over the world in modern times was that they held the advanced technology," he said. Outwardly, becoming a leader in strategically important technologies like artificial intelligence would help China compete with the United States. Inwardly, it would help the Party build a new system of control that would ensure its own well-being. The social engineering schematic that Qian Xuesen, standing on Norbert Wiener's shoulders, had developed decades earlier would provide the framework.

Technology has been a fixation of the Chinese ruling class for generations.

Every Chinese child is taught in school how a court eunuch of the Eastern Han Dynasty invented paper in the second century and how ingenious Chinese in subsequent dynasties went on to pioneer printing, gunpowder, and the compass. Carved just as deeply in the collective psyche, though, are the country's technological failures. The Qing Dynasty's inability in the early nineteenth century to match the technological progress of the newly industrialized West, a consequence of imperial arrogance and institutional inertia, is widely blamed for ushering in the Century of Humiliation. The catastrophe of Mao's pursuit of industrial self-sufficiency during the Great Leap Forward, and the famine that followed, only buttressed the sense of China as having lost, perhaps permanently, the technological moxie that underpinned its former greatness.

The notion of China as a technological has-been destined to cower in the face of Western know-how persisted into the early years of the twenty-first century. Western elites believed it at least as strongly as their Chinese counterparts, buoyed by confidence in the explosion of information technology. In the same way Western powers had exploited modern rifles, cannons, and steamships to fatally weaken the Qing rulers in the late 1800s, many in the developed world believed they could use the internet to pry loose the Party's authoritarian grip. Then-president Bill Clinton delivered the most memorable expression of this idea during a speech at Johns Hopkins University in the year 2000. At the time, Clinton was pushing for China to be admitted into the World Trade Organization but faced opposition from those who were wary of inviting an authoritarian regime into the globalization clubhouse. Clinton argued that letting China in would open the country up further to the internet and, by extension, to the ideals of freedom and rule of law. The Communist Party might try to control cyberspace, he said with a wry smile, but doing so was "like trying to nail Jello to the wall."

The punch line quickly morphed into a catchphrase among foreign policy wonks in Washington for the conviction, almost ubiquitous at the time, that the internet was an unstoppable democratizing force. The White House, like the developed world writ large, was convinced Beijing didn't know what it was getting into. For a long time, it seemed they might be right.

Over the next decade, China's government poured billions of dollars and incalculable hours into building and upgrading its system of internet filters in an effort to nail the Jello in place. Inside what has since come be known colloquially as the Great Firewall, officials nurtured the creation of what was in effect a parallel internet populated with Chinese versions of Google (Baidu), Amazon (Alibaba), and Facebook and Twitter (Weibo), each beholden and ultimately subservient to Beijing. Despite that investment and effort, however, the Party often seemed like a greyhound sprinting after a target it was destined never to catch. As soon as Chinese censors figured out how to manage message boards, the internet invented blogs. After they got a handle on blogs, along came microblogs, video sites, and chat apps. The censors were "winning the battles everywhere," Isaac Mao, one of the country's blogging pioneers, said in a 2009 interview, "but losing the war." By the time Xi was ready to take over, the Party had built the most sophisticated censorship apparatus on earth— one that largely had succeeded in controlling access to information for hundreds of millions of internet users. But the furor over Wenzhou and explosions of social media angst showed it was still struggling to pin down the gelatinous blob of human activity online.

Xi changed the status quo by switching from defense to offense. In July 2013, a few months after he assumed the presidency, he traveled to the state-funded Chinese Academy of Sciences and urged the country's top researchers to focus their collective brainpower on marshaling the country's data. "Big data is a 'free resource' for industrialized societies," he told them. "Whoever gets control of the data controls the initiative." It was the first step in a new state-led strategy to seize on technological innovations and build them into the core of the China Dream.

The outline of that strategy came into sharper relief in 2016 when Xi unveiled a national plan to develop big data, and then again a year later when he did the same for artificial intelligence. The plans followed similar technological blueprints published by the United States under Barack Obama. Melding government funding with private investment, the Party aimed to build an AI industry worth close to $150 billion and transform China into the world's leader in the technology by the year 2030.

Both the American and Chinese plans cited the enhancement of national security as motivating forces. China's differed from the United States' by emphasizing the potential to use the technologies to optimize society. One of the country's most important goals, China's AI development plan revealed, was to build a matrix of smart cities, smart courts, smart schools, smart hospitals, and smart government agencies that would help solve "hot and difficult issues in social governance" and "make social operations more safe and efficient."

◉

One of the first places the Party put AI to use was in taming dissent online. Under pressure from Beijing, the country's internet companies built hybrid filtering systems that blended human "content managers" with machine censors. New algorithms fed with mountains of data were now able to scan messages by the millions and automatically flag any that might cross the Party's red lines. Crucially, they could also scan images, PDF files, and video—the sort of painstaking task that previously had to be done by hand. The machine censors could still miss sensitive content, especially if it involved a new topic they hadn't been trained to spot. In those instances, the human censors would step in to mop up. The cat-and-mouse game continued, but the Party was getting much better at it.

Xi also expanded technological controls in the real world. Almost immediately after he came to power, the Party's top security officials worked with police and the ministry in charge of information technology to accelerate the rollout of a vast surveillance program, called Project Skynet, that required the installation of batteries of high-definition video cameras for real-time monitoring in cities across the country. Over time, police departments in some cities connected the Skynet cameras to new facial recognition systems and used them to track down fugitives who had assumed fake identities. In 2016, the Party's Central Committee, evidently pleased with Skynet's results, approved Sharp Eyes, a new program that expanded the installation of cameras into rural areas.

While surveillance cameras were nothing new in China, the scale of the expansion under the two programs was staggering. Cameras multiplied, not just in Xinjiang but outside far-flung Tibetan monasteries and in remote hamlets scattered around the country. State media reported that police in Sichuan, the populous province known to most of the outside world for its spicy cuisine and pandas, had installed Sharp Eyes systems in 4,800 villages and other residential areas in the space of a year. Reports from other provinces suggested similar explosions. Sifting through public tender documents, researchers at the Asia Society discovered that by 2020 the government bill for Sharp Eyes projects alone added up to around $2.1 billion.

The government's aim was to install video surveillance in all of China's "key public spaces" by the end of 2020—a goal it would largely achieve. But the new networks were not just larger. They were also far better organized and interconnected, feeding into command centers where local authorities could collect and analyze surveillance footage covering broad areas with relatively little effort.

As China's surveillance capabilities expanded, Xi urged senior leaders to "fully exploit" advances in AI and the explosion of data "to improve our ability to sense, predict and prevent risks." It was the approach that Qian Xuesen had been advocating since the 1980s. Qian was long dead by then, and his protégé Song Jian was retired. But a new generation of scientists and scholars had emerged and stood ready to guide the Party into its new era.

◉

Crammed into his narrow office crowded with stacks of books and paper in a dusty corner of the Tsinghua University campus, Meng Tianguang sat forward and conjured the image of a shimmering future. It was early 2016, a year after the Party had unveiled its big data plan. Meng, a newly minted assistant professor of political science, was one of a bevy of promising young scholars at China's top universities who were scrambling to meet the government's demand for insight into how it could use data to predict everything from traffic problems and spikes in pension demands to shifts in the mood of internet users. "The government really wants to make policy based on predictions, and use predictions for contingency planning," he said, his eyes shining with excitement. "This is very important in China."

Bright-faced with a wide smile and thin-framed glasses, Meng was refreshingly open about his work, much of which involved advising the government. Growing hostility toward foreign media among the Communist Party leadership, especially in the wake of Western newspaper reporting on Xinjiang, has made it politically risky for Chinese scholars working on data and governance to grant interviews. As a result, it has become almost impossible to get inside the thoughts of the researchers now advising the Party on the uses of surveillance. At the time of our meeting, however, the atmosphere hadn't yet soured. Like others in the field, Meng was invigorated by the possibilities laid out before him and was happy to discuss them.

Meng's career started out on a conventional path. He earned his PhD in political science at Peking University, China's equivalent of Harvard, having spent one year conducting research at the actual Harvard as a visiting scholar. After earning his degree in 2013, he took up a postdoctoral position in the Tsinghua political science department. Early in his career he wrote papers on the theory of democratic transition and how social class affected political attitudes. But a year into his postdoc, Tsinghua joined other top universities in responding to the Party's new fascination with big data and set up a new Data Science Institute to recruit talent to the field. Meng got swept up in the wave and showed a talent for the work.

One facet of Meng's previous work—a focus on the notion of political trust—dovetailed nicely with the government's interest in data. The country's big internet companies, eager to curry favor with Beijing, had offered to make vast troves of social media data available to university researchers to study. Meng decided to use that data to measure how responsive China's "authoritarian system" (his phrase) was to fluctuations in online public opinion.

Though he came from a traditional political science background, this new direction required him to learn the social engineering approaches Qian Xuesen had helped popularize. The government's goal, Meng said, was to build systems that bolstered trust in the Party by automatically detecting signs of negative shifts in social media conversation and using that information to inform decisions. For example, such a system could scan Weibo for certain combinations of keywords previously associated with local environmental protests, like "corruption" and "pollution" and "factory," and alert provincial officials when they reached a certain threshold in posts from areas under their control. The officials could then step in to assuage local concerns before residents took to the streets.

American security analyst Samantha Hoffman made this new data-driven approach to social control the subject of an illuminating 2017 PhD dissertation she titled "Programming China." In her research, Hoffman found that the Party's ideal of "social management" had evolved over the course of the post-Mao era to include a sophisticated mix of carrots and sticks, or what she called "co-optation and coercion." The field of China studies tended to see the Party as alternating between periods of cracking down, when it moved to impose its will, and loosening up, when it tried to accommodate the desires of the people. Hoffman found that the Party's aspiration was more nuanced than that. "It is not one or the other at various points in time," she wrote. Instead, it was "both acting together in unison." At the same time, the Party was constantly monitoring the interplay of internal and external threats, watching how foreign ideas and activities could exacerbate problems.

During her search for a new framework to understand what she was seeing, Hoffman stumbled onto a paper about self-regulating "autonomic" computer systems. The systems had been developed by American technology giant IBM in the early 2000s in response to constant increases in the complexity of modern computing. The company couldn't find enough human IT managers capable of keeping the new systems running, so it began to develop computers that could optimize themselves by sensing and solving basic operational problems on their own. In cybernetic fashion, the idea drew inspiration from the human autonomic nervous system, which controls internal organs like the heart and triggers the "fight or flight" adrenaline rush when a person feels threatened.

The notion of autonomic error correction matched what Hoffman was seeing in China. One example she cited was the Social Credit System. A project the Party began to promote widely in 2014, it sought to combine regularly updated measures of financial, social, and political behavior into a single mechanism that would encourage trustworthiness in businesses and individuals through a mix of rewards and punishments. The system was complex and flawed (for more on this, see Chapter 11), but its conception encapsulated the Party's approach toward regulating society. In theory, Hoffman argued, it could be automated to incentivize obedience and preempt discord.

Hoffman traced the origins of this notion back to Qian Xuesen's promotion of social cybernetics and to Song Jian's argument in the early 1980s that social management could be automated through technology. Now that it had the tools and the data to put those ideas into practice, she argued, the Party was building something new. "What's happening in China," she wrote, "defies conventional categories." It was still authoritarianism, but a vastly more stable and nimble version.

By 2017, the Party's interest in AI and big data had already set off an explosion of research inside China. Meng said Tsinghua was recruiting upward of a hundred master's students a year from social science, public administration, and economic management departments to join its data science lab. All of the other top universities were doing the same thing. Chinese researchers waxed lyrical about the new worlds big data promised to open up. "The entirety of human history will eventually exist in the form of data," one professor at the Central Party School, the elite training academy where Tahir Hamut had worked in the 1990s, had written in a research paper in 2015. Another Party School professor, writing in the Chinese journal *E-Government*, predicted a near future in which "everything in the world" would be digitized, and it would become possible to combine data with mathematical models to optimize every mechanism of society.

Some of the most enthusiastic contributions came from scholars working in the field of political and ideological education, which were concerned with how to compel the country's youth to embrace Marxism and the political writings of China's leaders.

One such pair of scholars at the University of Electronic Science and Technology in the southwestern city of Chengdu argued that mass collection of social media and other data would allow schools to create a "precision profile" of each student's political leanings and use it to craft personalized messages more likely to persuade them of socialism's superiority. They also imagined the use of data visualization to map out students' opinions of classes, interests, and areas of intellectual confusion.

Meng wasn't certain that big data could do all the Party hoped it would, but he was still a believer in the overall direction. The marriage of data and governance opened up such a world of possibilities. "In any case," he said, "it's better than the traditional era, when we had no data and policy was based on the judgment of individuals."

At some level, his argument felt hard to refute. So many of the problems the Party encountered—so many of the protests that erupted either online or in the streets—were a response to abuses of power, greed, corruption, and criminal negligence among local officials, encouraged by a regime that allows political manipulation of the legal system. Building the political equivalent of an autonomic nervous system might be something of a fantasy, but even a partly functioning version of it would allow the Party to manage the country with vastly greater efficiency than it had in the past.

◉

Xi Jinping marked the arrival of 2018 by delivering a videotaped greeting on New Year's Eve from his personal office. As in years past, he sat in the center of the frame in a dark suit with a red tie, his folded hands resting on an immense wooden desk polished to a mirror-like shine. A Chinese flag rose up behind his right shoulder, while an ink brush painting of the Great Wall occupied the space directly behind him, a camera-friendly background for his robustly combed hair. The only significant difference appeared on the shelves to either side of the painting.

In recent years, state media had highlighted the books that Xi, a purported bibliophile, had on his shelf to start the year. That year the book selection was telling. Next to Marxist texts *Das Kapital* and *The Communist Manifesto* sat two books on artificial intelligence: *Augmented: Life in the Smart Lane* by futurist Brett King, a forward look at what life will be like in the coming age of predictive technology, and *The Master Algorithm*, a layman's introduction to machine learning by computer scientist Pedro Domingos that imagines a universal learning algorithm capable of deriving all past, present, and future knowledge from data. (Domingos later told the German magazine *Der Spiegel* it was "both exciting and scary" to learn his book was on Xi's shelf. King was less equivocal, writing on Twitter, "It's a good day when you find out that the Chinese President reads your books.") If it wasn't evident before, the books sent a clear signal: Xi was determined to graft the technologies of the future onto the Party's revolutionary roots.

It's hard to know whether Xi believed as fervently as some of the Party's political scientists and Marxist theorists in the power of data to know and control everything. Nevertheless, a year into his second term as president, officials under him had responded enthusiastically to his call to exploit this "free resource." The state had poured billions of dollars into AI research centers and new training programs for data scientists. Central planners were experimenting with using algorithms to predict pressure on social welfare programs. Local governments had also started to build data collection platforms to be used in compiling social credit records.

The security agencies had gone even further. A few weeks before Xi's New Year's speech, state media reported that more than 2 million new cameras had been installed in four years under Skynet alone, "leaving criminals with no way to hide their tracks." In addition to the cameras, authorities were using AI and big data to do predictive policing, it added. "Not only has it spread throughout the country, it also leads the world."

The claim to world leadership was not an empty boast. Chinese data scientists both inside China and overseas were involved in, and often directing, the best research into the subfields of AI that were most useful in surveillance, like facial and voice recognition. With close to 800 million internet users at the time, the country was producing oceans of data every day for those scientists to study.

The world's largest authoritarian country appeared to be marching forward with confidence in its tech-powered model of social control, seemingly having killed once and for all the fantasy that technology would one day transform it into a freedom-loving, multiparty state. That confidence was bolstered by the struggles of the world's most powerful democracies as they tried to confront the iniquities of globalization and warp-speed distortions produced by social media. In their book *Superpower Showdown*, about intensifying US-China conflict at the time, *Wall Street Journal* reporters Bob Davis and Lingling Wei reported that Xi Jinping started referring to America's political system in the Trump era as "a sheet of loose sand," too destabilized by partisan conflict to achieve any meaningful progress.

Though Xi's revival of Mao-era politics had caught some people by surprise, upon stepping back it was clear the Party had been moving in the direction of greater state control for some time. While the West was pulling itself out of the pit of the 2008 financial crisis, Chinese leaders had been busy behind the Great Firewall building a sealed-off world of Chinese search engines, video sites, and social media platforms that offered the illusion of choice. Rebecca MacKinnon, a vice president in charge of global advocacy at the Wikimedia Foundation and CNN's former bureau chief in Beijing, argued that this project of the Party's had given birth to a novel form of political control, which she called "networked authoritarianism." Chinese internet users, she wrote, "are managing to have more fun, feel more free, and be less fearful of their government than was the case even a mere decade ago." At the same time, she wrote, the Party had retained control and been able to exploit the internet to sniff out signs of opposition.

In a 2020 essay, political scientist Francis Fukuyama suggested that the Party under Xi was taking the next step. "The starting point is to recognize that we are dealing with an aspiring totalitarian country like the mid-20th century Soviet Union," he wrote. The difference, he continued, was that Xi made better use of positive incentives and "has at his disposal technological tools that were simply unavailable to 20th-century totalitarians."

China's leaders wanted to redefine government using the same tools that Google, Facebook, and Amazon had used to remake capitalism. In an ideal future, with enough data and the right algorithms, they wouldn't have to impose their will with violence the way Stalin, Mussolini, and other twentieth-century tyrants did. Instead, like a Google advertiser, the Party would be able to divine when and how to nudge its subjects to behave in ways it prefers. They could engineer away dissent. Instead of freedom or oppression, China would have optimization.

It was unlikely the Party would ever achieve such a flawless idea of control, but as Xi Jinping entered the middle of his second term he seemed determined to travel as far down the path as possible. How close he got would depend to a large degree on powerful entities not entirely within the Party's control.

5

LITTLE BROTHERS

On a smoggy autumn day in October 2016, dozens of senior officials from China's Central Political and Legal Affairs Commission, the powerful organ of the Communist Party that oversees police and the courts, gathered in a cavernous hall in Beijing to hear from a guest speaker. The speech was part of a series of seminars that Meng Jianzhu, then the secretary of the commission and a former minister of public security, had introduced in April that year to keep members up to date with new trends in law enforcement. This was the fourth time in six months that Meng had called them together but the first time they would hear from someone outside the government.

Following an introduction by Meng, the speaker stepped to the dais, dressed sharply in a blue collared shirt and black slacks. He was all of five foot three, with a boyish haircut that belied his fifty-plus years and an elfish demeanor that was instantly familiar to anyone who had been following the stunning rise of China's tech industry. Nearly everyone in China, certainly everyone in the room, recognized Jack Ma.

A brash and ebullient former English teacher, Ma was the founder of

Alibaba Group Holding, which he started as an e-commerce website out of an apartment in 1999 and quickly built into a titan standing astride the Chinese tech world. The company raised $21.8 billion when it listed in New York in 2014—the biggest US IPO in history at the time. A little over two decades after its founding, more than 900 million Chinese consumers shopped on the company's online retail platforms, including its most popular e-commerce platform, Taobao, which sold everything from kitchen appliances to origami decorations. Alibaba also boasted a food delivery network, ran a widely used mobile payments affiliate, and operated the country's most successful cloud-computing business. By 2020 its valuation would hit $800 billion—a dizzying number that reflected, among other things, the company's vast repository of data on the preferences, habits, activities, and finances of hundreds of millions of consumers.

Outside of China, Ma served as the face of the "new" breed of Chinese businesspeople, breaking the mold of stuffy middle-aged men in shapeless collared black jackets running bloated state-owned enterprises. He loved to play to the crowd. In 2009 he famously strutted onstage in dark red lipstick and a white wig with a feather mohawk to sing "Can You Feel the Love Tonight?" in front of thousands of adoring employees. A year later he appeared on another stage, decked out *Terminator*-style in a black leather jacket and sunglasses, to meet with California governor Arnold Schwarzenegger. He traveled regularly on his private jet to attend global conferences like the World Economic Forum in Davos, Switzerland, wowing the global elite with his self-taught English and making splashy donations to causes like entrepreneurship in Africa and earthquake relief in Nepal.

He had a different audience in Beijing—one that was vastly more important. Listening attentively that Friday were some of China's most powerful officials, including Guo Shengkun, the head of China's police force, who would soon take over for Meng as head of the Political and Legal Affairs Commission; Zhou Qiang, the head of China's Supreme People's Court; and Cao Jianming, the country's top prosecutor. His speech was also being live-streamed online to more than 1.5 million police, judges, and prosecutors across the country.

The topic of Ma's speech was big data. The vast accumulation of data collected by companies like his, he told the audience, was disrupting every aspect of society. Law enforcement was no exception. Police officers exhausted themselves physically chasing after petty thieves every day, Ma observed, but what if they monitored a suspect's data instead of his footsteps? "Big data leaves a trail, even if humans can't see it," he said, and it was often easier to trace. Even better, he told the rapt officials, big data meant that police were no longer stuck trying to solve past crimes. "Whoever owns enough data and computing ability can predict problems, predict the future, and judge the future," he said.

To illustrate this last point, Ma brought up the example of a would-be terrorist preparing a bomb attack. "It is normal for a person to buy a pressure cooker, it's normal for a person to buy a clock, it's normal even for a person to buy gunpowder and ball bearings, but if one buys all those things together, then it is not normal," he said. Algorithms could be built to spot those suspicious purchasing patterns and flag them to authorities. "The political and legal system of the future is inseparable from the internet, inseparable from big data," he said. "Bad guys won't even be able to walk into the square." Whether by "the square" Ma meant to evoke Tiananmen Square was uncertain, but the substance of his message was clear: Alibaba's data could help prevent existential threats to the Party's power.

Ma's speech left an impression. Following him onstage, Meng proclaimed big data would open the "third eye" of humans and change the way people view the world. The commission needed to embrace these disruptive technologies, he warned, or be in danger of falling behind.

Eight months later, the commission would hear from another tech entrepreneur, Pony Ma. Unrelated to Jack but one of his fiercest competitors, Pony was the founder of Tencent Holdings, which began life as a copycat instant-messaging start-up in the early days of the Chinese internet but had since grown into a behemoth with interests in gaming, music, video, and social media. Its most popular offering was WeChat, a do-everything app that combined text, video, and audio chat with public-facing pages and mobile payments, like WhatsApp, Instagram, and Apple Pay rolled into one. At the time of Pony Ma's speech in 2017,

WeChat had close to a billion users, most of whom used it on a near-daily basis.

Personality-wise, Pony Ma was Jack's opposite, reserved and low-key almost to the point of invisibility. But his message was the same. "Data is a force for production. The more you let data do the legwork, the less police have to run about," he said. "If we have enough data and use proper algorithms, we can dig into and use big data to analyze abnormal behaviors, and finally find suspects." Delivered in the delphic jargon of the data engineer, his speech might have been less rousing than Jack Ma's, though for the people in the room that wasn't important. What mattered was the mere fact of his appearance, and the willingness to collaborate that it signaled.

For as powerful as the Communist Party is, its ambitions for social control depend heavily on companies in the one sector of the Chinese economy not dominated by the state. Nurtured inside a walled garden, China's tech giants are unique. They often boast deeper insight into the lives of their users than Facebook, Google, and Amazon, those pioneers of what author Shoshana Zuboff memorably dubbed "surveillance capitalism." They also have a much closer relationship to the state than their Silicon Valley counterparts, depending on government support for development and, ultimately, survival.

At the same time, like all creatures of global capitalism, they are driven by a powerful thirst for profit—one that doesn't always align with the state's interests. To the Party, that makes them both an invaluable asset and a source of profound anxiety.

The extraordinary relationship between the Party and China's tech companies is a product of China's internet, which functions unlike any other. China has by far the world's largest population of internet users, with more than 1 billion people who log on regularly. (For comparison, India, with a similar-sized total population, has about 825 million internet users.) Close to 97 percent of China's online population accesses the internet primarily through mobile devices. But unlike American smartphone users, who carry virtually the entire World Wide Web in their pockets, Chinese internet users live inside a virtual world that is almost exclusively Chinese, sealed off from the rest of cyberspace by the digital equivalent of a cell membrane with meticulous criteria for what gets in and out.

The Communist Party started to lay the foundations of this bizarre environment early on in the evolution of the internet with a mix of censorship and lax intellectual property enforcement. As the Great Firewall held American internet giants at bay, China's government fed the most promising of its homegrown copycats with tax breaks, easy financing, and discounts on rent. When Google decided to stop offering censored search services in China in 2010 following a series of hacking attacks, it had already fallen far behind Baidu as the Chinese search engine of choice.

Revelations in 2013 from former NSA contractor Edward Snowden that American government hackers had pilfered millions of text messages from Chinese telecom carriers and broken into computers connected to a critical network backbone at Tsinghua University in Beijing played a key role in the next phase of Chinese tech development. Stunned, the Party set out to rebuild the country's internet infrastructure according to a new mantra, "secure and controllable," and moved even more aggressively to defend Chinese cyberspace from foreign influence. A new effort was launched to root out products from companies such as IBM, Cisco, and Microsoft, which the Party described as American "Guardian Warriors," and replace them with Chinese alternatives. When American cloud-computing companies came knocking a few years later, they found a steel door dead-bolted with data security and investment rules that ensured only Chinese companies would handle the country's data.

Inside the Great Firewall, the Party granted tech companies surprising leeway. As long as they obeyed censorship orders, internet companies were left pretty much to do as they pleased—a jarring contrast to other key areas of the economy, like energy or transportation, which the Party made sure were monopolized by state-owned companies under its direct control. The result was a gladiatorial competition that left countless copycat start-ups bleeding in the dirt and created enough pressure to eventually produce genuine innovation. Blending creativity and ruthless business acumen, Alibaba and Tencent came to dominate the arena.

The companies had little to do with each other at first. Alibaba stuck to e-commerce, while Tencent concentrated its efforts on QQ, the desktop instant messenger product it had blatantly copied from AOL in the late 1990s. But as each company expanded its empire into new areas, the competition grew fiercer. With a few exceptions, nearly every promising new Chinese tech company would sooner or later get drawn into the orbit of, or be outright swallowed up by, one of the two giants as the two Mas scrambled to claim as much of the Chinese internet for themselves as they could. Ultimately, the companies found themselves in a pitched fight to control a single resource—user data.

❖

The battle for insight into the behavior of China's consumers played out largely through mobile payments. Alibaba launched a mobile version of its online payment system, Alipay, in 2008, striking deals with utility providers so that consumers could use it to buy a new shower head on Taobao and pay their water bill all on the same app. The next big innovation came from Tencent, which in 2013 married WeChat, then a simple but popular messaging app, with its PayPal knockoff TenPay. The new and improved WeChat allowed users to make purchases and transfer money by scanning QR codes. That meant vendors could accept mobile payments simply by printing a code on a piece of paper and taping it up somewhere customers could scan it. In a cash-bound country that had never embraced credit cards, it was a transformational development.

Nearly everyone in nearly every city, township, or village in China now conducts their business through Alipay or WeChat, whether it's buying street food, booking flights, or investing in money-market funds. In 2020 alone, Chinese people used mobile payment systems to conduct more than 123 billion transactions worth $67.5 trillion, nearly eleven times the total global credit and debit payment volumes recorded by MasterCard that year.

As valuable as the technology is to China's economy, its contribution to surveillance is likely greater. The way people spend money is the most reliable and revealing window into their desires and beliefs. In the United States, Amazon is alone among the Silicon Valley titans in owning large troves of data on consumer spending. But even Amazon can only see how money is spent on its own platforms. Tencent and Alibaba, meanwhile, can see how users spend money across China. Through their other services, they can also see where users spend time, who their relatives and friends are, what movies they like, how much electricity they use, and what they like to do on vacation—a degree of behavioral insight that is breathtaking in its breadth and clarity.

The experience of one local resident in Alibaba's home city of Hangzhou, Ethan Feng, illustrates the enormous influence the country's internet giants exert on the lives of Chinese people. Feng was thirty years old when we met him in 2019. He grew up a short drive from Alibaba's campus. By the time he reached adulthood, the company touched virtually every aspect of his life. When he got into his car to drive to his job as a manager at a local logistics company, he turned on Autonavi, an Alibaba-owned mapping app that guided him along the most efficient route through the city's notorious traffic. When he bought clothing or gifts for his son and daughter, his first stop was Tmall, an e-commerce app spun off from Taobao. When he took his wife and the kids on a short vacation at the end of 2018 to Qiandaohu, a scenic lake two hours' drive from Hangzhou, he used Alibaba's Kayak-like travel app to book the hotel.

Of all the apps on Feng's device, by far the most important was Alipay, which by then was operated by an Alibaba affiliate called Ant Group. Feng used it to pay for nearly everything: his morning coffee, Ralph Lauren shirts at the nearby outlet mall, snacks from a vending machine near the entrance to his office. On days when he didn't feel like driving, he used it to take the bus or subway. Like anyone in China over the age of ten, he remembered as a child having to stand in line with his parents for an hour or more at the bank so they could hand stacks of cash to the teller to pay for their water and gas. With Alipay, he was able to pay both bills each month with a few taps on his touchscreen. His wallet bounced around, forgotten, at the bottom of his backpack.

Alibaba knew Feng better in some respects than his family members did. Because of Alipay, it knew that his favorite Japanese restaurant was the one five minutes from his office and that he needed a caffeine fix every afternoon. It knew that he had a lead foot because he used Alipay to pay his speeding tickets. Autonavi told the company where he drove and when. Thanks to its food-delivery app, it also knew when he went on one of his frequent work trips to the southern city of Guangzhou. Privacy consciousness was growing in Chinese cities at the time (as we explore at length in Chapter 10), but Feng wasn't perturbed. The personal exposure was worth the frictionless convenience. "Chinese don't have the same sensitivity to privacy as people in the West," he said. "Many people can't grasp the concept of privacy, and it's hard to get worked up over it if you don't understand it."

As the Party began to roll out its surveillance state in earnest in the late 2010s, the tech giants' comprehension of the desires, anxieties, and conflicts swirling through Chinese society would prove critical. "The data in private hands is vastly larger than what the government can acquire," said one Chinese big data researcher at Peking University who asked to remain anonymous because of the sensitivity of the topic. "That's the crucial question for state governance in the internet age: how to build a good, cooperative relationship with these superplatforms. Because the government recognizes that its own capacity isn't sufficient."

Xi delivered his strongest indication of the state's attitude toward its internet companies in a sweeping speech he gave in April 2016 as part of a forum on cybersecurity in Beijing. Peppered with idiomatic expressions, the speech emphasized the need for China to harness the full Chinese internet to improve the lives of its people and overtake competitors in cutting-edge technologies, just as "a car overtakes another in a turn." Doing so required clearing away bureaucratic roadblocks that might hamper the growth of internet companies, he said. But there were limits, he warned: "A company's fate is intertwined with a nation's growth. Once a firm lacks state and crowd support, once it stops serving its country and citizens, it will be very difficult for the firm to grow big and strong."

◉

By the time we started reporting on China's surveillance state in 2017, China's tech giants were happy to trumpet their willingness to help the government maintain social order but stayed steadfastly silent on what that help looked like. While public pressure has compelled American companies like Apple, Facebook, and Alphabet Inc.'s Google to routinely outline their government cooperation in transparency reports, their Chinese counterparts felt no such obligation.

Digging into the relationship between the Party and Chinese internet companies, we looked at criminal case files as one of our first steps. Before a mass purging of records in 2021, China's public court database contained thousands of files that showed prosecutors using mobile payment data and other information from Alibaba and Tencent platforms to convict people of crimes. In some cases, police had pulled the data directly from the suspects' phones. But others were mysteriously vague about where it had come from. We called the defense lawyers from a dozen of those cases. None knew how police had acquired the data.

As we continued reporting, we stumbled on a little-noticed promotional video from Alibaba that described a team within the company called Shendun, or "Magic Shield." According to the video, the team used algorithms to scan Alibaba's e-commerce sites for prohibited items, like weapons and pornography, as well as suspicious behavior. "Guns, drugs, nuclear bombs," the narrator said. "As long as it's illegal, it will not escape our control." The team had assisted police in thousands of cases, it said. Current and former members of the team told us that Magic Shield agents would review items flagged by the algorithm and remove any that violated the company's rules. If they found items or behavior that appeared criminal, they would alert the police. But the video said nothing about how the company communicated with police, and Alibaba employees we spoke to were not able or willing to talk.

After weeks of fruitless searching, we received a tip from a former Alibaba staffer about a dedicated outpost on the company's main campus where police met with staff to request data for their investigations. We found another former Alibaba employee who recalled being summoned to the outpost to provide user information for an investigation into content that was "terrorism-related," a phrase typically used by Chinese authorities to refer to Uyghur separatism. Alibaba confirmed that the outpost existed, saying police only visited "occasionally." Former employees told us police were regularly there, and one later told us that the campus had added at least one more outpost. (Alibaba's security team has since changed its name to Alibaba Safety.)

In October 2017, as we were learning about the police outpost, Joseph Tsai, Alibaba's executive vice chairman, spoke at a *Wall Street Journal* technology conference in Laguna Beach, California, and he pushed back on the idea that his company was sharing large amounts of data with the Chinese authorities. "I would disagree with the premise that the central government has access to all this corporate data. That's just not true," he told a packed conference room, after a member of the audience asked about Alibaba's relationship and data-sharing with Chinese authorities. "If they want data from you, just like in the US, they have to have a reason." The company repeated the same idea to us weeks later.

Chinese police do have to submit something akin to a warrant to request data from internet companies, but unlike in the United States, they don't need a judge's signature. All that's required is the approval of a senior police officer. Also unlike in the United States, Chinese companies have no effective legal means to resist. A suite of vaguely worded laws enacted between 2015 and 2017 compel corporations to share data with the government. One of them, the Cybersecurity Law, demands that companies running internet platforms in China help authorities ferret out content that "endangers national security, national honor, and interests," a category that covers everything from suicide bomb threats to social media posts questioning the Party's view of history. Party cells embedded in each company add another layer of assurance that its interests will be honored.

Another major difference between China and the United States manifests in platform liability. Chinese laws dictate that internet content firms must monitor and control the information posted on their websites, or else they risk losing their license to conduct business. Those rules exert significant pressure on internet companies to develop systems capable of fine-grained monitoring and filtering content. "If I say something illegal or bad using Gmail, then I am responsible for it, not Google," said Lokman Tsui, a former journalism professor at the Chinese University of Hong Kong who previously served as Google's Head of Free Expression in Asia and the Pacific. "In China, it's the opposite."

Tencent is subject to the same demands, though like its founder, the company is discreet. From time to time, video and photos have circulated on Chinese social media purporting to show security agents scrolling through what appears to be a back-end portal into WeChat, but none have ever been verified. Tencent has vehemently denied suggestions that it gives police unfettered access to WeChat's treasure trove of behavioral data. Before the mass deletion in 2021, China's court database was lousy with examples of WeChat users charged with "picking quarrels and provoking trouble," a vague crime often used to punish political dissent, for messages they posted in private chat groups, though it was never clear who or what had flagged the messages to police. The experiences of Chinese human rights activists suggest Tencent is at least as cooperative as Alibaba in handing over information on its users' activities.

One of those activists, Hu Jia, a relentless political dissident and advocate for HIV patients, offered an example. As a result of his work, Hu was often confined to his home in Beijing or taken on forced vacations out of the city by state security agents around the time when sensitive political events were being held. Bored during one confinement ahead of a Communist Party meeting in 2017, Hu took a friend's advice and bought a slingshot online for target practice in the yard of his apartment complex. He used WeChat Pay. A day later, he recalled in a phone conversation, a state security agent asked why he'd bought a slingshot. "They thought I was going to use it to shoot out their cameras," he said.

"They understand what you spend money on, where you spend it." The example was mundane, but that was the point. Even something as harmless as buying a slingshot was enough to get flagged. Everyone, Hu said, now had a spy in their pocket.

◉

The partnership was not perfect, and it grew more complicated as the value of user data in predicting human behavior became more apparent. As Tsai's comments in Laguna Beach suggested, Alibaba, Tencent, and other Chinese tech companies didn't always share data with the government as readily as the latter would like. The resistance boiled down to competition: The companies had fought hard to accumulate their troves of data. It was by far their most valuable and important asset. The unique insights into Chinese society they could mine from it gave them leverage over the government as well as each other.

The friction was largely hidden from view but could occasionally burst into the open, as it did in 2018 when the People's Bank of China (PBOC) revoked provisional licenses it had granted to Alibaba's payments affiliate Ant, Tencent, and six other companies to develop credit scoring systems. The decision was the outcome of long-simmering frustration at the central bank. For decades, the PBOC has struggled to build a reliable mechanism for judging the financial credit of Chinese consumers. That was in part because Chinese people never embraced credit cards but instead jumped straight from cash to mobile finance. In 2015, the bank turned to the companies responsible for mobile payments, inviting them to develop systems using their data that could fill the gap.

Ant came the closest, creating a rating system called Sesame Credit that drew from Alibaba's stores of data, third-party data providers like telecom service providers, and government databases to give users a rating between 350 and 950. Users were evaluated according to an unconventional constellation of factors, including the value of assets in their account, what items they'd purchased and when, their investments, whether they were registered as rural or urban residents, their involvement in civil litigation, where they traveled, and their education level. In one famous interview, an Alibaba executive explained that someone whose data showed they bought a lot of diapers would earn a higher score than a user who spent their money on video games, as the average parent was assumed to be more responsible than the average gamer.

Bank officials were intrigued, but also wary. They worried that the scores were designed more to incentivize consumers to spend money on the companies' platforms and less to gauge actual creditworthiness. The companies also weren't willing to share enough of their data to put regulators' minds at ease. As a result, the bank decided to scrap plans for private credit scoring and invalidated the eight licenses. Instead, it set up a new government-led credit scoring company, gave each of the eight companies an 8 percent stake, and invited them to contribute data to a joint effort. Alibaba and Tencent both balked at sharing data with the new company, which in effect meant sharing it with each other and other stakeholders. A years-long stand-off ensued and would become part of a reckoning for the country's tech industry in 2021 (a period we address in Chapter 11).

In the meantime, however, the Party and China's tech giants found other ways to cooperate. Evidence of the immense potential of that partnership began to surface in cities scattered throughout the country's wealthy coastal regions. In Alibaba's hometown of Hangzhou, in particular, the Party demonstrated how it could use the tech industry's surveillance tools to sand down society's friction points.

6

DATATOPIA

If cities in Xinjiang like Urumqi and Kashgar are where the Party's fervor for mass surveillance descends into dystopian nightmare, then Hangzhou, the capital of Zhejiang province, is where it soars to its most utopian heights.

Hangzhou is a lyrical city straddling the Qiantang River just as it prepares to flow into the East China Sea south of Shanghai. Mountains cradle it on three sides, and waterways crisscross in between. Its most famous feature, the West Lake, spreads out over an area almost twice the size of New York City's Central Park, a tranquil mirror reflecting a pageant of pagodas, gardens, and undulating pathways that traipse along its shores. Writing about his visit to the city in the 1860s, British missionary Arthur Evans Moule evoked a common Chinese saying that likened Hangzhou to heaven on earth. As he approached it for the first time, Moule wrote, the city did indeed look "like a glimpse of celestial regions."

Hangzhou retains its luster in modern times. Where once the city's silk-clad gentry were carried around the lake in sedan chairs, now its nouveau riche drape themselves in Louis Vuitton and zip along the shore in European sports cars. Now, as then, it attracts hordes of sightseers who come to take in not just the scenery but the atmosphere of wealth. The city notched close to 10 percent economic growth throughout the 2010s, even as economies elsewhere in China began to slow. In 2020, its GDP was equivalent to the entire economy of Portugal.

Just like Xinjiang, Hangzhou is rife with cameras—including more than a hundred over a two-mile stretch of road along the West Lake near the city center. But this dense network of sensors is meant to improve residents' lives as much as control them. They feed data into algorithms that alleviate traffic congestion, monitor food safety, and help escort first responders to a scene more quickly.

What also sets Hangzhou apart from many other Chinese cities is how closely its government works with local technology firms. The heart of the city's modern economy is a cluster of carefully nurtured, unusually successful technology companies. They include both the e-commerce behemoth Alibaba Group and Hikvision, the world's number-one maker of surveillance cameras. Thanks to their presence, Hangzhou's business districts—freshly constructed areas with names like Future Sci-Tech City and Internet of Things Street—now thrum with a youthful, world-conquering energy recognizable to anyone who has spent time in American tech hubs.

Hangzhou doesn't just promote, protect, and fund its tech champions. Starting around 2016, it made them partners in running the city itself. This is especially true of Alibaba, which in 2016 built an AI-powered platform, City Brain, to help the government optimize everything from traffic to water management. To ease Hangzhou's legendary traffic snarls, Alibaba designed a system to crunch data from video intersections and real-time GPS locations, allowing the city's traffic authorities to optimize traffic signals and reduce congestion on its aging road networks. Alibaba's other products and platforms make it easier for city residents to pay their utility bills, take the bus, get a loan, even sue local companies in online court. Hikvision and its in-town rival Dahua are also deeply involved, providing high-definition cameras and AI systems to give the government a window into what's happening, and what might happen, on the streets and in public squares. Taken together, these collaborations have turned Hangzhou into the "smartest" of Chinese cities and a model that others around the country are rushing to emulate.

Roughly 300 cities across China have been given the nod to experiment with systems that would automate planning decisions using data vacuumed up from thousands of sensors, part of state planners' push to realize a "new model of smart cities." Beijing, Shanghai, and Shenzhen (the last of these a buzzing southern metropolis just across the border from Hong Kong) all rushed to cover their streets with cameras and centralize their data on new cloud systems that aimed to code away the problems of urban management. None, however, quite matched Hangzhou, which soon boasted one of the most wired municipal governments in the world.

Beyond Alibaba's City Brain, Hangzhou's camera surveillance network has been credited with finding abducted children. Over the decades, China's birth limits had spawned a black market in stolen children that gave parents around the country fits of anxiety. Offering AI-powered cameras that could track down a lost son or daughter earned the government immense goodwill, even if only a scattering of families would ever need to rely on them. Other data helped the city manage the flow of tourists at crowded attractions, optimize parking spaces, and design new road networks. More than any other place in China, Hangzhou was the picture-postcard version of the Party's vision for a new, digital authoritarianism.

◉

In 2019, we got a rare peek at how this smart city project worked in a tidy Hangzhou neighborhood known as Little River Street. A residential patchwork of old, squat apartment buildings in the shape of shoeboxes, Little River Street straddles the intersection of three canals just north of the West Lake. In a few places, newer, taller complexes with European touches and generous balconies poke proudly into the sky. At street level, the storefronts are mostly family-run: fruit shops, convenience stores, home-renovation suppliers, a local barber who offers head massages before each trim. The district that contains Little River

Street, Gongshu, is home to more than a million people. Many are migrants to the city who have been granted residency, or what longtime locals refer to, with a wisp of derision, as "New Hangzhou People."

While researching smart cities, we had come across news reports of an initiative in Little River Street called City Eye. The reports described it as an AI-enabled, modern method of city management by the local branch of the *chengguan*, an urban management force akin to junior varsity police. We sent in a request to the local *chengguan* branch to visit and learn more about how the system worked. To our surprise, they said yes.

Known formally as the Urban Administrative and Law Enforcement Bureau, the *chengguan* are responsible for enforcing rules that govern the everyday running of cities. In practice, they spend most of their time taking care of tasks that police don't want to bother with: chasing away street peddlers, punishing unauthorized trash dumps, tracking down vandals, and handing out parking tickets. Over the years, the *chengguan* have become the object of close-to-universal loathing across China, and not without reason. Chinese social media is crawling with videos that show vicious attacks by *chengguan* on street vendors, frequently among the poorest and weakest members of Chinese society.

We arrived at Little River Street on a brisk autumn day. China is filled with similar neighborhoods, where people are either on the verge of moving up into the middle class or trying hard not to fall out of it— where well-being feels widespread but fleeting. It's these in-between places, where laundry dangling between apartment windows obscures peeling paint behind billowing rainbows of T-shirts and underwear, that worry the Party the most. The rich don't have an incentive to make trouble, and the destitute don't have the power. The people in the middle have just enough of both. And the pressures they face trying to make their way in modern China—merciless work hours, bad health care, constantly rising prices, pollution and food-safety scares, a capricious stock market—make them more likely to lash out. As a result, local officials often have to tread a fine line, exerting enough force to keep the streets in order and the economy growing, but not so much that they trigger an unpleasant reaction.

We found our destination on the third floor of a low-rise administrative building with an unassuming beige exterior. A blue sign reading CITY EYE OPERATION CENTER was visible from a hundred yards away. Inside the main control room on the second floor, two rows of desktop computers bathed in the flickering glow of twelve interconnected LED screens, each flashing one of dozens of time-stamped camera feeds from the surrounding neighborhood. It looked like the kind of facility that a decade earlier would have been reserved for state security agents and other top-level defenders of the national order. Two men and a woman sat at the computers eyeing the screens. The woman wore a bright yellow pullover with the word GUCCY written across the back. The men were both dressed all in black, though one had opted for a sweatshirt dotted with white dollar signs.

Some of the screens streamed live video from the entrances of local schools and kindergartens. Others were trained on side streets. A parade of residents strolled past the cameras either unaware or unbothered: families dropping off their children at school, commuters parking their cars, delivery people zipping to and fro on electric scooters loaded with parcels—all in crisp, high-definition detail.

In an area off to the side, we found Qiu Liqun, the official in charge of the command center, seated at a long mahogany table. Qiu, a tall and thickset fifty-year-old with a loud baritone voice, was a sixteen-year veteran of the *chengguan*. It was rare for anyone in his position to grant outsiders an inside look at a system like City Eye. Since Xi Jinping rose to power, more and more of the daily workings of government had withdrawn behind a veil of secrecy. But Qiu and his team were proud of the way the system had transformed the neighborhood and eager to publicize the changes. "Previously, we needed a lot of manpower to do our job in these districts," he said proudly. "Now, it's all machine-led."

Like many Chinese across the country, the people in Hangzhou shared the same disdain for *chengguan* as everyone else, Qiu said. "Residents only see the street management part of the job," he complained. Even in the wealthiest Chinese cities, sidewalks are vulnerable to appropriation by the messy, insistent, and occasionally desperate forces of developing-world economics. Farmers selling fruit from the backs of beat-up minivans. Migrant vendors hocking socks, cheap knockoff handbags, or the region's famous stinky tofu out of unlicensed carts. Beggars blocking foot traffic with stories of personal tragedy scrawled on scraps of scavenged cardboard. Qiu and his team were responsible for keeping Gongshu's streets free of those phenomena. It was true, they sometimes had to get physical, he said, but that was only in extreme cases. No one saw the effort they put in behind the scenes trying to reason with violators.

City Eye had revolutionized their work, according to Qiu. The system had been installed in Little River Street on a provisional basis following a meeting in 2017 between the local Party boss and representatives from China Electronics Technology Group Corporation, the same state-owned military contractor that built the centralized data platform that police used to track and categorize Muslims in Xinjiang. The company had deep connections to Hangzhou through its most successful subsidiary, the world-dominating camera maker Hikvision, which had worked with the Party boss on a project to install police surveillance cameras—roughly 1,600 of them—around the neighborhood. The company had been searching for a place to train a new AI system that would enable its cameras to quietly spot and flag minor infractions. Hikvision said they would let Little River Street try it out for free for a period of time in exchange for access to all of the data it collected to train and refine its own algorithms.

City Eye linked surveillance cameras with AI technology that kept a twenty-four-hour watch on the streets and sent an automatic alert with a screenshot any time it saw something out of order. Among the things it was trained to notice were piles of garbage on the street and mobile street vendors selling their wares on unauthorized corners. Officers would then decide whether it merited a response. The trial was a success, and Gongshu officials decided to expand the system to cover the entire district. Government bid documents published just before our visit showed Gongshu paid $2.5 million to CETC and a second data management company to run and service the system for three years.

The system, Qiu explained, was an upgraded version of grid management.

Visitors walking up to the City Eye command center pass a map that shows Little River Street divided into dozens of subunits, each of which is assigned a grid manager selected by local officials. Just as in other neighborhoods in other cities, Little River Street's grid managers are tasked with resolving disputes, distributing propaganda, and keeping an ear to the ground for discontent that might mushroom into unrest. The difference is in the tools Little River Street's grid managers used to carry out their mission.

Together with the grid managers, Qiu's team had set up chat groups on WeChat where the grid managers, *chengguan* officers, local officials, social workers, and owners of the area's roughly 360 local businesses could exchange information. Whenever the City Eye cameras spotted a potential violation—an illegally parked car or a pile-up of deliveries blocking the sidewalk—they sent notifications through an app to the *chengguan* and the grid manager in charge of the area. The grid managers then used WeChat to find and notify the offender. In cases where the grid manager couldn't persuade the person to fix the problem, the *chengguan* would get involved.

The system also relied on public shaming. Once a week, the *chengguan* gathered data on violations in each of the district's nine residential areas and published them through a public account on WeChat that anyone could see. Below the data table, Qiu's team inserted a list of the most common violations in each area—invariably one form of illegal parking or another—and screenshots of surveillance feeds of the biggest problem areas, with red squares marking each instance of illegal behavior.

The week before our visit, the app showed the Tanghe Residential Compound had been the worst offender with 226 violations. The most common was "mis-parked bicycles" (149), followed by "mis-parked vehicles" and "business conducted outside of shops" (29 each), "drying laundry along the street" (10), "illegal advertising" (6), and "rubbish piles" (2). Notably, not a single residential area had recorded an instance of the last item on the list: "abnormal gathering of people," a category that included protest. (Later, Qiu's team would use the WeChat account to assign stores in the area red, yellow, or green tags, with red tags indicating frequent rule breakers.)

The AI didn't always get things right, and its mistakes sometimes led to wasted effort. Especially in the early days, the machines would mistake fallen leaves or fresh snowfall for trash. Other times they would flag something that was technically a violation but that wasn't a big enough problem to act on. To demonstrate, Qiu thumbed through the app and pulled up a picture of a three-wheeled motorcycle left under a tree. The AI correctly recognized that it had been parked illegally, but the time stamp showed the alert had come in at 11:00 P.M. the previous night. "If it's 11:00 P.M., it's fine. We're not that inhuman," Qiu said. "By the morning it's usually gone." He clicked on another picture, this one stamped 7:00 A.M. It showed the tree with no motorcycle under it.

But the system got better the more data it collected, Qiu said, and the benefits far outweighed the nuisance of the false alarms. To prove his point, he brought up numbers from a PowerPoint presentation he'd given a few months earlier. Between January and July 2019, his human street patrols had singled out 2,600 potential violations. Over the same time period, City Eye's AI had flagged 19,000. More importantly, the scrutiny had produced results: Qiu's team had recorded a fall in monthly instances of unlicensed vending in Little River Street from more than 1,100 in August 2018 to just 30 a year later. "You catch one each time they pop up," he said of the illegal vendors, waving a hand dismissively through the air. Qiu gestured to the three officers in the other room watching the video screens. "In reality, we don't need people to monitor the screens," he said.

Qiu's superiors were evidently pleased also. A wall behind the conference table was hung with local state-media stories extolling the system's effectiveness, photos of law enforcement delegations sent from other cities to study what they'd done, and a framed message of praise from Hangzhou's deputy mayor. Residents likewise seemed happy. The pedestrian experience in particular had improved, they said. Streets, previously cluttered, were now clean and free from trash. Electric bikes were parked neatly within allocated white lines on the pavement instead of randomly on the sidewalk.

Judging the response among the business owners of Little River Street was trickier. None complained outright—there was nothing to be gained from openly criticizing a government initiative. Some praised the system, though with less enthusiasm than the residents they served. The owner of a local electric scooter shop said he and his employees used to assemble and repair bikes on the sidewalk—"a total mess," he conceded. After the new system was put in place and complaints began to pour in through WeChat, he brought the repairs inside. "The sidewalk in front of our store is like our face. If we keep it clean and tidy, our customers will feel good about our goods," he said. "In the past, we were too busy to notice where we were repairing bikes. But now, I get someone to remind me each time." Nearby, a twenty-nine-year-old watching over his family's window business recalled City Eye spotting a car parked illegally on the sidewalk near his shop and notifying *chengguan* officers in the area to track down the car owner to get the vehicle removed. Of course, those most directly affected by the system—the unlicensed vendors Qiu's team chased away—weren't around to say how they felt.

To Qiu, one of the most important influences of the City Eye system appeared in the way it smoothed out misunderstandings between *chengguan* and people in the neighborhood. In the past, he believed, the *chengguan* had two problems: first, residents couldn't see the long process that led officers to take action at street level; and second, some officers were able to act with impunity because their managers didn't know what they were doing. "A lot of it stems from this information asymmetry," he said. When Google first began selling Google Glass, one *chengguan* in the city of Cangzhou made headlines by plopping down $2,166—a fortune at his salary—to buy a pair of the video-recording eyeglasses in the hope that he could use them to avoid misunderstandings. To Qiu, City Eye—a supersized and more sophisticated version of Google Glass—had all but eliminated those problems. With everything recorded by the cameras and noted in WeChat, the *chengguan* had a record to prove that they came into the streets only when other options had been exhausted. The cameras also kept the *chengguan* honest and cut down on bribes. "The machines are unbiased. They flag everything," he said. The cameras didn't care about preexisting relationships between officer and offenders.

In Qiu's eyes, digital surveillance had transformed him and his fellow *chengguan* from loathed emblems of state brutality into respected protectors of social order in Little River Street. Yes, the technology could be used to crush a local protest over abuse of power. But to local officials, it could preempt the conflicts that lead to protest.

◉

While CETC introduced new levels of efficiency at the neighborhood level with City Eye, the task of optimizing life in Hangzhou as a whole fell to Alibaba.

The company's tree-lined headquarters, Taobao City, is a full-sized, twenty-first-century futurama located in Yuhang District, covering nearly 3 million square feet on the northern edge of Hangzhou. As of 2019 (the most recent year for which data exists), it housed 20,000 employees. Like Google's sprawling campus in Silicon Valley, it is a world unto itself, equipped with enough amenities—a gym, basketball courts, a hair salon, four cafeterias, a classical Chinese garden, and China's busiest Starbucks—that an employee never need leave. Autonomous robots zoom around the grounds delivering packages and groceries, and cameras at the cafeteria payment kiosks automatically recognize what dishes employees have taken from the buffet, charging them accordingly. At a "hotel of the future," guests can check in, access the elevators, and unlock their rooms with just their faces. Down the street, a mall for employees features virtual reality mirrors that allow shoppers to try on outfits without having to bother with dressing rooms. Of all of Alibaba's technological experiments though, City Brain was the company's most ambitious—and arguably its most successful.

The City Brain was built on a vision for smart cities introduced to China in 2009 by IBM. Hammered by the global financial crisis, IBM was trying to move into software and consulting, which offered higher profit margins than the hardware it was known for. China, with its massive cities, was a fat target. IBM executives traveled all over the country in a bid to woo local governments, offering to help them weave together different technologies in ways that would raise the quality of life, increase efficiency, and lower costs.

China's government was eager to hear what IBM had to say. Waves of migrant workers from poor areas of the country were flooding into urban areas, straining resources and increasing crime. The idea also came along just as officials were trying to find ways to spend a $590 billion stimulus package the Communist Party had approved to power the country through the global downturn. To a local government looking to justify massive new infrastructure spending, "smart city" had a nice, modern ring.

For all the sci-fi imagery they evoked, China's early smart city efforts were rudimentary, with many involving little more than installation of 4G mobile internet networks. Alibaba announced its intention to change that in the fall of 2016. In a speech peppered with the vague but beguiling jargon of techno-utopianism, Wang Jian, the head of Alibaba's Technology Steering Committee, unveiled plans to optimize the city's operations using cloud computing. Combined with AI, Wang said, Alibaba's cloud systems would be able to "conduct overall real-time analysis of the city, automatically deploy public resources and amend defects in urban operations." For Alibaba, it meant a lucrative and long-lasting government contract. For Hangzhou, it offered a path to becoming the city of the future.

Not long after announcing its launch, Alibaba built a cloud platform to suck in data from traffic and surveillance cameras around the city. Pairing that information with data from Autonavi, the company's smartphone map app, the company created a real-time virtual recreation of the city's roads that it said was capable of monitoring traffic down to the individual car. The potential uses for this data were enormous. Alibaba trained AI algorithms that could spot traffic accidents and violations and push alerts to apps on the phones of traffic police within twenty seconds. It developed another algorithm to automatically control traffic lights to optimize the flow of cars. Two years later, Alibaba's data showed that notoriously car-clogged Hangzhou had fallen from fifth place on the country's list of most-congested cities to fifty-seventh.

Easing residents' paths through life is one aim of the City Brain. Helping to save them is another. One feature of the system is an AI-powered navigation tool provided to ambulances that manipulates traffic lights to clear a path through traffic. In October 2019, we noticed a local news report about the speedy ambulance rescue of an elderly resident in the village of Xiaoshan, a rural district that sprawls south from the Qiantang River, that mentioned the system. According to the report, a seventy-seven-year-old Xiaoshan resident named Wang Fengqin was washing laundry near a creek when she lost her balance and fell in the water. A sanitation worker pulling weeds from the bank of the creek saw the woman fall and shouted for help. A nearby villager ran to the bank, saw Wang's crop of white hair floating on the surface of the water, and jumped in to pull her out. Medics arrived and saw the situation was dire. Loading her into the ambulance, they activated the City Brain navigation tool, the report said. As the ambulance powered down the road toward Xiaoshan No. 1 People's Hospital, the algorithm ensured that green lights appeared at each of the fourteen intersections they had to pass.

In the past, the police would have to issue radio broadcasts or send officers to the intersections to try to clear a path—tactics that didn't always work. On a good day in the past, the journey from where Wang had fallen to the hospital could have taken close to half an hour. This time, according to the report, it took twelve minutes. The medics wheeled her into the emergency room, where doctors found she still had water in her lungs. They drained it out.

We tracked down Wang's son, Li Dong, who said that he had arrived at the creek to find his mother lying on the ground soaking wet, her eyes closed and jaw clamped shut. Her face was turning black. Someone called emergency services, who talked Li and another villager through CPR compressions over the phone. Shortly before the ambulance arrived, a panicked Li pried open his mother's jaw and jammed his fingers down her throat. She coughed and a gush of creek water poured out.

After his mom came home from the hospital, Li treated twenty of her fellow villagers to a banquet and distributed $50 fruit baskets to thank them for their help. It wasn't until later that he found out City Brain had played a role in saving his mother. He was so preoccupied with his mom's breathing that he didn't notice the lights turning green, though he did remember thinking the ride had been surprisingly smooth. He used computers to automate machining tools at his job in a factory in another province and had read that China was making a lot of progress in AI. "I never expected AI would affect my life in this way," he said.

The Xiaoshan system has quickly become a centerpiece of the City Brain. At the time of Wang's accident, it covered 400 junctions and 600 traffic lights spread over the entirety of the district. By the end of 2019, it was deployed in eight hospitals and eighteen emergency stations, and had been used more than 400 times, cutting emergency travel times down by an average of 50 percent. In response to an email seeking comment, the Hangzhou police sent an uncharacteristically detailed answer spanning several printed pages. Their excitement at the system's results was palpable, even filtered through the rigid officialese of a Chinese government email. Smoothing a path for ambulances "provides hospitals and ER doctors with more precious time for saving lives," they wrote. "It has given city residents a deeply true experience of the help City Brain can provide the masses in their daily lives."

The ambition of Chinese cities to make their residents' lives easier is real. Local governments and companies spent $24 billion on smart city technology in China in 2020, a figure that was likely to rise to about $40 billion by the end of 2024, according to estimates by the tech-market analysis firm International Data Corporation. In Hangzhou, Alibaba has pumped money into a City Brain Lab dedicated to honing and expanding its smart city platform. With advanced processing, the company predicts, the City Brain will eventually broaden its algorithms to cover urban planning, electricity consumption, and firefighting. In the longer term, China's state planners are pushing for smart city systems to soak up data from a more diverse web of sensors: not just cameras and smartphones but also QR code readers, point-of-sale machines, air quality monitors, and radio frequency identification chips used to store biometric information in advanced ID cards.

As next-generation 5G mobile internet networks become more widespread, the list of potential data sources is likely to expand exponentially. Connected devices ranging from surveillance drones to smart toasters are set to produce new streams of data for city governments to tap. If everything goes as planned, officials will be able to crunch the information from those censors to revolutionize everything from sewage treatment and health care to crowd control.

Like Xinjiang, Hangzhou serves as a pilot zone for social control, giving the Party a view into what works and what doesn't. The experiments in both places also help prove that the same technologies the Party uses to terrorize and remold people who buck its authority can be deployed to coddle and reassure others who are willing to play along—a dynamic that has held true as its model of surveillance flows beyond China's borders.

PART III

TRADE WINDS

7

DIGITAL SILK ROAD

On a cool, overcast September day in 2015, a crowd of roughly 500 people filed into the headquarters of the Kampala Capital City Authority in central Kampala to witness an unveiling. The group included senior officials from the Ugandan government, Chinese business executives, and several Chinese diplomats. Among them was Beijing's ambassador to Uganda, Zhao Yali, who was dressed sharply for the occasion in a dark blue suit with a bright yellow tie and a red Chinese flag pinned to the lapel. As photographers gathered around, Zhao positioned himself next to a Ugandan man in his early seventies, also gussied up in an oversized gray pinstriped suit and a wide-brimmed hat with the chin strap hanging down.

The headwear gave the man away as Yoweri Museveni, Uganda's president since the days of Ronald Reagan. The aging strongman had been invited to the gathering by the Ugandan subsidiary of Huawei Technologies Co. Ltd., the world's largest maker of telecommunications equipment. Huawei had operated in Uganda for almost a decade and a half, expanding and upgrading the sub-Saharan country's phone and internet networks. Now it wanted to make a donation to Museveni's government—a gesture of thanks for past contracts and an advertisement for a new product the company hoped would lead to business.

Zhao and Museveni stood with other important guests in the center of a drab room observing three flat-screen monitors hung on the wall opposite them. One showed a street scene outside, the other a map, and the third a diagram that explained what they were looking at: a Safe City system built by Huawei to help the government keep better track of what was happening in the capital. The screens were connected to twenty cameras that Huawei had installed at ten "key surveillance points" around Kampala. Zhao looked on, a broad smile spreading across his face, as Museveni grabbed a walkie-talkie and issued the order to officially bring the system online.

According to an account later posted online by the Chinese embassy, the Ugandan leader thanked Huawei for "fulfilling its corporate social responsibility." The starter surveillance network, worth roughly $750,000, was a modest investment that would pay off big down the road for Huawei and Museveni alike.

Uganda's capital, Kampala, is an undulating patchwork of red-roofed houses, pale high-rises, and emerald vegetation. The city churns through its days in an atmosphere of unfulfilled potential. Bathed in sunlight, its districts spread over a cluster of more than twenty hills north of Lake Victoria, with dense ribbons of car traffic weaving past stands of palm trees. The city's wealthier neighborhoods feel almost Californian: crisscrossed by wide roads; dotted with high-end hotels, innovation hubs, and air-conditioned malls; abuzz with entrepreneurial conversation. Its ghettos, meanwhile, have a feeling all their own: hot, crowded, and unpaved; short on electricity and running water; forgotten by policymakers but kept under close watch by police. That contrast is mirrored across Uganda, which has one of sub-Saharan Africa's most robust and energetic economies but has struggled with rising inequality. In combination with corruption, the wealth gap holds the country back from realizing what many on and outside the continent see as its great promise.

The weight of those unfulfilled expectations had begun to press down on Museveni. A former cattle herder, he maintained power by mixing enticements and prods. He tapped neglected oil reserves, brought in foreign investment, and spun a glittering vision of Uganda's future as a pioneer in African prosperity. He also put a premium on security, cowing his enemies and critics with threats, harassment, and violence. The elites grazing at Kampala's tapas bars and Japanese izakayas supported Museveni, even if they found his methods distasteful. But to ghetto residents surviving on cheap plates of chapati and beans, he seemed a relic whose retirement was long overdue.

Public frustrations came pouring out when Museveni ran for reelection in 2016 after three decades in power. As he campaigned, he was bombarded by complaints over corruption, high youth unemployment, and the country's rickety health system and neglected schools. He won nevertheless, pulling in 60 percent of the vote after placing his opponent under house arrest and imposing a social media blackout. At least twenty-two people died in clashes after the result was announced. Opposition activists accused the government of orchestrating the violence.

The following year, Museveni moved to abolish age limits on the presidency, clearing a path for him to serve as leader for life. When opposition politicians led a flood of people into the streets to protest, Museveni decided he needed to sharpen the government's ability to detect threats. He knew just where to turn for help.

Over the course of a year, Huawei, with help from the Chinese embassy, worked with Ugandan security officials to design a full-sized Safe City system to suit the government's needs. The company had competition. Genetec, a Canadian security and surveillance firm, traveled to Kampala in September 2018 to pitch a rival system. But a few months later, Uganda's police posted a photo on its Twitter feed showing China's new ambassador and Uganda's security chief meeting with a delegation from the Chinese Ministry of Public Security in Kampala to discuss a technology training program for Ugandan police officers. The next spring, Huawei emerged as the winner from a classified bidding process. The $126 million deal included a new six-story, $30 million surveillance hub in Kampala that would link to hundreds of cameras capable of doing real-time facial recognition. The project would start by connecting 83 police stations in the capital in its first phase, then expand to another 271 through the rest of the country. Uganda would pay a little more than $16 million up front, with the rest financed by a loan from the Standard Chartered banking company.

In public, Huawei and the Ugandan government touted the system as a way to target criminals. In practice, Museveni's regime followed the Chinese example and used it to track political threats, including one in particular with roots in the Kampala ghettos.

◉

China, for all of its associations with authoritarianism, has done more than any other country to democratize state surveillance around the globe. It has accomplished this by helping its companies sell useful and affordable digital tracking systems to governments and by offering to train local police in how to get the most out of the technology. As a result, almost any regime can now get their hands on advanced surveillance tools to do with as they see fit.

The global market for mass surveillance is young. Like many markets, it was invented in the West. Prior to 9/11, retail sales of surveillance technology were virtually nonexistent. The Global War on Terror gave rise to new companies from the United States, Israel, Germany, France, and Canada— many of them founded by former spies and soldiers—that sought to profit by selling military-grade tracking tools developed to hunt terrorists to the highest bidders. The firms' products, mostly spyware intended for breaking into protected communications, were enticing to criminal groups and governments alike. They were also expensive, narrowly focused, and hard to use. In 2011, *The Wall Street Journal* reported that the retail surveillance market had grown from "nearly zero" in 2001 to a robust but still modest $5 billion a decade later.

Chinese companies entered, and changed, the field with a new type of product: "safe city" systems. They resemble the smart city platforms that Alibaba built in Hangzhou but with an emphasis on security. They promised to help governments track not just a handful of suspicious individuals but entire populations. Huawei began marketing the systems abroad as early as 2010. The company's domestic rival ZTE followed suit a few years later. Early versions were rudimentary and had few takers. But starting in the mid-2010s, exponential growth in the availability of data and the capabilities of artificial intelligence made it possible for the companies to offer governments a new menu of much more powerful tools like facial recognition and crowd analysis.

Since then, Chinese surveillance systems have expanded across the globe with breathtaking speed. As of 2019, Huawei said it had installed Safe City systems in 700 cities across more than 100 countries and regions. ZTE claimed to have built similar systems in 160 cities spread across 45 countries. Tallies conducted by independent scholars are smaller but still striking. Sheena Greitens, a professor of political science at the University of Texas, found that Chinese surveillance and public-security technology systems had been adopted in more than eighty countries worldwide by 2020. With the exceptions of Australia and Antarctica, every continent now sees Chinese surveillance technology aiding its police forces.

Democracies host several of the Chinese systems. Hangzhou-based camera maker Dahua has installed its own "safe city" products to help monitor public transportation in multiple cities in Mexico. Huawei has refurbished video surveillance systems in the French village of Valenciennes, built smart city systems in Italy's Sardinia to monitor public safety threats and extreme weather, and begun installing a camera network in central Belgrade that can identify faces, track license plates, and alert police to suspicious behavior.

Estimates by market research firm IDC put the value of the market for video surveillance alone at more than $23 billion in 2019, and predicted it would more than double to nearly $50 billion by 2025. China is a driving force in that growth. This is due in large part to the ingenuity and drive of Chinese tech companies, but also to state support. While all governments play a role in supporting the business interests of domestic companies abroad, Beijing has gone further than most, offering generous loans to other governments to partner with Chinese firms without the demands for political or economic reforms that Western governments typically attach.

In recent years, the Chinese government's role has mushroomed and grown more muscular. The reason is Xi Jinping's Belt and Road

Initiative. In the same way that the United States launched the Marshall Plan to rebuild war-ravaged Western Europe as a bulwark against Soviet expansion in the 1940s, Xi wants to use the Belt and Road Initiative to rebuild the global trading system in ways that protect China's interests. One part of the trillion-dollar plan involves creating what Beijing describes as a "Digital Silk Road." By seeding other countries with Chinese technology in three areas—communications infrastructure, cross-border e-commerce, and smart (or safe) cities—the Communist Party hopes to rewire cyberspace according to its own vision.

Since the launch of the Belt and Road Initiative, Chinese diplomats have morphed into full-blown salespeople for built-by-China information technology projects abroad, brokering deals with the promise of easy financing that governments find difficult to reject. As of 2019, such projects accounted for an estimated $79 billion in investments around the world. Most of that money has gone into infrastructure like internet cables and 4G base stations, but surveillance has made up an ever larger slice of the pie.

As the scope of China's ambition became apparent in the late 2010s, concern began to bubble up in technology and policy circles about its implications, particularly in cutting-edge fields such as AI. By 2018, Chinese start-ups were vanquishing Silicon Valley giants in facial recognition tests, and AI research papers written by Chinese scientists held their own against their peers in global conferences. With both Washington and Beijing zeroing in on the technology as an area of competition, observers envisioned a near-future world divided between US and Chinese spheres of AI influence.

In October 2018, *Wired* magazine ran a cover story that captured the anxiety coursing through Western societies over China's growing tech prowess. Its title: "The AI Cold War That Could Doom Us All." In the story, the magazine's editor in chief, Nicholas Thomson, and political scientist Ian Bremmer fretted that China's Sputnik moment had come at the worst time. The world was beginning to doubt the durability of democracy. Far from spreading democratic ideals, information technology had helped put Donald Trump, an authoritarian, in the White House—and now it was helping China's Communist Party spread its influence around the globe. "Is the arc of the digital revolution bending toward tyranny, and is there any way to stop it?" they asked. Their answer to both questions: a resounding "maybe."

Evocations of the Cold War reflect the enormousness of the stakes, but as events in Uganda demonstrate, they paint a mistaken picture of the dynamics. China might be the United States' most formidable challenger since the Soviet Union, and the notion of a world divided certainly had a familiar ring to anyone old enough to remember the fall of the Berlin Wall. But for all its genuflecting to Marx and Lenin, the Party had demonstrated little interest in leading a global insurrection of the proletariat. The "China model" is not something Beijing necessarily expects anyone to be able to replicate. The point in promoting it is to show to the world and to China's own citizens that alternatives to liberal democracy exist and should be considered legitimate. In helping its companies to sell surveillance systems abroad, China's government is equipping countries with the tools and knowledge to develop their own alternatives, whatever those might be.

◉

For a time, Uganda shined in the eyes of the United States and other Western governments as a beacon of democratic potential in Africa. That was thanks in part to Museveni. A brash young leader from the longhorn ranchland of southwestern Uganda, he helped depose two dictators on his way to assuming the country's presidency. When he was sworn in as president in Kampala in 1986, dressed humbly in undecorated military fatigues, Museveni had promised a new era of democracy in which power would return to the people. "Nobody is to think that what is happening today is a mere change of guards," he said.

A year after being sworn in, Museveni flew to Washington for a White House meeting with Ronald Reagan. Human rights groups criticized abuses by troops as Museveni put down scattered insurgencies in the country's north, but they credited him for his relative tolerance of dissent. Ugandans themselves seemed to approve: he won reelection in a vote in 1996 that observers described as fair. Bill Clinton, concluding a visit to Africa two years later, praised the continent's "new breed" of leaders who professed dedication to liberal democratic ideas, a group that included Museveni. Subsequent election victories appeared substantially less legitimate, but Washington continued to see Museveni as the sort of temperate autocrat it could work with. After 9/11, Uganda's leader would become an enthusiastic partner in the US War on Terror, and an even more enthusiastic recipient of billions of dollars in American aid.

China also saw potential in Uganda. The Communist Party has maintained a keen interest in cultivating African allies since shortly after it took power in China. In the 1960s, it threw its support behind African liberation movements, shipping young revolutionaries and copies of Mao's "Little Red Book" to Dar es Salaam, the Tanzanian cauldron of leftist politics where Museveni spent his formative years. As China's wealth grew in the post-Mao years, the Party pushed to rival the United States as a supplier of aid to African nations, offering financial and other support free of the demands for political reform that Washington attached to its own largesse. In 2001, China donated $6.5 million to build a new headquarters for Uganda's Ministry of Foreign Affairs. It also canceled $17 million in debt and financed a half-billion-dollar four-lane expressway linking Kampala with Uganda's main airport in Entebbe.

Beijing's support freed Museveni to indulge his more autocratic impulses. In a 2012 operation called Fungua Macho (Swahili for "open your eyes"), Ugandan police installed spyware from the German company Finfisher on the Wi-Fi networks of twenty-one high-end hotels to compromise the devices of opposition figures and of the journalists and activists who visited them. ("Hotels are known meeting points for people with depraved plans," a leaked government memo on the operation noted.) In 2014, the Ugandan leader banned homosexuality.

The Obama administration, along with several other Western governments, cut funding following the homosexuality ban. China kept the money flowing. When Museveni encountered political trouble a couple of years later, the Party found itself with another opportunity to expand its influence.

The Chinese presence in Kampala is subtle but expansive. The new

Chinese-built highway, completed in 2018, provides a butter-smooth connection between downtown and the airport twenty-five miles to the south. A miniature strip mall near downtown houses a Chinese grocery store run by a former farmer from Jiangsu province, a Chinese hair salon called A Dong, and Big Thumb, a pan-Chinese restaurant with outdoor tables covered in flowery red tablecloths owned by a family from Jilin province in China's industrial northeast. A Beijing-sponsored Confucius Institute teaches Mandarin to students on the hilltop campus of Maker-ere University, where giant ill-tempered marabou storks cast a hungry eye over the city from the towering branches of flat-crown trees.

African countries, many of which had little to no previous telecom-munications infrastructure, were a critical proving ground for Huawei. The company started doing business in Kenya in 1998 and expanded from there, laying cable through some of the continent's most treacher-ous regions. In Uganda, where it first entered in 2001, the company oc-cupies the top floors of The Cube, a quasi-futuristic glass-fronted blue and red building that rises above the restaurants, bars, and embassies of Kampala's wealthy Kololo District. Framed photos of Museveni hang on the walls to either side of the company's main reception desk on the eighth floor. Three floors higher, elevators open onto a roof garden for Huawei staff. The garden is equipped with a ping-pong table, barbecue grills, and scaffolding that bears the company's name and logo, visible from miles away.

In a 2006 speech to employees stationed in Sudan and the Congo, founder Ren Zhengfei, a former engineer in the People's Liberation Army, drew on his military roots in lauding the company's fortitude. "'When the enemy retreats, we pursue' is Mao Zedong's rule for guerrilla war, is it not?" he said, pointing to Western companies that had given up on Africa after the first dot-com bubble burst in the year 2000. "It is only because we persisted in Africa that we are where we are today."

In addition to building and maintaining Uganda's communications networks, Huawei also ran training programs in computer science and telecommunications for Ugandans at Makerere University and at its main headquarters in Shenzhen, and it was helping the country develop quality standards for telecommunications equipment. All were critical contributions to Digital Uganda, a Museveni initiative that aimed to turn his country into a tech powerhouse on the continent.

The Ugandan leader's plans dovetailed almost perfectly with the Party's ambitions under the Digital Silk Road. In the years following the Snowden revelations, Beijing and Moscow had teamed up to promote the notion of "internet sovereignty." Where the United States and most of the developed world envisioned the global internet as a single, global network governed according to liberal democratic ideals of transparency and freedom, Chinese and Russian leaders argued that the governments should be allowed to govern the cyberspace inside their borders in whatever way they chose. The Digital Silk Road aimed to link together countries that shared the same view. It also aimed to expand the notion of sovereignty to cover not just the internet but digital technologies in general. In Museveni, a leader with an already demonstrated interest in social media controls and state surveillance, the Party had a willing partner.

In the spring of 2017, with opposition against his bid for a forever presidency heating up, Museveni ordered his police chief to approach the Chinese government for help in building out a police surveillance system. In doing so, he was following what had by then become standard practice around the continent. In his recent book *The Rise of Digital Repression*, former State Department Africa specialist Steven Feldstein recalls a conversation with a government intelligence contact in Ethiopia who contrasted the hard-sell approach of Israeli surveillance companies with China's sit-back style. "They know that you will come to them. They know that demand," he told Feldstein. Rather than approach suppliers directly, his agency always went through government officials. "And ta-da! They [the Chinese] would send their experts."

That May, shortly after being contacted by Museveni's government, the acting ambassador in Kampala, Chu Maoming, boarded a plane bound for Beijing with dozens of Ugandan police officers. In the Chinese capital, Chu escorted the Ugandans to a complex of severe buildings just east of Tiananmen Square that houses the Ministry of Public Security, where police officials demonstrated how Chinese surveillance systems could be used to automatically identify and track individuals using networks of high-definition cameras. After three days, Chu flew with the delegation to Huawei's headquarters in Shenzhen, where they discussed with company executives what type of Safe City system would satisfy Museveni's needs. The work paid dividends when the formal bidding process began the following year. Between the attention from Beijing and Huawei's incumbent advantage, the other companies never had a chance.

◉

Early on in its history, Huawei developed a reputation for legendary customer service, taking pride in cultivating employees who would go anywhere and do anything to satisfy a customer's needs. As the company installed the first phase of Uganda's new Safe City system, the country's police would learn firsthand how accommodating Huawei employees could be.

Toward the end of 2018, the six members of an elite Ugandan police intelligence unit had started listening to the wiretapped phone conversations of a pop-star-turned-politician named Robert Kyagulanyi Ssentamu, better known by his stage name, Bobi Wine. The thirty-six-year-old had built a successful musical career blending reggae and Afrobeats with strands of social commentary. In 2016, Museveni had tried to pressure Uganda's most popular musicians into backing him for reelection, and Wine refused. Instead, the singer sheared off his dreadlocks, donned a red beret, and walked door-to-door campaigning for a seat in the Ugandan parliament. He won by a wide margin.

Wine was a threat to Museveni. The singer was born and raised in Kamwokya, a dusty maze of tin shacks in central Kampala bisected by an open sewer that residents cross using makeshift bridges. He was beloved in the city's poorer neighborhoods and among its youth. More than just speak their language, he had invented some of it: *kikomando*, the Kampalan name for the ghetto staple chapati and beans, came from the title of a song he released in the 2000s. When Museveni imposed a new tax on the use of mobile data—a transparent bid to stifle online criticism of the government coming from the country's poor—Wine led people into the streets to protest. Later, he drew tens of thousands of fans to a series of concerts where he called for Museveni to step down. After Wine wrote on social media in August 2018 that his driver had been shot and killed by Ugandan security forces at a political event in the border town of Arua, the singer was arrested and charged with treason. Two weeks later, he was released and traveled to the United States in a wheelchair, saying he had been beaten in prison and needed treatment for a dislocated back.

The trip to the United States, where he met with members of Congress, gave Wine the heft to unbalance the Ugandan status quo. After his return to Kampala, Senators Marco Rubio of Florida and Cory Booker of New Jersey sent letters to the Ugandan embassy protesting Museveni's suppression of political dissent. The European Parliament also weighed in, passing a resolution urging the Ugandan government to drop "what appear to be trumped-up charges" against Wine. That's when the Ugandan police intelligence team picked up phone conversations between Wine and his entourage, the Fire Base Crew. Based on the calls, Wine was planning another concert, and by the sound of it, this one would be even bigger than the others, intended to increase pressure on Museveni even further.

But that was all the intelligence officers could surmise. Wine had been in politics long enough by then to know that the country's phone lines were compromised. Whenever they started talking about key details, he and the rest of the Fire Base Crew switched to a coded street slang the intelligence officers didn't understand. Other times the crew exchanged messages using the encrypted chat app WhatsApp, which the intelligence officers would only be able to read by breaking into Wine's device, an iPhone. Apple's security was virtually impossible to crack using traditional methods, which meant it was pointless to try to get their hands on the phone. Instead they turned to spyware that Ugandan security forces had recently purchased from an Israeli firm.

The spyware was modeled on Pegasus, a tool developed by a team of former Israeli intelligence operatives known as the NSO Group, that exploits flaws in iPhone security to give operators a level of control over the device normally reserved for Apple itself. Pegasus and other programs like it had been used to target the devices of activists, lawyers, journalists, and politicians in the Middle East, Europe, and North America. The intelligence team used a text message to trick Wine into downloading the spyware on his phone. Israeli experts had flown out to Kampala to teach the intelligence officers how to use the spyware to access emails and texts, but not encrypted messages. The team spent days huddled around a computer trying to get it to work. They failed.

For months, the police intelligence team had been sharing their command center with technicians from Huawei, whose logo—eight bright red flower petals arranged like a fan—was emblazoned across one of the walls. Desperate, the intelligence officers walked across the room to where the Chinese men sat and asked if they could help.

In keeping with their Huawei training, the technicians dropped what they were doing and took control of the spyware. Within two days, they had full access to Wine's phone.

The Huawei technicians in Kampala weren't alone in providing such services. Months later, some of their colleagues working with a cyber-surveillance unit of the Zambian telecom regulator called the Cyber-crime Crack Squad would help the government access the phones and Facebook pages of a group of opposition bloggers who had been hammering Zambian president Edgar Lungu over corruption, police violence, and censorship. In an interview with *The Wall Street Journal*, Zambian senior security officials would describe how two Huawei experts pinpointed the bloggers' locations and fed the data to police units deployed to arrest them in the northwestern city of Solwezi.

The results were similar in Kampala. Once inside the device, the police were able to read all of Wine's WhatsApp messages. In one private group, named FireBaseCrew, they found a list of eleven senior opposition political figures whom Wine had invited to speak onstage at the concert.

Wine had planned to host the event at One Love Beach, a property he owned on the shores of Lake Victoria. He had arranged to hold it early in the day to throw off the police and ensure that at least some of the speakers would be able to take their turn onstage before it got shut down. However, hundreds of police flooded the One Love Beach just as the show was getting underway. They arrested dozens of organizers and attendees. Some of the scheduled speakers never even made it to the venue but were instead arrested en route.

Wine and his team were stunned. In the aftermath, they racked their brains trying to figure out how the information had leaked out. Over time, they would realize it was only the start of a new phase in Museveni's campaign to suffocate their movement.

◉

A little over four months after the Huawei technicians helped hack Wine's phone, in April 2019, we met with Dorothy Mukasa, a diminutive but unrelenting former journalist turned privacy activist based in Kampala. Mukasa ran an anti-censorship nonprofit named Unwanted Witness that had just put out a lengthy report detailing the evolution of state surveillance in Uganda. Huawei had changed things, she told us. Where other foreign firms had sold Museveni single tools, the Chinese company was furnishing an entire system. "When it comes to surveillance, they're the big players," she said. "We copy a lot from China."

Huawei's Safe City was quickly taking shape. New utility poles had begun to pop up at intersections, near markets, and in villages on the city's outskirts, wrapped in garlands of anti-theft spikes that glinted with ill intent in the East African sun. Near the top of each pole, a crossbar held aloft clusters of new surveillance cameras that would have been familiar to any of Xinjiang's Uyghurs. Like many people in the developing world, most Ugandans couldn't afford the luxury of worrying about abstractions like privacy. "They say, 'You know, I'm not a criminal.' Why should they care?" Mukasa said. But for opposition politicians who only used to have to worry about being physically tailed, the cameras meant they now also had to be careful not to linger too long in public.

Ingrid Turinawe, a leader of Uganda's main opposition party, worried about the effects of increased pressure from the added scrutiny. She told us police had recently installed a camera at the end of her street. Strange clicks and echoes on her phone—signs, she assumed, that the call was being tapped—had been multiplying. The police had started blockading her in her home when she was about to set off for events, reciting her plans in disturbingly accurate detail. Similar tactics had led some in the opposition to chicken out, she said. "Some people are not too resilient," she explained, her tone as dry as dust, as she recounted stories of government critics being pressured into spying for Museveni. Others, like her, were determined to keep fighting, though hope for peaceful change was dwindling. Increasingly, there was talk of revolution. "I don't know how it will happen or how it will end," Turinawe said, staring grimly ahead. "But some of us believe that's the only option."

The sense the game had changed was palpable when we visited Bobi Wine at his home in the low-slung suburban town of Kasangati, north of central Kampala. Hidden at the end of a rutted dirt path the color of rust that snakes through a newly built suburb, the compound is hard to find and well guarded. It is surrounded by two concentric ten-foot walls of concrete with a gnarled band of untamed bushland between them. On the day we visited, at least a dozen members of Wine's entourage patrolled the front and rear gates and inside the compound itself.

Inside the walls, the compound at first looked like an oasis. Palm trees lined a driveway that ended in a roundabout in the center. On one side of the roundabout stretched a grassy yard dominated by a towering mango tree. On the other sat Wine's house, painted a pristine white with large windows looking out from behind stacked rows of colonnades and spirals of wrought iron encircling a generous second-floor balcony. When we pulled up, Wine was sitting on the floor just inside the entrance, posing with his wife, Barbie, and the couple's three children for photos that he later planned to post on Twitter.

Trim and energetic with a wide smile, Wine cut a sharp contrast with Museveni, who had thickened and grown stern with age. Instinctually, the singer played the part of the celebrity. He had created the sanctuary for his family when most of the neighborhood was still undeveloped, he explained, sweeping his arm in a semicircle with practiced nonchalance. "We built this from nothing, man," he said. "At the time, everything was bush." But whispers of doubt gradually mixed in with the bravado. The house, the singer explained, was a relic of a past life. He'd built the Kasangati compound, and another on the shores of Lake Victoria south of Kampala, with money he'd made performing. "But a lot of that is gone now," he said. "The police won't let me hold concerts anymore." He had money saved, but he wasn't sure how long it would last.

The sense of insecurity had intensified since police broke up his last concert. Not long after, Wine had tried multiple times to meet with members of his crew to plan a protest against the social media tax. Security forces broke up those gatherings as well. The crew fell into a state of paranoia, gripped with fear that one of their own might have sold them out. The rings of security Wine had erected around his home began to feel flimsy. Soon it seemed impossible to plan anything at all.

It wasn't until two months before our visit that Wine discovered what had happened. That's when *The Wall Street Journal* approached him to ask about screenshots Ugandan security officials had shown one of its journalists of his "FireBaseCrew" WhatsApp group discussing details of the concert. Sources in the government had warned him that the police had acquired new spying tools, he told us. The *Journal*'s phone call confirmed that they were being used against him. The singer and his team immediately stopped using the chat app and started saving sensitive discussions for face-to-face meetings.

Walking inside the house, Wine displayed his other method for escaping detection: a stack of four phones, some loaded with SIM cards registered under other people's names. "We're playing a cat-and-mouse game here," he said. "They might have two phones tracked, and I could decide to send all these phones in different directions of the country, you know, to confuse them." The constant evasion was exhausting and took time away from planning, but he and his crew had no choice.

That still didn't help the Fire Base Crew with the other methods of control Museveni was exploiting, including the Safe City camera systems. Wine's answer for those: a mix of speed and crowds.

We saw that strategy in action a couple of days later, when Wine set out to provoke a confrontation with Museveni. The singer had earlier applied for permission to put on an Easter concert at One Love Beach, his lakeside property. The holiday is one of the biggest of the year in Uganda, which is roughly 40 percent Catholic, and it is a time when many of the country's top musicians hold concerts. Police had nevertheless rejected his application, saying they couldn't guarantee the safety of attendees. Instead, Wine planned to hold a press conference to slam the decision and call out Museveni for being a coward. The police would almost certainly try to arrest him.

The plan was risky, but Wine felt he didn't have any choice. For months, the police had kept him hemmed in. He needed to be in the streets and on a stage, riding the power of the crowd.

Gathering in Wine's compound under rainy skies, the Fire Base Crew was anxious. If Wine was going to be arrested, he needed to be arrested in a loud way, surrounded by TV crews and as many supporters as they could muster along the way to the other property. If they didn't move quickly and strategically, the police could pick up on their movements and scuttle the plan by blocking their way out of Kasangati.

Wine emerged from his house dressed for action in jeans, a denim jacket, and a new pair of Nike sneakers. His infectious grin was gone. Instead he kept his lips pressed together, a mask of grave resolve. On his head he sported his customary red beret, adorned with a patch in the front showing a black clenched fist against a white map of Uganda. He conferred in hushed tones with members of his security detail, then offered businesslike handshakes to a handful of local reporters he had invited to tag along. As the Fire Base Crew moved toward their vehicles, the tension climbed higher. The security team warned the reporters not to get between them and Wine's SUV.

As soon as the convoy was through the gate, it tore off down the road, kicking up a cloud of dust that enveloped the reporters' vehicles trailing behind. It sped through turns and intersections, heedless of traffic lights and anyone who fell behind. In Kamwokya, Wine's SUV rolled to a stop, and he did a short live interview with the trailing journalists through the window. Soon, the convoy was surrounded by a dozen supporters, several of them on motorcycles. As the vehicles continued south, more cars and motorcycles joined, converging into a column that stretched the length of a football field. Pedestrians cheered and raised their fists. By the time they reached the city's southern suburbs, Wine had gathered enough of a crowd that it was safe for him to slow down. People poured out of their homes and lined both sides of the road to cheer. Hundreds ran alongside the convoy, arms raised in the air, lofted fists bouncing to the rhythm of their footfalls as the men on motorcycles buzzed back and forth, whipping up the enthusiasm with shouts of "People power!"

The procession ran into a police blockade a little more than a mile north of One Love Beach. For a moment, it seemed Wine might succeed in punching through, but the police presence was overwhelming. An armored police truck fitted with a water cannon pounded the crowd with three high-velocity bursts in quick succession. The water, mixed with pepper spray, produced screams from the crowd, some of whom backed away. A dozen police in helmets and bulletproof vests moved in, smashed the window of the SUV, and forced Wine out of the vehicle, dragging him away as they fended off his supporters with riot shields. The reporters stood by, capturing all of it—the heaving crowds, the thuggishness of the police—on their cameras. Wine believed he had won: another high-profile arrest, another leap in his stature.

A few months later, *The Wall Street Journal* published a story about Huawei employees helping African governments track opposition political figures, including Wine. In a letter to the *Journal* published online after the story was published, Huawei's lawyers said several of the story's statements about Huawei's involvement with government cybersecurity forces in Africa were "demonstrably false" and accused the newspaper of defamation. The letter challenged the reliability of the *Journal's* sources but didn't offer evidence to rebut claims in the story. To our knowledge, the company never pursued a legal claim against the *Journal*.

On November 29, 2019, Museveni posted photos of himself on Twitter presiding over the official launch of phase one of the Huawei surveillance project, officially called the National CCTV System, at the new command center in Ugandan police headquarters. The Ugandan leader was wearing an outfit almost identical to the one he had sported five years earlier at the donation ceremony for Kampala's first mini–Safe City system, including the ever-present hat. This time, however, the screens in front of him covered the entirety of a giant wall and were connected to a much more comprehensive network of cameras. In Kampala alone, he said, there were 83 monitoring centers staffed by 500 operators and overseen by 50 commanders. "It is evident that we are well on our way to tightening the noose on criminals who had become daring," he wrote, "including those who unfortunately thought they would use crime to discredit the NRM" (Uganda's ruling National Resistance Movement). He promised more to come in phase two.

Wine's showdown with Museveni began in earnest twelve months later, when the singer officially submitted his paperwork to stand in the general election. The year before he had been named to *Time* magazine's 100 Next, a list of "rising stars" intended as a companion to its annual roster of the world's 100 most influential figures. On his way to attend the ceremony in New York City, he had met with members of the Ugandan expatriate community, who reassured him he would have the financial resources to make a serious run against Museveni.

Wine was detained almost immediately after handing in his application and later told news media that security forces had assaulted him inside a van for several hours before dumping him at his home. He was arrested again at a political rally a few weeks later for violating rules against public gatherings amid the Covid-19 pandemic. Thousands of his supporters poured into the streets, kicking off days of violent protest. The unrest conjured Ingrid Turinawe's warnings about the possibility of revolution. "Could Bobi Wine's arrest be the start of a civil uprising?" one African media organization asked in an ominous headline.

But if Wine's arrest was a spark capable of lighting the Ugandan prairie ablaze, Museveni was quick to extinguish it—with help, once again, from Huawei. The singer was charged and released two days after his arrest. Museveni intimated, not for the first time, that Wine was a foreign agent. "Some of these groups are being used by outsiders, homosexuals—I don't know, groups outside there—who don't like the stability of Uganda, the independence of Uganda," he said in a speech to supporters of the NRM. "But they will discover what they are looking for." As the violence ebbed, Ugandan security forces fanned out across the country, using data from license plate readers and facial recognition—all connected through Huawei's networks—to identify and detain protesters caught on the Chinese company's cameras. A week after the protests kicked off, Ugandan police delivered a final tally of 45 killed and 836 arrested.

Even before Museveni deployed his new system to crush the protests, his partnership with Huawei had already helped focus Western attention on the rapid spread of Chinese surveillance exports. The *Journal*'s story detailing the relationship circulated among national security officials in the Trump administration as evidence of the need for more aggressive moves to counter the Chinese Communist Party's technological ambitions. Think tanks from Washington, DC, to Canberra cited Uganda in reports that echoed earlier warnings of a coming tech cold war, describing a comprehensive strategy drawn up in Beijing to spread the "China model" throughout the developing world—and maybe, if people weren't careful, some of the developed world too.

Others were less certain that Chinese surveillance exports were intended to create mini-Chinas around the globe. Testifying before Congress during a hearing on the rise of China's digital authoritarianism in 2019, Jessica Chen Weiss, a Cornell University scholar who studies nationalism and international relations, argued that the story of Chinese surveillance exports was more complicated than it was often made out to be. Chinese tracking tools may help other governments control their populations, she said, but the way the technology is deployed is determined by local politics. She pointed to one of the earliest known examples, a Chinese surveillance system installed in Ecuador in 2011 that had failed to reduce crime because of a lack of personnel and has since been scrutinized by a new administration with less authoritarian tendencies. Her takeaway: "The diffusion of digital authoritarianism is not the same thing as an intentional effort to remake other governments in China's image."

For all of the work Xi was doing to promote the China Solution, Chen Weiss pointed to other instances in which the Chinese leader highlighted the uniqueness of the country's rise and indicated the Party wouldn't ask others to emulate it. "Neither China's economic nor its political model is well suited for export," she wrote in an essay that served as the template for her congressional testimony. China's miraculous growth in the post-Mao era was the product of a rare blend of factors that few countries could replicate: a massive and compliant population, strong leadership, and a generous dose of good timing.

China's success with surveillance is likewise the result of a concurrence of advantages—a large and disciplined bureaucracy, massive stores of data, and deep financial resources—that few other countries can match. Chinese citizens have been issued with detailed identification cards since the mid-1980s, notes Iginio Gagliardone, a scholar of China-Africa relations at the University of Witwatersrand in South Africa. In Africa and other parts of the developing world, public records are poor, he points out, and in nations like Sierra Leone, complete records may not even exist. Many of the people a developing-world government might want to target with surveillance exist on the fringes of society—and outside government databases. To a country with limited resources, successfully copying the China model was no less an improbability than replicating the American one.

Both Chen Weiss and Steven Feldstein, the former State Department Africa specialist, argued that China's surveillance exports were driven by opportunism as much as ideology. "In none of the countries I visited did I encounter evidence of an overt Chinese push to establish an alternate governance model through the export of repressive technology," Feldstein wrote in *The Rise of Digital Repression*. "The biggest selling point for Chinese technology was its low cost and accessibility—with few strings attached."

So what was China trying to achieve? Despite presiding over the world's second-largest economy, the Party has remained connected to its origins as an underground organization—and to the paranoia that helped it endure many attempts by more powerful forces to snuff it out in its early days. In promoting the China Solution and exporting surveillance, the Party was trying to undermine the notion that democracy is the only legitimate form of government to which a country can aspire. In Chen Weiss's words, its ultimate aim was "to make the world safe for autocracy" and, by extension, itself.

The Ugandan elections were an example of that strategy bearing fruit. On January 13, 2021, the eve of the vote, Museveni imposed an internet blackout, as Chinese officials had done in Xinjiang a dozen years earlier after the riots in Urumqi. Two days later, with exit polls showing Museveni in the lead, Bobi Wine accused the military of stuffing ballot boxes and chasing his supporters away from polling places, proclaiming that "every legal option is on the table" for contesting the results. Not long after, security forces surrounded the singer's compound in Kasangati, putting him under de facto house arrest. "He is not an ordinary person anymore," said a military spokeswoman, explaining that Wine should "appreciate" the security forces, which she insisted were there for his protection. The US ambassador to Uganda was blocked from visiting Wine, who stayed trapped in his compound for eleven days until the Ugandan High Court ordered the security forces to disperse.

The official results of the election showed Museveni winning 59 percent of the vote to 35 percent for Wine. Museveni called it "the most cheating-free" election in the country's history. Unsatisfied, Wine filed a legal challenge in the Ugandan courts but dropped the case three weeks later, accusing the Supreme Court judges of being biased in favor of Museveni. "We have decided to move the case from [the Supreme] Court and bring it back to the court of the people," he told supporters. In the weeks that followed, he pleaded with Western countries to back up words with action. The main target of his comments was undoubtedly the United States, which had issued a statement condemning the detention of opposition politicians but still declined to cut ties with Museveni.

During a swing through Africa in late February 2021, China's top foreign affairs official, Yang Jiechi, met with Museveni to congratulate him on the victory. He relayed warm greetings from Xi Jinping. "Under the personal care and promotion of the two leaders, China-Uganda relations have developed smoothly," he said. "China supports Uganda pursuing the path of development that suits its own national conditions." That path wasn't likely to follow China's. For Museveni to cling to legitimacy, Uganda had to at least keep up the illusion of democracy. That meant accepting far more dissent than the Communist Party would ever tolerate. Nor was it likely that Uganda's relatively ragtag police could operate their surveillance system with the same ruthless efficiency as China's security agencies, even if they wanted to. But none of that mattered. It was enough that China had provided Museveni with the means to stay in power and, in doing so, to move a country still described on the US State Department's website as a "reliable partner" further outside the bounds of Western norms.

Research by Sheena Greitens and Edward Goldring, a scholar of authoritarian politics at the University of York, showed that Beijing's approach has been both infectious and effective in eroding democratic values. Sifting data on Chinese technology sales abroad, the pair found that having two neighboring countries acquire Chinese surveillance technology made a country 1,200 percent more likely to also acquire it—a dynamic that recalls the "network effects" that helped Facebook, Google, and Twitter achieve scale. And while Chinese surveillance systems generally failed to reduce crime, the scholars discovered, they were associated with a significant increase in human rights abuses.

A large part of the Party's success in setting the United States back on its heels stemmed from its ability to exploit the capitalist market forces that American leaders since Richard Nixon had been encouraging Beijing to embrace. The profit drive of Chinese tech companies like Huawei transformed them into efficient, ruthless soldiers in Beijing's guerrilla assault on the status quo. But they were hardly alone. Mesmerized by the immense potential of the China market, American technologies played just as important a role.

8

PARTNERS IN PRE-CRIME

For a long time, Intel Corporation's grip on the global market for micro-processors seemed unshakable. The tiny chips, made by weaving together electronic circuits on a minuscule piece of semiconductor material like silicon, are the building blocks of modern technology. In the 1990s, as anyone who watched American television at the time knew, there was "Intel inside" nearly every personal computer and most of the computer servers sold in the United States. But as the decade unfolded, the company struggled to defend itself against rivals who were either more nimble or more affordable. By the late 2000s, the once invincible chip giant was lurching into the future, one slingshot blow from tumbling to the ground.

Like a lot of American companies at the time, Intel sought salvation in China. In 2007, it announced plans to build a $2.5 billion factory in the northeastern Chinese city of Dalian, bringing the company's total investment in the country to just under $4 billion. "China is our fastest-growing major market and we believe it's critical that we invest in markets that will provide for future growth to better serve our customers," Intel's then-CEO Paul Otellini said when announcing the deal. The company's investment arm, Intel Capital, armed itself with $500 million and went on the hunt for opportunities in new tech sectors that its competitors had yet to discover.

At the time of Intel Capital's shopping spree, China had just usurped Japan as the world's second-largest economy. As incomes rose, Chinese people became voracious consumers of the latest electronics. The Chinese government had likewise developed a taste for cutting-edge technology and mirrored Chinese consumers in its relentless pursuit of upgrades.

Otellini, an Intel veteran who served as CEO for eight years and died in 2017, had been a fierce proponent of the Asian emerging market. When word circulated that Google would pull its search business out of China over conflicts with the Communist Party, the charismatic Californian dismissed them. "Nothing's ever final in China. And you can't really leave the world's largest market at the end of the day," he said in a 2010 interview on PBS. "So there has to be a rapprochement." Google eventually gave up on search in China. Intel, like most other Western tech companies, chose to remain behind. With its immense size, China was a market that had captivated Western businesses for centuries. Presented with the opportunity to reap untold profits from the world's most populous country, few could resist the allure.

Intel Capital found one opportunity in a small but promising start-up that specialized in stringing together security cameras—an early version of the techniques that would be used years later to weave the web of surveillance devices in Xinjiang. Founded in Beijing in the year 2000, NetPosa Technologies Ltd. launched itself into the video business just as the industry in China was switching from analog to digital. The evolution of the technology created demand for companies that could develop systems to connect networks of cameras that could be monitored and controlled from a single location. By the time Intel discovered the company, NetPosa had already shown promise by linking together a network of 10,000 cameras in eastern Beijing that the government used to maintain security during the 2008 Summer Olympics. It had provided similar systems for the Shanghai Expo in 2010.

Investing in NetPosa had its risks. Digital video was still relatively new, and the field was crowded with start-ups. The company had done well, but it had yet to develop a product that separated it from other leaders in the field. Still, Intel decided to take a flyer. In 2010, it bought a 6 percent stake in NetPosa for a little over $4.5 million, becoming the start-up's fifth-largest shareholder. "Our software group sponsored this investment," Richard Hsu, Intel Capital's managing director for China, said in an interview at the time. "They saw the investment with these guys as very, very interesting going forward."

Hsu said the company saw the deal from a "computing perspective," rather than a security or political one. The surveillance industry would inevitably require huge numbers of high-performance chips, he explained, which would benefit "Intel's core business." The amount was small enough that Intel would barely feel the loss if the Chinese company went under. If the company did well, then Intel would have a nice foothold in an intriguing and growing industry.

Measured in returns and the expansion of Intel's business, the Net-Posa investment would end up being one of the company's most lucrative moves in China. With Intel's help, NetPosa established itself as a player in Chinese surveillance just as the industry was about to skyrocket. By 2019, China accounted for almost half of revenues in the $20 billion global video surveillance market, according to the industry research firm Omdia. A willing supplier to China's police forces, NetPosa would see its value double many times over in that span. The company would also go on to play a role in Xinjiang's public security market, selling cutting-edge video management systems, facial recognition capability, and vans that doubled as command posts to police bureaus there. More importantly, Intel's partnership with NetPosa helped establish the American company as a chip provider of choice for companies looking to match the start-up's success.

Intel was not alone. Several other Silicon Valley brand names—including Cisco Systems and Sun Microsystems—had also sniffed out the potential in China's surveillance market early on. More continued to pile in as the market grew, helping to further expand and refine it. In November 2018, the China Security and Protection Industry Association, a surveillance industry group based in Beijing, recognized thirty-seven Chinese companies for outstanding contributions to the country's "safe city" industry. Of those, roughly half had financial, commercial, or supply-chain relationships with American technology companies.

The appeal went beyond pure profits. In the same way that fast-growing Chinese cities like Beijing and Shanghai became playgrounds for the world's architects in the 2010s, China's surveillance market had developed into a laboratory for Western security companies to test technologies that would raise eyebrows back home. In 2018 at Security China, the country's largest security expo, Israeli AI start-up Faception went onstage to advertise its system, which it said could identify terrorists based on their facial features. To demonstrate, the company's CEO, Shai Gilboa, ran spectators through a demonstration using images of what he claimed were Xinjiang terror suspects, saying its algorithm identified them with 95 percent accuracy. Hours later, a Canadian start-up, NuraLogix, took the mic to tout technology it said could read stress levels by capturing blood pressure and heart rate data from capillaries in the face from smartphone footage, which it pitched as useful in interrogations. After the presentation, Marzio Pozzuoli, the company's CEO, said NuraLogix had decided to concentrate on China after growing frustrated with Western governments' long, regulation-heavy processes for testing new technology. "We went to Hangzhou and talked to government people there and they said, 'How soon can we put this stuff to use?'" Pozzuoli said, his bearded face cracking a wide smile. "It's amazing what you can do in China."

Over time, the enticements of the Communist Party's hunger for new and better ways to track China's population also pulled in the computer science departments of elite American universities and a few top researchers in fields on the outer orbit of surveillance, including genetics. By the time Huawei was pushing the expansion of the Chinese surveillance state abroad, American tech companies, investors, and academics had already played vital roles in nurturing it inside China's borders. Many of them profited from it, some handsomely.

The experiences of Intel and others illustrated the trade-offs faced by foreign corporations eager to tap into China's burgeoning market in the last decades. By 2010, as China consistently delivered economic growth rates of close to 10 percent, multinationals without a foot in the market faced uncomfortable questions from shareholders. Yet, operating in the nation meant firms were forced to play by a set of rules very different from those in the West. For providers of hardware or internet services, that meant not just dealing with an authoritarian state that led the world in censorship and was often accused of being a serial abuser of human rights but potentially enabling it.

As firms sought to balance their commercial interests with the need to present a socially responsible exterior, they increasingly took refuge in complexity. They produced statements of principle gilded with references to democratic values but said the machinations of global supply chains combined with their own immense operations made it impossible to know when one of their products or services was being used in violation of those beliefs. The approach helped some of the biggest names in tech sidestep scandals on multiple occasions, though it would face its stiffest test as outrage continued to build over Xinjiang.

◉

Intel was by no means the first to profit from helping Chinese leaders spy on their own people. The Western business world, it turns out, has midwifed the Party's surveillance state since its embryonic beginnings in the late 1990s.

China's surveillance industry traces its roots to the "Golden" projects the Party launched in the years following the 1989 Tiananmen Square crackdown to upgrade the country's "e-government" infrastructure. With the Golden Shield project, the Ministry of State Security wanted to upgrade the Great Firewall, at the time a crude gateway with rudimentary internet filters that couldn't keep up with the economy's growing hunger for information. Rather than simply block large swaths of the internet, the MSS wanted to fine-tune its censorship systems to manage—and track—access at the individual level. China at the dawn of the twenty-first century didn't have the necessary technology to pull that off, so it had no choice but to reach beyond its borders for help. When it did, as cybersecurity researcher Greg Walton documented in a groundbreaking 2001 report, it found several willing hands extending enthusiastically toward it.

The extent of that enthusiasm was visible in the who's who of Western network equipment companies that flocked to an industry gathering held in Beijing in the year 2000, described in detail by Walton. The event, Security China, was the second of what has since evolved into one of the world's premier security technology expositions. The list of attendees that year included America's Cisco Systems, Motorola, and Sun Microsystems, German technology firm Siemens, and Canada's Nortel Networks. China's minister of public security was listed among the guests of honor. Compared to the previous expo held two years earlier, the number of international exhibitors registered to sell their services and wares at Security China 2000 had increased by 50 percent.

China was then already buying close to $20 billion a year in telecommunications equipment from foreign firms, according to Walton's calculations. Sun Microsystems, one of Silicon Valley's original computer and software success stories, helped the Ministry of Public Security build a national fingerprint database. Nortel, one of North America's dominant makers of networking gear at the time, provided state-owned Shanghai Telecom with state-of-the-art equipment that allowed the Chinese company to filter out unwanted URLs at the point where individual subscribers accessed the internet, allowing for fine-tuned censorship.

Another company that would play a critical, and ultimately controversial, part in the wiring of the Party's earliest digital control mechanism was Cisco Systems. Like Sun Microsystems, Cisco was a product of Stanford University and a Silicon Valley pillar; its name was taken from San Francisco, the city to the north of the Stanford campus, and its logo was an abstract rendering of the Golden Gate bridge. The company was the world's largest supplier of internet networking equipment, including sophisticated firewalls that allowed for "granular" filtering of internet traffic. As China built out its internet infrastructure, Cisco joined Nortel in supplying state-owned telecom companies with equipment that would help the Party revamp the Great Firewall. The company's routers made it possible for China to use lists of banned keywords to block specific web pages within websites without blocking the entire site, a capability it used for years to block specific Google search results.

Congress called Cisco to testify twice, in 2006 and 2008, about its sales of equipment to China. A leaked internal Cisco presentation from 2002 noted that one of China's goals with the Golden Shield project was to "combat Falun Gong evil religion and other hostiles." Cisco's general counsel, Mark Chandler, told Congress that he was "appalled" by the presentation but that it didn't represent the company's policy and wasn't used in marketing. In his testimony and a later blog post, Chandler wrote that firewalls are a necessary part of any network. "Cisco sells the same products globally, and does not modify its products for any government," he wrote. In 2011, members of the Falun Gong sued Cisco, saying the company's customized technology had enabled the Chinese government to track down and torture individuals associated with the group by monitoring their internet activity. The case was subsequently dismissed by a federal judge, who said there was no proof that Cisco knew the customized features would lead to that outcome, though press coverage of the dispute further hurt the company's public reputation.

Despite the barrage of negative publicity, Cisco explored an expansion beyond internet filtering into other areas of Chinese surveillance. In 2011, *The Wall Street Journal* uncovered Chinese government plans to install a network of up to 500,000 surveillance cameras covering 400 square miles in and around the inland megacity of Chongqing. The contractor for the project, the Hangzhou video surveillance giant Hikvision, said it would tap Cisco to supply the networking equipment. American companies had been prohibited from selling crime-control technology to China since the Tiananmen Square crackdown. In its report, the *Journal* noted that American officials were nevertheless powerless to stop Cisco's participation in the project, named Peaceful Chongqing by the Chinese, because of a key loophole in US export restrictions: the export limits, put in place in the

1990s, covered traditional items like fingerprint kits but not new products like digital security cameras. In response to the article, Chandler said that Cisco had been invited to participate in Peaceful Chongqing but turned down the opportunity. Even if that were true, former CNN Beijing bureau chief Rebecca MacKinnon later wrote in her book *Consent of the Networked*, "it is also clear that Cisco has sought business opportunities with law enforcement authorities in China"—a country, she noted, where religious and political dissent were considered crimes.

Cisco's defense of its presence in China played on the belief that technology would, if not bring democracy to China, at least loosen the Party's grip on Chinese society. Hewlett-Packard (HP), another American technology giant that had planned to bid on the Peaceful Chongqing project, offered a blunter response. "We take them at their word as to the usage," Todd Bradley, an executive vice president who oversaw HP's China strategy, told the newspaper. "It's not my job to really understand what they're going to use it for." As the shape and aims of the Party's surveillance state came into clearer focus and appeals to the inherent democratizing power of the internet crumpled under the weight of reality, arguments like Bradley's were left as the only credible alternative: when China's government offered a lucrative opportunity, companies had a duty to shareholders to pursue it.

◉

A gathering at the five-star Manchester Grand Hyatt Hotel in San Diego offered a peek at the returns Intel's stockholders reaped from the company's involvement in the Chinese surveillance industry. Over three cloudy and balmy October days in 2016, more than a thousand prominent tech executives and investors convened in the hotel for the company's annual venture capital bash—a coveted opportunity in the tech world for networking with potential clients and getting a sense of future trends. That year, attendees sat in on fireside chats by the CEOs of Salesforce and Verizon and PayPal's chairman as the executives prophesied growth areas such as big data analytics, robotics, and health. Participants could talk business during scheduled coffee breaks in a foyer with unblocked views of San Diego's deepwater bay, or indulge in the menu of recreational activities Intel had prepared, including go-karting and Segway riding at venues around the city.

The event culminated in Intel Capital's unveiling of its CEO of the year. Hundreds watched as Cheng Feng, NetPosa co-founder and CEO, walked onstage in a sleek leather jacket and fitted black pants to accept that year's award. After receiving his plaque, the bespectacled entrepreneur smiled broadly for the cameras. He had just become the first head of a Chinese company to earn the honor.

Cheng, who kept a low profile and rarely talked to the press, didn't speak publicly about the award. In a press release, NetPosa said it had received the award from Intel in recognition of its "rapid development over the years and future development." NetPosa had listed on the Shenzhen stock exchange four years after Intel's investment, the release noted. Within a year of going public, it exceeded 1.5 billion yuan in market value, nearly $250 million at that time, making it one of China's fastest-growing surveillance companies. The release didn't mention the critical role Intel had played in its growth. Neither did it mention the nature of the market that had driven NetPosa's growth, or the windfall Intel had reaped from it.

Making a functional microprocessor is complicated. Designing one that can process large amounts of data without consuming lots of power or running too hot is extremely difficult. When Intel made its initial investment in NetPosa in 2010, the Chinese microprocessor industry was more than a decade behind that of the United States. Chips were then, and still are, among China's two largest imports alongside petroleum.

At the time, NetPosa was struggling to develop a successful and affordable network video recorder, a key piece of equipment in making the next generation of surveillance technology available on a wider scale. Recorders are necessary to collect feeds from cameras in a network and transfer them to a storage device. NetPosa needed a chip that was both efficient and inexpensive to run the recorder. Intel's Atom processor fit the bill. When NetPosa's engineers couldn't figure out how to build a motherboard around the Atom, Intel dispatched its own experts to help. The revamped recorder catapulted NetPosa into the upper tier of Chinese video surveillance companies, helping it gain the separation from competitors that it had long sought.

In return, NetPosa helped introduce Intel to the Chinese surveillance industry as a worthy partner. At China's largest public security exhibition in Beijing, shortly after Intel's investment, NetPosa set up a booth with the slogan COME BUILD WITH US displayed over the logos of both companies. The partners went on to host joint industry forums on security technologies, where together with Intel they met senior Chinese police officials and academics from research institutes linked to the Ministry of Public Security. At a forum in the eastern city of Nanjing, the head of Intel's smart systems business unit, Wang Donghua, demonstrated the use of Intel's tech in surveillance and law enforcement between speeches by a high-ranking provincial police officer and a NetPosa executive. "Our joint activities have helped Intel win support from the industry," Net-Posa co-founder Liu Guang said in an interview transcript posted on the company's website. Intel sold its stake in NetPosa for six times the amount it had invested about two years after NetPosa's listing in 2014. The entrée NetPosa had provided into the world of Chinese surveillance proved more valuable.

The timing of NetPosa's listing could not have been better. Chinese leader Xi Jinping was pushing hard to upgrade the technology at the disposal of China's security forces, with a strong focus on video. In an exultant presentation on its investment successes in China in 2014, Intel Capital highlighted how NetPosa was poised to take advantage of that development: "NetPosa's solutions are now being implemented across China as part of the Safe Cities project, in which DDS [dynamic digital surveillance] solutions in over 600 cities will provide real-time alarms to prevent and deter crimes." By then, Intel had helped expand NetPosa's offerings to include cloud storage, which enhanced its ability to manage and analyze video footage.

Xinjiang would soon emerge as one of NetPosa's most promising markets. The firm built its initial links with the region's police by providing surveillance video management systems for the 2011 China Eurasia Expo, a major trade fair held every year in the Xinjiang capital, Urumqi. Not long after Intel Capital honored Cheng Feng in San Diego, Xinjiang's new Party boss, Chen Quanguo, launched the government campaign to reengineer Muslim identity in the region. NetPosa was ready to pounce, supplying local police with cloud-based video surveillance systems. It also sold them windowless black vans that it had developed to serve as mobile command centers.

As time went on, NetPosa started funding Chinese surveillance start-ups on its own. One of them was DeepGlint, a facial recognition company involved in several Xinjiang projects that advertised on its website an algorithm capable of recognizing the region's Uyghur Muslims. Another, a facial recognition and crowd analysis joint venture called SenseNets, also did extensive work in Xinjiang. In early 2019, a European cybersecurity researcher uncovered a SenseNets database online that contained the personal information and location data of more than 2.5 million people in the region. Intel had sold its stake in NetPosa by then, but the company continued to supply hardware to Cheng Feng's company and the other Chinese firms NetPosa supported. That included DeepGlint, which the California company promoted as a provider of "market-ready partners solutions" to clients interested in facial recognition.

Again, Intel was not alone among American corporations in profiting from the Communist Party's social engineering project in Xinjiang. A joint venture 49 percent owned by Hewlett-Packard Enterprise supplied internet switches to the government of Aksu, home to multiple internment camps for Muslims. As we documented in a story for *The Wall Street Journal* in 2019, digital storage giants Seagate and Western Digital supplied the overwhelming majority of the inexpensive hard disk drives Chinese police needed to save and process surveillance footage, including in Xinjiang. Contractors for two new surveillance projects in the region told us they preferred drives from the two American companies because of their superior quality. "For the most part it's Seagate or Western Digital. We don't buy domestic," said one. According to an estimate by one industry analyst, Seagate and Western Digital both pulled in more than $1 billion in revenue from China every year.

The participation by these companies in systematic government oppression of a religious minority inevitably recalled one of the more appalling episodes in American corporate history: IBM's collaboration with the Nazi regime in the lead-up to and during World War II. In the early days of Adolf Hitler's ethnic-cleansing campaign, the Nazis struggled to identify the large proportion of European Jews who had assimilated and could effectively "hide" their Jewishness. To overcome this, Nazi demographers would have had to conduct detailed surveys that traced the lineages of entire populations back several generations. The ferreting out of obscured cultural identities was the opposite of the Communist Party's goal in Xinjiang of erasing cultural difference, but it involved an identical technical challenge. As journalist Edwin Black documented in his book *IBM and the Holocaust*, IBM had technology perfectly suited to satisfy Hitler's "data lust": a machine that automated the tabulating of census data by reading and sorting punch cards marked to record an individual's traits.

The punch card system was patented in 1884 by IBM co-founder Herman Hollerith, a seminal figure in the development of data processing. The technology, Black wrote, "was nothing less than a nineteenth-century barcode for human beings." With their "magical ability to identify and quantify," the Hollerith machines were the ancestor of the algorithms employed today by Google, Amazon, and Alibaba, speeding up and improving the exploitation of data by orders of magnitude. Nazi Germany leased hundreds of them and bought punch cards in the hundreds of millions.

IBM's involvement in the Holocaust didn't stop at helping the Third Reich count Jews. As Hitler's project moved from identification to ghettoization, forced labor, and eventually genocide, the American corporation adapted its machines to each new task. Through a German subsidiary, IBM helped automate the scheduling of trains that crisscrossed Europe, carrying supplies to German troops and Jews to concentration camps. The machines became critical to the operations of the camps themselves and, toward the end of the war, to the enormous logistical challenge of gassing and shooting as much of Europe's Jewish population as possible. "The technology had enabled Nazi Germany to orchestrate the death of millions without skipping a note," Black noted. At the same time, the company touted its patriotic leasing of other machines to the US government, which used them to organize its own troop movements and corral Japanese-Americans into internment camps.

As Hitler's horrifying endgame came into clearer focus, IBM executives in the corporation's New York headquarters shielded themselves from the details of how their machines were being used in Europe. Long after the war ended, the company continued to deny responsibility for the way its machines were used in Germany. Documents Black examined showed that Hollerith machines leased by commercial clients were indeed sometimes transferred to Nazi installations without the company's knowledge, though the mere effort of trying to keep the operations of its German subsidiary at arm's length was indication enough that the company knew it was abetting terrible acts. In the end, Black wrote, "it did not matter whether IBM did or did not know exactly which machine was used at which death camp. All that mattered was that the money would be waiting—once the smoke cleared." Long before the Golden Shield project or Xinjiang, IBM established the American template for using strategic corporate ignorance as a lubricant to the collection of profits from activities that violate democratic values.

If the parallels between IBM's enabling of the Holocaust and American involvement in the Communist Party's surveillance state are instructive, however, so are the differences. Many of those differences are products of the wave of globalization unleashed in the wake of World War II. The stretching of supply chains across borders means that fewer tech companies provide entire systems the way IBM did with the Hollerith machines. Instead, like Intel, they supply discrete parts and knowledge. Meanwhile, the globalization of finance and the growth of venture capital allows American corporations to earn revenue from foreign markets without setting foot on foreign soil. Both developments have made it possible for American businesses and investors to reap rewards from assisting oppressive regimes while keeping their hands relatively clean. The result has been a massive expansion in efforts to do just that.

Most early investors in China's digital surveillance industry followed Intel's example and put their money into companies that built physical systems. By 2017, the smart money had moved to a new breed of company that specialized not in the eyes of the surveillance state but in its brains. The most prominent among this new group was a start-up known as SenseTime, founded by a small group of Chinese computer scientists and engineers doing innovative work with neural networks at the Chinese University of Hong Kong.

Inspired by the processing activity of the human brain, a neural network is capable of learning patterns and regularities in data. Spam filters in email are an example: When someone marks a message as spam, the neural network studies its content and learns to classify similar emails as spam. The more feedback it gets about its choices—from a user telling it when it has misclassified a message—the better it gets at filtering out unwanted emails. This type of data processing, known as deep learning, is particularly useful in the fields of computer vision and image analysis. And SenseTime's advancement of image recognition algorithms was particularly impressive, helping it push computer vision to levels of accuracy that hadn't been seen before.

SenseTime's success attracted a horde of suitors hoping to invest. One of the first American investment firms to fund the start-up was IDG Capital, which bought a stake with $10 million pooled from the University of Michigan, early Facebook investor Jim Breyer, the Rockefeller Foundation, and other limited partners. When we first visited the SenseTime offices in Beijing in 2017, it was in the middle of raising $410 million—a record funding round for an AI company at the time—from IDG and a handful of Chinese firms. The next year, it raised an additional $1.2 billion, including funds from Fidelity International in Boston and Silver Lake Partners, a powerhouse Silicon Valley private equity firm whose largest backers include the California Public Employees' Retirement System and the Teacher Retirement System of Texas. A 2019 investigation by Buzzfeed News found that six American universities and at least nineteen public pension plans or retirement systems held indirect investments in SenseTime or its domestic rival Megvii Technology.

For those who got in with SenseTime early, the payoff was gargan-tuan: by the time of the Buzzfeed story, the company was valued at $4.5 billion. Later that year it climbed to $7.5 billion, greater than the gross domestic products of sixty countries.

Investors' enthusiasm for SenseTime was easy to grasp. Its technology felt both revolutionary and practical. Banks had already started using it to verify their customers' identities. It helped users of live-streaming video platforms "enhance" their virtual appearance by adding cartoon animal ears or whitening the tone of their skin. More ominously, it offered some of the most advanced facial recognition systems for the country's well-funded police.

Before the topic became sensitive, Chinese surveillance start-ups were happy to talk about their collaboration with public security forces. In 2017, SenseTime's CEO, Xu Li, told us that the company had recently installed two automated facial recognition systems in Chongqing, where government officials had approached Cisco for help in building a surveillance network in 2011. "We still need to push the envelope. The technology isn't completely there," Xu said. "But it's already very, very useful." Within forty days, the Chongqing systems had identified sixty-nine suspects and led to fifteen detentions. The municipal government had sent them a thank-you letter, which Xu forwarded. The Chongqing police wouldn't tell us whom it had targeted with the new system, or whether any of them were dissidents. Xu seemed more concerned with the numbers than the people they represented.

Before SenseTime arrived, the then-thirty-five-year-old noted with boyish excitement, the city's old police surveillance system had pro-duced only a few detentions a year. The results put SenseTime far ahead of its competitors in real-world success. The company was collecting new examples all the time and promised even more sophisticated sys-tems in the future. "In the future, all of these controls will be handled by a centralized brain," Xu said, a smile spreading across his face. China was set to leapfrog into a new era of technology, and SenseTime was in the perfect place to help get it there.

One of SenseTime's financial backers was Qualcomm, an early pi-oneer in wireless technology and the maker of advanced processors dominant in the mobile device industry. At the time of its SenseTime investment in 2017, Qualcomm derived almost two-thirds of its revenue from China. In the run-up to the decision, Qualcomm, like many other foreign high-tech firms, faced pressure from the Chinese government to move production of its more advanced processors to the mainland, where executives feared the technology would be easier to steal. Qualcomm encountered further hiccups after being investigated by Chinese regulators on suspicion of unfairly charging high prices for their mobile phone chips, settling the accusations with a $975 million fine—about 7 percent of its annual revenue in China then—after a fifteen-month investigation. Investing in start-ups like SenseTime was one way for American companies to demonstrate commitment to the Chinese market and to mollify the Communist Party without handing over their most valuable intellectual property.

Other American chipmakers also benefited from the rise of Sense-Time and other AI companies enabling Chinese state surveillance. The neural networks required for deep learning needed immense amounts of processing power. Chipmakers, particularly manufacturers of graphics processing units or GPUs, originally designed for gaming, proved an ideal fit for deep-learning applications like facial recognition. With no formidable Chinese competitors, Santa Clara–based Nvidia was selling vast quantities of chips to surveillance companies all over the country.

As China's surveillance companies continued to grow, they began sending money out to fund research partnerships with universities abroad. While they could import chips, Chinese AI firms had a harder time importing talent. When Andrew Ng, a British-born Chinese American out of the University of California, Berkeley, who had been among the first to apply deep learning to computer vision, decided to leave Google for Baidu in 2014, it was an encouraging sign that Chinese tech companies were able to attract the best talent. But Ng left Baidu after only three years on the job. Many of the other top ethnic Chinese AI scientists, most of whom studied at American institutions, preferred to remain in the United States, where cleaner air and the rule of law made for a better quality of life. To tap that resource from afar, Huawei committed $1 million in 2016 to fund AI research at Berkeley and set up other research partnerships at Stanford and MIT. In 2018, SenseTime partnered with MIT, the alma mater of founder Tang Xiao'ou. In announcing the new "MIT-SenseTime Alliance on Artificial Intelligence," MIT said its aim was to "open up new avenues of discovery" in computer vision, algorithms inspired by human intelligence, medical imaging, and robotics. The school didn't disclose how much money SenseTime had pledged to the project.

Few of these partnerships raised alarm at the time. For decades, China and the United States had engaged in cooperative research across the whole range of scientific fields. In the vast majority of cases, there was no evidence of ill intent. In many cases the collaborations had been fruitful for the United States, leading to advances in everything from nanotechnology to nuclear physics. Even when surveillance companies benefited from some of the partnerships, it was often through peer-reviewed research available to others in the field. On occasion, though, the Party exploited the openness of American academia in more troubling, and unexpected, ways.

◉

In 2014, Dr. Kenneth Kidd received an email from a physician named Li Caixia, who worked for the Chinese Ministry of Public Security's Institute of Forensic Science. She wanted to know whether he had any space in his lab. Kidd, a professor in population genetics at Yale University known as a trailblazer in persuading American courts to allow DNA samples as evidence, had recently rekindled a long-burning interest in China. He'd first visited the country in 1982, at the dawn of the reform era, when bicycle-riding residents in quilted Mao-style jackets shared the roads with carts pulled by mules. A medical condition forced him to cut short the trip, implanting a desire in the back of his mind to someday return. He kept abreast of Chinese work in genetics through a Yale colleague who had connections at Fudan University in Shanghai, and in 2010 he had returned to Beijing at the invitation of the Chinese government, which was eager for him to give a talk on his research. Li Caixia had served as his translator on that trip.

Kidd remembered being impressed with Li's helpfulness and intelligence while in Beijing. The two had exchanged occasional messages after he returned to Yale. In this latest email, Li wrote that she had won a Chinese government scholarship to go to an overseas lab for a year to conduct her own DNA research and hoped he could take her in. Kidd couldn't think of a reason not to invite her. She arrived a few months later at the Yale campus in New Haven, Connecticut, and took up a space in Kidd's lab three rows from the entrance, not far from where a group researching monkey DNA had installed a plush Curious George toy. She was quiet and reserved, a diligent researcher who also worked hard at improving her English, interrupting conversations with her peers occasionally to write down new words in her notebook.

After eleven months, Li went back to Beijing, taking with her DNA samples and notes on the genetic markers of ethnic groups from around the world. Not long after, Kidd was invited back to China, this time to the ancient capital of Xi'an, which he had been scheduled to visit on his first trip before he got sick. There he spoke alongside Chinese and foreign geneticists at a genomics conference, underwritten in part by Thermo Fisher Scientific, a Massachusetts-based maker of advanced DNA mapping machines. By that time, China's Ministry of Public Security—the same agency that employed Li Caixia and sponsored Kidd's visit to Beijing in 2010—had already published a study demonstrating methods for genetic identification of Uyghurs; to develop them, the researchers had compared forty Uyghur DNA samples against samples from other ethnic groups collected in Kidd's lab.

In 2017, *The Wall Street Journal* discovered that Thermo Fisher, the company that had co-sponsored the conference Kidd attended in Xi'an, had supplied DNA sequencers to police in Xinjiang and elsewhere in China who were working to build the world's largest database of human genetic records. Following up on that story in 2019, *The New York Times* discovered patent applications filed by MPS researchers that described the sorting of ethnic groups by DNA. One application filed in 2017 described a system that would help in "inferring the geographical origin from the DNA of suspects at crime scenes" and noted they had used samples provided by Kidd's lab to the Allele Frequency Database, or ALFRED, an open platform for genetic research containing data from more than 700 populations around the world. *The Times* also found that Chinese researchers had contributed gene sequences to the ALFRED database. After seeking comment from Kidd, the newspaper published the story in early 2019, linking the use of Kidd's data to the widespread collection of blood samples from Uyghurs in Xinjiang.

The criticism came swift and hard. Among the critics was Sophie Richardson, China director at Human Rights Watch, who told the Yale student publication *The Politic* that Kidd should have been more aware of the people he was dealing with. "Now, I realize Professor Kidd's area of expertise is in genetics, but it is not very hard to know—especially if you have gone through standard research ethics review protocols—that we're talking about a place that is effectively a police state."

The story raised alarms in part because of the opaque nature of China's DNA collection efforts, particularly in Xinjiang. Just as Tahir and Marhaba had their DNA samples and iris prints recorded in the police station, many other Uyghurs had theirs gathered in similarly dubious circumstances. Uyghurs and human rights groups told *The New York Times* that the DNA collection took place as part of a program called Physicals for All in which authorities offered free medical checkups in the province. Between 2016 and 2017, nearly 36 million people had taken part, according to Chinese state media. During our own trip to Xinjiang in late 2017, we had come across around a hundred Uyghur residents lined up in tidy rows in a children's playground opposite a clinic in Kashgar waiting to undergo their physicals, but we were blocked by police from interviewing any of them. It wasn't until later that we discovered they had been about to have their genetic data collected.

Though China's government has been open about its ambitions to build a world-leading DNA database, it has been less forthcoming about why. Local officials in some parts of China have spoken explicitly about linking the DNA database to existing surveillance programs like Sharp Eyes without saying how the information would be used. Scholars and human rights groups have also speculated it could be used to add a layer of genetic certainty to collective punishment, enabling police to use DNA analysis to find and harass the extended families of people accused of political crimes. The database might also be connected to experiments Chinese forensic scientists have been doing since the late 2010s using a process known as DNA phenotyping, which can extrapolate biographical traits such as hair and eye color, age, and skin pigmentation from a genetic sample. The technology, which has also been deployed in some instances in the United States, theoretically allows police to reconstruct the image of a person's face based on a blood sample.

Kidd was in his late seventies and on the verge of retirement in 2019 when he met with us in his office at Yale's School of Medicine, a short walk from downtown New Haven, on a sunny September morning in 2019. Diminutive and grandfatherly, with a white-blond beard and a Julius Pringles handlebar mustache, Kidd spoke softly and squeezed his eyes closed as he recalled the details of his ordeal. "I had a pretty significant reputation, when they asked me to come and give them advice," he said, referring to the MPS's Institute of Forensic Science.

Evidence of that reputation was arrayed across the windowsill behind him: a line of awards and commendations from the National Institute of Justice, the FBI, and the US Department of Labor. Over the years, Kidd had become a world-class expert in matching human genetic variation to geography. After the World Trade Center attacks in 2001, the FBI called Kidd to help identify bodies by tracing the ancestry of their DNA. He had run the ALFRED database, which was partly funded by the Department of Justice, since its founding roughly two decades earlier.

Comfortable working with the research arms of law enforcement, Kidd hadn't stopped to consider what it meant to have invited an employee of China's police ministry into his lab. "Should I have recognized that she was part of the Ministry of Public Security?" he said of Li Caixia. "But she's with the Institute of Forensics, it's not a police arm. She was a researcher in the department doing the DNA work, obviously bright and well educated." Li had never once spoken to him about Chinese politics or given any indication that she was working on Uyghur DNA, Kidd said. By the time he realized what she had been up to, it was too late.

Kidd said he was so absorbed in his research that it didn't occur to him his Chinese partners might have more sinister motives. Between 2010 and 2014, the time between his visit to Beijing and Li's email, the Party's assimilation campaign in Xinjiang had yet to ramp up and Uyghurs were rarely in the headlines. Academic collaboration with China was also common: in 2011, American academics co-authored more scholarly papers with Chinese partners than with colleagues from the United Kingdom, Germany, or Japan. "The worst I would say of myself is that I was naive," he said. Yale had a long history of collaboration with Fudan University, and a faculty member Kidd knew in the school's genetics department often flew to Shanghai to conduct research. Kidd said he assumed, wrongly, that the DNA data the Chinese had submitted to ALFRED was collected using international scientific norms.

The head of Yale's Institutional Review Board, or IRB, which typically reviews research by Yale affiliates who work on research involving human subjects, stood up for Kidd after the *New York Times* story ran, saying genetic material wasn't subject to ethics review because it didn't constitute personally identifiable information. Even if it had reviewed the case, there would still have been only a slim chance of predicting such an outcome, said Stephen Latham, chair of Yale's IRB on Social and Behavioral Research. American legal structures are designed to deal with harms to individuals, he added. "It's quite possible, in this case, that if you didn't think about what China might be doing to the whole pool of human subjects that you're dealing with, there's no mechanism that would catch that automatically." Latham's statement did little to calm the outrage. In the months after the report came out, Kidd said, he received a barrage of phone calls and emails attacking his character and, in some instances, threatening his safety. He reported the threats to the police.

Gripping the sides of his swivel chair, Kidd said he realized his mistake but felt wounded by the reaction. The geneticist also did what he could to limit the damage, he said. He removed from ALFRED all the Uyghur data contributed by the Chinese and emailed his contacts at the MPS to tell them to stop using his DNA data in their work. "I am doing honest, fair, ethical research, and to read about all this that I've supposedly done to the Uyghur is painful," he said, his face and voice twisted with anguish. "I'm not in favor of the kinds of surveillance and such that's being done to the Uyghur, but there's nothing I can do about it."

Whether Kidd was negligent or just naive, his story sparked an overdue debate about the level of involvement American academics and institutions should have in research that was at risk of exacerbating Chinese human rights violations. The discussion was especially fraught at math and science powerhouses like MIT and UC Berkeley that had partnered with Chinese tech companies on cutting-edge AI research. The universities defended the funding the companies provided, saying it paid for fundamental, open-source research that would ultimately be available to anyone to use. Critics countered that the money was tainted by its association with the Chinese surveillance state and that the partnerships helped the companies identify top talent to recruit. Under pressure, Berkeley cut ties with Huawei, which had provided the university with $8 million in funding in 2017 and 2018. MIT ended its cooperation with Huawei and ZTE, and said it would review its relationship with SenseTime, and vowed to apply new standards in evaluating projects involving China, Russia, and Saudi Arabia.

◉

Increasing global awareness of what's happening in Xinjiang has also complicated matters for American companies, many of which have faced questions about their involvement in the Party's campaign against the Uyghurs. When questioned, the tech firms have fallen back on a familiar explanation: their products were used by a variety of customers in a variety of ways, and they didn't sell items directly to the Chinese government.

The companies' responses highlight the difficulty the US government faces in trying to prevent American technology from powering China's surveillance state. So many of the products involved, from chips to hard drives, are used in a vast range of systems, the overwhelming majority of which are innocuous. On top of that, supply chains have grown so complicated—with components often traveling through multiple layers of intermediaries before landing in the hands of Chinese police—that

companies could plausibly claim they had no idea who their end customers were.

Under the Trump administration, American officials tried to pro-
hibit sales of advanced American technology to Chinese surveillance
companies, with limited success. The only guaranteed way to starve the
Party of the American technology it needs is to issue a blanket ban on
exports of critical components to anyone in China, but doing so would
strip billions of dollars from the balance sheets of corporate America.
Given American politicians' reliance on the financial largesse of the
country's business titans, that option feels untenable.

In a certain sense, the damage has already been done. The most important American exports—ideas about state surveillance—were delivered long ago. The tracking of groups like Uyghurs based on where
they live and pray and how old they are is an example of what people
in law enforcement circles call "birds of a feather" analysis—a guilt-
by-association surveillance technique pioneered by the American intelligence community for tracking terrorists online in the 1990s. The
American creation of an expansive "homeland security" concept in
the wake of 9/11 likewise exerted a profound influence in China (and
many other places around the globe). The intense politicization of what
constitutes terrorism, the elevation of security as the driving force in
domestic policy, and the aggressive pursuit of security partnerships
between the state and private industry that characterized the United
States in the post-9/11 period are all prominent features of China's own
homeland security apparatus.

As American officials debate how to contend with US complicity in
the Communist Party's abuse of surveillance, they also have to confront
a new phenomenon: the spread of state surveillance inside the United
States itself.

9

HOMELAND SECURITY

Kaitlin Jackson was on arraignment duty at the Bronx Criminal Court on April 10, 2018, when she picked up the case: a local man arrested for stealing a package of socks from a T.J. Maxx department store. The police complaint said the suspect had brandished a box cutter at a security guard who'd tried to confront him, which elevated the theft from a misdemeanor to a felony. At first, it seemed indistinguishable from any of the dozens of other felony robbery allegations Jackson had handled as a public defender in the Bronx, except that she couldn't piece together how police had zeroed in on her client as a suspect. She called the assistant district attorney to ask how her client had caught the eye of the New York Police Department.

That's when things took an unexpected turn.

"It's so strange, Kaitlin, this is my first facial recognition case," the assistant DA, Larry Carter, said. "Have you ever had one before?"

Jackson knew that facial recognition systems existed. Facebook was using the technology to automatically tag photos, and Apple had recently introduced face scanning as a way to unlock iPhones. She thought of it as the latest in gee-whiz gadgetry. She had no idea that law enforcement was using it, or that anyone thought of it as a serious forensic tool.

The police report said her client had been identified as the thief by a T.J. Maxx security guard named Lawrence Jordan. It didn't say anything about his face being scanned by a machine. Confused, Jackson sent investigators to talk to Jordan about how he'd come to identify her client as the thief. The security guard recalled that he'd been watching the T.J. Maxx surveillance monitors when he saw someone steal a package of socks. He said he followed the thief to the escalator and confronted him over the socks; at that point the thief brandished a yellow box cutter and then fled down into the street.

Jordan told Jackson's investigator that he had spotted the same guy on one of the store's surveillance cameras once before (he wasn't sure when) stealing a $19.99 handbag. He hadn't reported that theft to police because he was dealing with other thefts at the time. After the sock incident, he said, police came in and took screenshots of the surveillance footage, telling him they had "high-tech" facial recognition technology that could identify people from video. A police detective later sent a message to Jordan's phone with a mugshot of Jackson's client.

"Is this the guy you know from going into the store many times before?" the detective wrote.

Jordan typed out a reply: "That's the guy."

Police arrested Jackson's client a little more than six weeks later. A grand jury indicted him on seven counts, including robbery, menacing, and criminal possession of a weapon. The client had a long rap sheet filled with petty larcenies. Jordan said he had no doubt the client was the one who'd stolen the socks. The case felt open-and-shut. But as she pored over the police report, Jackson found a glaring weakness.

The only evidence tying Jackson's client to the theft was the witness identification provided by Jordan. The DA had nothing else. On top of that, it was a questionable ID. The prosecutors tried to argue that Jordan knew Jackson's client, but Jordan claimed to have only seen him before in video footage. That made them strangers. Police lineups were invented because human memory is unreliable and identifications by strangers are notoriously vulnerable to suggestion. It's unusual for a police officer to send suspect photos to a witness by text message because it allows the witness to repeatedly view the images, which can distort memory. Sending a single photo is worse because it strongly suggests the suspect is guilty. How had the police zeroed in on her client as the only suspect?

To tackle the case properly, Jackson decided she had to do a crash course in facial recognition. What she found disturbed her. The technology seemed powerful, but also deeply flawed, with the potential to mislead law enforcement into victimizing innocent people. Despite those risks, police departments around the country were not just experimenting with it but using it in real-life criminal investigations—and on a startlingly large scale.

The discovery in the late 2010s of futuristic, China-associated surveillance systems lurking inside American police stations unsettled lawyers and privacy activists, but to those familiar with the dynamics of the Chinese surveillance state it wasn't entirely a surprise. Like China's Communist Party, American police departments are preoccupied with security. Not coincidentally, they have shown the same affinity for new tools that promise to help maintain social order, and the same willingness to downplay the dangers that come with untested technology.

Unlike Chinese police, however, American law enforcement is subject to robust scrutiny by the press, lawmakers, and defense lawyers.

◉

One of the sources Jackson consulted as she was trying to understand facial recognition systems was a report produced by Georgetown Law School's Center on Privacy and Technology. Titled "The Perpetual Lineup" and published in late 2016, it was the first major report to document the explosion of facial recognition systems in American law enforcement. Based on dozens of public-records requests, it found that sixteen states had granted the FBI access to their databases of driver's license photos for use in facial recognition scans. They also found more than two dozen states that allowed police to conduct facial recognition searches on driver's license databases.

By the middle of 2016, they calculated, at least 117 million Americans over the age of eighteen—more than 50 percent of the adult population—had been placed in a virtual, never-ending police lineup, often without their knowledge. The report's conclusion: a new era in state surveillance had arrived in the United States with barely anyone noticing.

Use of the technology has expanded since then. In 2019, the same Georgetown researchers found law enforcement agencies in Detroit, Chicago, New York City, Washington, DC, and Orlando had already launched tests of real-time facial recognition systems like those used on Chinese streets. The Department of Homeland Security, meanwhile, has been carrying out a plan to install face-scanning cameras to identify foreign travelers at the United States' top twenty airports (and, for a time at least, contemplated forcing American travelers to get their faces scanned as well). As of 2021, close to half of the US federal agencies that employ law enforcement officers reported owning or using back-end facial recognition systems for matching still images against databases of known individuals, with six saying they used the technology to identify people suspected of breaking the law during the civil unrest that followed the murder of George Floyd by police in Minneapolis.

Public scrutiny has restrained American law enforcement's love affair with digital tracking technologies, keeping it from growing even more rapidly. But the scrutiny has had another effect: unlike their Chinese counterparts, who are happy to trumpet their new surveillance tools, American police tend to shroud their arsenals in secrecy. The more powerful the tool is, the more care they often take to shield it from view. The transparency built into the American system in some instances makes it harder to see how the police are watching.

This paradox traces back two decades to the indelible image of people jumping to their deaths from the smoldering upper floors of the World Trade Center's twin towers on the cloudless morning of September 11, 2001. A month and a half later, with much of lower Manhattan still coated in ash and the country reeling over the almost 3,000 lives lost, the USA Patriot Act passed through both chambers of Congress with barely a whisper of opposition. The new law introduced "enhanced surveillance procedures" that allowed intelligence agencies to conduct roving wiretaps and access previously off-limits information about American citizens, like library records, so long as there was a suspected connection to overseas terrorist groups. All that was required was permission from the secret (and, it would turn out, permissive) Foreign Intelligence Surveillance Court. Lawmakers and the Bush administration justified the secrecy in the name of national security. Most Americans bought the argument: a year after it passed, only 15 percent thought the Patriot Act went too far, while more than 80 percent either thought it was just right or didn't go far enough. By 2005, as panic over terrorism began to subside, 30 percent said they thought it went too far.

The notion at the heart of the Patriot Act—that civil protections against privacy invasions by the state were expendable in the face of national security threats—would go on to influence the thinking of other governments around the world as George W. Bush pursued the Global War on Terror. But the United States' pioneering influence on the development of state surveillance is not a recent phenomenon.

In *The Soft Cage*, his book on the history of American surveillance, Christian Parenti describes how colonists in Virginia invented an embryonic form of the modern ID card with rules that required Native Americans, indentured Irish servants, and, later, plantation slaves to carry passes when traveling in or out of the territory. (The US government resurrected and modernized the pass system following the arrival in the late 1900s of exclusion laws aimed at Chinese immigrants. To help them keep out new arrivals, border agents built a registry and ordered all Chinese residents to carry identification papers with their name, age, occupation, last place of residence, and "physical marks and peculiarities"—a stunning extension of state visibility into a population. In turn, the Chinese community launched a decades-long effort to undermine the system using fake paperwork that became, in Parenti's description, "the largest informal anti-surveillance movement in United States history.")

Tension between the public desire for transparency and the demands of secrecy has intensified alongside improvements in technology and expansions in the scale of surveillance. Twelve years after 9/11,

Edward Snowden's revelations about the National Security Agency's mass data collection through PRISM and other shadowy programs offered a shocking window into what the government was doing behind closed doors. The fire and fury of the debate about how Snowden should be judged, hero or traitor, was equally revealing of the complexity of American feelings about the balance between security and civil liberties.

The new surveillance capabilities unleashed in the era of advanced AI have heightened those tensions even further. They have also fundamentally changed the dynamic: The targets of state surveillance are no longer limited to the small population of American citizens with real or imagined connections to overseas terrorist groups. They now include a large swath of regular Americans.

The impact of the new generation of surveillance tools in the United States is best explained, according to privacy activist and lawyer Albert Fox Cahn, in terms of a single factor: money. In 2019, after experience doing pro bono work with New York City's Muslim community introduced him to the sweep of the NYPD's intelligence gathering, Cahn founded a nonprofit group called the Surveillance Technology Oversight Project, or STOP, out of a small office on Rector Street, a few blocks south of the 9/11 Memorial. "The most effective check on surveillance hasn't been laws. It hasn't been the media. It's been economics: surveillance has always been expensive," Cahn told us a few months after he set up STOP. The algorithmic tools now at the disposal of the NYPD and other police departments had reduced the time it takes officers to identify someone from days or weeks to a matter of hours or even minutes, he pointed out. "Facial recognition makes surveillance cheap, which reduces the friction."

A combination of cost reductions and expanding budgets has given police departments across the United States access to a long list of what used to be considered military-grade spy tech tools, all of which reduce friction in one way or another: automatic gunshot detection systems that pinpoint the location and type of gunfire; "Stingray" cell-site simulators that can siphon data off mobile phones and intercept, or even alter, communications; social media profiling services that sift through the online activities of a population for early warnings about potential incidents.

Money has helped drive the expansion of state surveillance in other ways. In the United States, as in China, mass monitoring by law enforcement turns out to be an alluring market. Amazon's cloud division, AWS, markets its data storage and analytics services to police and has a contract with the Department of Homeland Security to store biometric data—mostly fingerprints, but also face prints and iris scans—for 230 million people. In addition, it has developed its own affordable facial recognition platform, Rekognition, which *The New York Times* once used to build a surveillance system that detected 2,750 faces over nine hours in New York City's Bryant Park, returning several likely identifications, for a total cost of $60.

Law enforcement agencies have also proven to be lucrative clients for data aggregators like Thomson Reuters that offer to create detailed profiles of individual Americans using information gathered from credit agencies, social media sites, property records, marriage records, cellphone records, bankruptcy filings, and more. The same holds true for data fusion companies like Palantir, co-founded by the investor Peter Thiel, which engineer sophisticated platforms—similar to the one the Communist Party uses to monitor Uyghurs in Xinjiang—that make it easy to search, compare, and analyze information from disparate databases. Combined together, the two services put immense power in the hands of government agencies to understand and track people across time and space.

◉

The New York City Police Department, America's largest municipal law enforcement agency and its best-funded at $5 billion a year, offers a comprehensive view into the forces promoting this shift, as well as the pitfalls that worry privacy advocates and other surveillance critics. Since just after the 9/11 attacks, when New York City's deputy police commissioner scrapped restraints on police investigation of street protests and political gatherings, the city has pursued a perpetual cycle of improvements to its police surveillance systems.

One of the biggest concerns in the United States, Albert Fox Cahn argues, is what activists and law enforcement officials alike refer to as mission creep. This happens when government agencies agree to use a surveillance system for a specific, narrow purpose but slowly add new applications over time. Often it occurs in ways that escape notice until the new uses have become locked in as common practice. Cahn pointed to the cameras installed in New York City's subway systems after 9/11 to look for potential terrorists, which police are now using to track homeless people who seek shelter in the stations (and in the case of those with outstanding warrants, arrest them).

In a sense, New York City's entire surveillance apparatus was an example of mission creep. Five years after 9/11, the NYPD unveiled plans for a $100 million Lower Manhattan Security Initiative, which called for the installation of 3,000 security cameras and 100 automatic license plate readers, along with mobile roadblocks and radiation detectors. A few years later, the NYPD and Department of Homeland Security announced Operation Sentinel, a program that would photograph every vehicle entering and leaving the city along bridges and through tunnels. Sold to the public as counterterror measures, the projects soon became integral to the NYPD's regular crime-fighting efforts.

As technology continued to improve, the NYPD enlisted the help of Microsoft to expand, revamp, and rebrand the entire apparatus, which they renamed the Domain Awareness System. The partnership called for Microsoft to take a 30 percent cut anytime the NYPD sold the system to another city, whether in the United States or abroad. The Domain Awareness System has grown to cover all five of the city's boroughs. Data from close to 9,000 privately owned and public cameras and 500 license-plate readers now flows into an always running central command center in lower Manhattan, where police can run searches for suspects driving certain types of cars or wearing a certain color of jacket. The system also has algorithms that are trained to identify suspicious patterns of behavior, sending alerts to the tablets and smartphones police use to access the system remotely.

One of the system's more popular features among police is Patternizr, software that sifts through historical data on hundreds of thousands of burglaries, robberies, assaults, and other offenses to help detectives spot patterns in criminal activity across precincts. The platform also includes a secretive predictive policing system, which uses similar data to attempt to identify areas where future crimes are likely to occur.

Facial recognition is handled by the Facial Identification Section, or FIS. The section was launched in 2011 to make use of nascent face-matching technology in identifying criminal suspects from crime scene images. In its early days, the rudimentary system only worked when fed near-perfect photos. By the latter half of the decade, the FIS had acquired a new system powered by more sophisticated algorithms that would produce matches from off-center snapshots and video stills.

The new technology was more powerful but also more vulnerable to misuse. Clare Garvie, one of the leading surveillance researchers at Georgetown Law School, witnessed this firsthand in 2018 when she paid $1,600 for a ticket to the Global ID Summit, a conference on bio-metric identification co-hosted in New York by the international police agency Interpol. During a presentation on facial recognition, NYPD officers told the story of a suspect caught on camera stealing beer from a CVS. A facial recognition search turned up no matches, but one of the detectives remarked that the suspect bore a resemblance to Woody Harrelson, so they tried using the actor's image as a "probe photo" (the image, usually taken from a crime scene, that the system compares with images in its database). The police got a set of "matches," which they used to arrest someone for the crime. Digging deeper, she discovered that the NYPD had entered a probe photo of NBA basketball player J. R. Smith into the system in a similar situation and used photo-editing software to alter suspect probe photos if they failed to return matches, pasting open eyes over closed eyelids or adding pixels to an image that was too low-quality. Not a single facial recognition company Garvie spoke to said these practices were condoned.

◉

When she picked up the T.J. Maxx case, Kaitlin Jackson was in her sec-ond year working for the Bronx Defenders, one of the two nonprofit or-ganizations that together handle the vast majority of public defense work in the Bronx. Founded in 1997, the group employs around 100 criminal attorneys and many more family, civil, and immigration lawyers. They occupy three buildings on either side of 161st Street, a brisk five-minute walk to the Bronx courthouse. In any given month, its lawyers handle more than a thousand criminal cases, from murder to shoplifting.

Jackson came to the Bronx Defenders after working as a public defender on Long Island and doing a short stint with a nonprofit group that studies criminal exonerations. The child of parents with a strong belief in public interest work, she had decided during her first year of law school that criminal justice was the area that afforded her the best chance to make a positive impact on people's lives. In the Bronx, progress had come in small increments, case by case, as she worked to mitigate the damage the criminal justice system often visited on the borough's poorer families, most of them Black and Brown. The T.J. Maxx case offered Jackson an opportunity to multiply the impact of her work. Facial recognition was so new to criminal law in the United States that a victory would instantly inform the playbook for other lawyers. But it was also going to be a major challenge.

To build a defense, Jackson asked to see footage from the surveillance cameras inside the T.J. Maxx. It showed an African American man roughly the same height and weight as her client grabbing a pair of socks before waving something yellow at Jordan, the security guard, and then running away down the escalator. Watching it, Jackson grew more suspicious of the DA's case. Research showed that eyewitnesses tend to fixate on guns and knives when confronted with them, a phenomenon known as "weapon focus," which impairs their ability to recall other details. If in fact the thief had brandished a weapon, that would throw the strength of Jordan's identification into even further doubt.

As she mulled over how to proceed, Jackson stumbled onto a critical piece of new information. While going over the case with her client, he mentioned that February 5, 2018, the day of the robbery, was his infant son's birthday. He had been at St. Barnabas Hospital for the birth. His signature was on the birth certificate, and he had a photo of himself in a hospital gown holding the child just after he was born.

The alibi wasn't perfect. Her client's son had been born an hour and a half after the sock theft, and Jackson couldn't prove he was in the hospital at the time of the theft. There was no sign-in log, and by the time Jackson sent investigators around to look into it, the security camera footage had been erased. Hospital staff said they couldn't think of any way to verify he was there before the birth. Still, the discovery filled her with confidence: What jury would believe that a man whose pregnant girlfriend was in labor would rush out to steal a package of socks ninety minutes before his child was born?

In researching facial recognition, Jackson had been surprised to discover how little case law there was that discussed the technology. She had scoured the internet and legal databases and come up with nothing. She had called around to nonprofit groups that specialized in criminal justice, but they weren't able to help. She was about to find out why.

Excited by what her client had told her, Jackson immediately went to the DA. She was certain he would decide to drop the case. Instead, he said he planned to press ahead with it. Jackson was astounded, and deeply curious. Was he really that confident in the NYPD's facial recognition system? She peppered him with questions about it: Who made it? How did it work? Whom else did it flag as a potential match?

He refused to answer.

We met Jackson at the Bronx Defenders offices on a rainy October day in 2019. She said her client had turned down previous interview requests and didn't want her to reveal his name but had given her permission to talk about his case. It's rare for public defenders to talk to journalists. They seldom take on the sort of cases that profit from media coverage. But in this instance, Jackson felt others would benefit from hearing the story.

Jackson's voice carries a wisp of her upbringing in southern Missouri. She's confident and direct, with a pierced nose and shoulder-length brown hair that frames a steady gaze. When she's thinking, she leans back in her chair, eyes pinned on the ceiling and hands behind her head with her elbows thrown out wide. Once she finds the answer, she swings forward to deliver it, eyes straight ahead, to make sure her point is getting through.

During our meeting, she leaned back to consider her battle with the

New York Police Department and why they'd fought her so hard to protect the new surveillance program they had used against her client. "It makes their job so much easier," she said, leaning forward. "Unless you're an asshole, you want to believe you have the right people. No one wants to get the wrong guy. They really want to believe this stuff is magic."

Because they are based on math, the algorithms at the heart of technologies like facial recognition shimmer in the public imagination as instruments of futuristic objectivity. Jackson's research suggested to her that this was far from the case. The Georgetown report said systems could identify the right person 95 percent of the time in ideal conditions—vastly better than anything police had used before. But accuracy rates fell in dark conditions, when images were blurry or out of focus, or when the people weren't directly facing the camera—in short, when the systems had to deal with real-life situations. Worse, tests by the National Institute of Standards and Technology, a Commerce Department laboratory tasked with technological quality control, indicated that facial recognition algorithms were less accurate at identifying dark-skinned people.

Cathy O'Neil, a mathematician who worked for years building trading algorithms for a Wall Street hedge fund, explained the problem in a 2016 book, *Weapons of Math Destruction: How Big Data Increases Inequality and Threatens Democracy*. Algorithmic systems, she explained, use math to build abstract models of the world to predict hypothetical outcomes. They draw on the ideas about information and control that Norbert Wiener developed in *Cybernetics* and that Qian Xuesen took back with him to China. Algorithms try to predict an outcome by digesting past data about the world they are meant to describe, the same way that the human brain creates models of the world based on past information and experience. Because humans design algorithms and choose which training data to feed them, they are never perfect. "A model's blind spots reflect the judgments and priorities of its creators," O'Neil wrote. Far from being impartial, algorithmic models "are opinions embedded in mathematics." A computer brain, in other words, can be just as prejudiced as a human one.

Such flaws explain how facial recognition systems could be worse at identifying minorities. Joy Buolamwini, a computer scientist then at MIT's

Media Lab, helped conduct studies that found that facial recognition models built by companies like IBM, Amazon, Microsoft, and China's Megvii consistently misidentified people of color and women—in one case misidentifying Oprah Winfrey as a man. The flaws, she determined, were the result of what she called "pale male datasets." The collections of images used to train the algorithms were filled with faces that mirrored the mostly white male Silicon Valley engineers who built them.

An experiment by the American Civil Liberties Union illustrated the racial bias in facial recognition systems to powerful effect. In 2018, the civil rights organization used Amazon's facial recognition tool Rekognition to run images of members of Congress as probe photos against a database of 25,000 mugshots. The result: Rekognition misidentified twenty-eight lawmakers as criminal suspects. Eleven were people of color—roughly twice the proportion of nonwhite members of Congress as a whole. One of them was Georgia Democrat John Lewis, a civil rights icon and leader of the Congressional Black Caucus.

Lawrence Jordan, the T.J. Maxx security guard, had told both Jackson's investigator and the police that he recognized Jackson's client from his distinctive face and walk. Jackson felt that little about her client was outwardly noticeable. He was average height and weight and not particularly dark- or light-skinned. As a check against her own bias, Jackson took the surveillance footage screen grab that police said showed her client's face and passed it around the Bronx Defenders with a photo of the client, asking if her coworkers thought the two images showed the same person. The verdict: maybe, maybe not.

Jackson was convinced that Jordan had been induced by the circumstances into misidentifying her client as the thief. Not only had the police not presented Jordan with a lineup (or a packet of photos) as they should have, they had also told him they were using "high-tech" tools to come up with suspects. "It's just about the most suggestive ID you can have," she said. Jackson didn't blame him. "Just like police, eyewitnesses don't want to get it wrong," she said. "How comforting must it be to think, 'Oh, facial recognition figured it out. I don't have to worry about my memory.'" (When we went to the T.J. Maxx to try to speak to Jordan in 2019, the manager said he no longer worked there. Relatives and acquaintances said he had left New York and offered to pass on a request to speak with him; he never responded.)

US law requires prosecutors to disclose to defense lawyers any information that might be favorable to their clients. In a year of research, the Georgetown researchers hadn't found a single case of facial recognition being disclosed by prosecutors, despite the technology existing in some police departments for years. Jackson suspected that police departments refrained from presenting facial recognition results in court because they would first have to submit the technology to stringent tests, the same way fingerprinting and DNA were tested before being accepted as evidence. Facial recognition technology wasn't mature enough yet to pass that test.

The NYPD, like most police departments in the United States, has a policy of using facial recognition search results only as investigative leads, not as evidence. Jackson suspected the NYPD was trying to do an end run around its own restrictions by laundering the facial recognition results through Jordan—in effect using him as a human front for the machine.

After the district attorney's office refused to answer her questions about NYPD's facial recognition system, Jackson filed a motion to either dismiss Jordan's testimony or compel the police to subject their system to the same scrutiny that would be applied to any new form of evidence. "FIS is the whole case—there is no information unrelated to FIS for the government to use," she wrote.

The pressure worked, at least at first. The judge sent the NYPD a subpoena for more information about the facial recognition system. A few days later, a lawyer for the NYPD emailed the judge directly to challenge the subpoena without copying either Jackson or the prosecutor on the message. The costs of "prejudice to current and future law enforcement investigations" of revealing what Jackson had asked for "vastly" outweighed any value the information would have in clarifying the facts of her client's case, he wrote. Sending a direct email to the judge without Jackson's knowledge was a breach of etiquette that the court batted back with a warning. The NYPD lawyer then filed a formal motion to quash the subpoena. It was the first time Jackson had seen police do anything like that.

As the case headed to trial, it was taken over by a new judge who told the prosecutor that the police would need to reply to the subpoena and hand over information about the NYPD's facial recognition system for the case to move forward. After lunch, the prosecution came back with a surprise plea deal: they would knock the charges down to a misdemeanor and essentially let Jackson's client go for time served. Jackson took it as a sign the NYPD was spooked.

Jackson wanted to take the case to court, where she was confident they would win. But by then her client's calculations had changed. He had been on probation at the time of his arrest. Two months after his family gathered enough money to get him out on bail, he was taken back to jail for violating probation. The Administration for Children's Services sent his newborn son to live with a foster family. (The child's mother had died two months after the birth under circumstances Jackson didn't feel free to discuss.) If her client didn't get out soon, there was a chance his son would be freed for adoption.

An examination of the admissibility of facial recognition in court would require complicated tests, the calling of experts, and a lot of back-and-forth with the judge and prosecutor. Jackson's client decided he didn't have that kind of time. She sat next to him in court and felt her heart sink as he pleaded guilty to a crime she was certain he hadn't committed. She'd won in a way—her client would get out soon and be reunited with his son. But it was an empty victory. She went home that night and cried.

Roughly a year after the T.J. Maxx case ended, New York's police commissioner, James O'Neill, wrote in an op-ed for *The New York Times* that detectives had submitted more than 7,000 requests to the Facial Identification Section, leading to more than 1,850 possible matches and just short of 1,000 arrests. The arrests included one man accused of raping a worker at a day spa and another who allegedly pushed a subway passenger onto the tracks. "It would be an injustice to the people we serve if we policed our 21st-century city without using 21st-century technology," he wrote. He denied that officers entered sketches into the system but acknowledged they sometimes used photo-editing software to "fill in missing or distorted data."

Not only did the technology help nab bad guys, O'Neill argued, it had also helped clear suspects by reducing reliance on unreliable witness identifications, which he said was the leading cause of wrongful convictions. "When facial recognition technology is used as a limited and preliminary step in an investigation—the way our department uses it—these miscarriages of justice are less likely."

Jackson understood why police were attracted to facial recognition, but O'Neill's op-ed rankled her. Facial recognition had not been used "as a limited and preliminary step" in her client's case. If anything, it had encouraged an unreliable witness identification, not prevented one. She was particularly incensed by a claim O'Neill made toward the end: "When cases using this technology have been prosecuted, our methods and findings are subject to examination in court." In 2019, Bronx Defenders lawyers handled half a dozen cases in which facial recognition was used, but in every case there was other evidence that allowed prosecutors to go ahead without disclosing the facial recognition results.

Even in cases where facial recognition did provide the main evidence, it would have to be a serious enough crime, something like murder, before police and prosecutors would have the incentive to risk testing the technology in court, Jackson explained. Otherwise, they could continue to shield it by having a case dismissed or offering a plea deal. In her career as a public defender, she only had one client decide to reject a time-served misdemeanor plea offer and risk spending years in prison to fight a felony charge in court. Even for the innocent, the risks of going head-to-head with the criminal justice system were just too great.

◉

Other types of digital state surveillance have spread through the United States under a similar veil of secrecy. In some cases, they've been used for purposes beyond fighting crime.

One of the government's most active surveillance agencies, Immigration and Customs Enforcement (ICE), has made extensive use of two powerful tools: license plate readers and data fusion products. One of ICE's partners, Vigilant Solutions, gives immigration officers access to 5 billion license plate detections collected by private businesses, like insurance companies and parking lots, plus another 1.5 billion records gathered by eighty law enforcement agencies in more than a dozen states. Another partner, Thomson Reuters, provides ICE with a massive cross-referenced collection of public and private data on individuals. Combined, the two companies allow ICE to run a "continuous monitoring and alert system" that tracks the life events and movements of 500,000 individuals per month, the overwhelming majority of them members of the Hispanic community.

The use of social media to track protests—an approach pioneered in China—has also grown in popularity among American law enforcement agencies. In 2016, the Baltimore Police Department worked with a Chicago-based social media monitoring firm to track protests that broke out after the killing of Freddie Gray, the twenty-five-year-old African American Baltimore resident who fell into a coma after suffering a spinal cord injury inside a police van, and arrest participants who had outstanding warrants. Police departments around the country continued to use the tactic with subsequent Black Lives Matter protests, as the ACLU and other groups have documented, including the nationwide demonstrations in 2020 over the murder of George Floyd.

Private surveillance has also exploded, with police encouragement, thanks to the popularity of Amazon's high-definition "video doorbell" system Ring. The company started working with law enforcement as early as 2015, when they partnered with police to distribute 500 free Ring cameras to homes in Wilshire Park and Country Club Park, a pair of historic residential neighborhoods in central Los Angeles, in a program that supposedly led to a 55 percent drop in burglaries. By 2019, the company had struck up partnerships with at least 400 police departments, relying on officers to market the devices in the neighborhoods they patrol in exchange for discounts and a built-in system that makes it easy for law enforcement to request footage from owners. The following year, American police departments made more than 20,000 requests for footage captured by Ring and other home security cameras. One researcher estimated that by 2021 more than 3 million Ring doorbells were online around the United States.

Aside from aiding police, Ring cameras have also introduced American neighborhoods to the psychological and behavioral reverberations of mass monitoring. *The Washington Post* explored this in 2021 when it interviewed Lesley Miller, a mother living near Santa Barbara, California, whose parenting came under fire on a neighborhood Facebook group after someone posted Ring footage of her seven-year-old son throwing a foam volleyball at a neighbor's security camera. "Every time you ride your bike down this block, there are probably 50 cameras that watch you going past," Miller recalled telling her son afterward. "If you make a bad choice, those cameras will catch you." She said she didn't want the fear of punishment to drive her child's choices. "But there is very little grace for mistakes when things are caught on camera."

The proliferation of these technologies in the United States went largely unnoticed for years, but the public pushback started to gain momentum toward the start of 2020. It was aided by a small surveillance start-up that had suddenly begun signing up police departments by the fistful. Called Clearview AI, the company paired facial recognition with a database of more than 3 billion images scraped from Facebook, YouTube, Twitter, Google, Venmo, and countless other public websites spread across the internet—a facial image database seven times larger than the FBI's. *The New York Times* analyzed the company's app and found code that would allow it to be paired with augmented-reality glasses, potentially allowing someone to pull up the social media history of anyone they saw on the street. "The weaponization possibilities of this are endless," the *Times* quoted Eric Goldman, co-director of the High Tech Law Institute at Santa Clara University, as saying.

One person in the world of data science who was taken aback by the capabilities of Clearview AI was Andreas Weigend, former chief scientist at Amazon and author of the book *Data for the People*. Weigend was a tireless evangelist for surveillance capitalism who believed that his father, who had spent six years in an East German prison after being accused of spying for the Americans, would have been left alone if only the Stasi had had access to more accurate data. Perhaps for that reason, he was approached by Clearview AI's CEO to write an op-ed defending the company. Given access to the platform, Weigend spent a week in June 2020 testing it out on strangers in San Francisco and online. After he showed the search results to one couple he had photographed in a restaurant, the woman snatched the phone from his hand and demanded he delete the images. In another instance, he entered a screenshot taken from the account of a man who posted pornographic content anonymously on the website OnlyFans and came up with search results from a Cornell University website that allowed him to find the performer's real name. "I'm absolutely shocked at how powerful this is," Weigend told us in a phone call days later. He said the notion of police having such a tool in their hands made him reconsider some of his previous assumptions. "The balance of power has shifted away from individuals to governments." He decided not to write the op-ed.

The chilling implications of Clearview AI's partnership with hundreds of police departments helped privacy activists sell the idea that facial recognition was such an invasive technology that it needed to be severely restrained. The fight was fiercest in California, where the ACLU teamed up with the Electronic Frontier Foundation, a group focused on digital privacy, to argue that the technology represented a radical assault on civil liberties and should be banned outright. The campaign set off arguments—between privacy activists and police, but also within the activist community itself—over how far the limits should go. Some activists pushed for regulation that would stop short of a ban, in a nod to police arguments that the technology had legitimate law enforcement uses.

Unexpectedly, supporters of a full ban began to notch victories. In 2019, San Francisco's city supervisors agreed to implement a ban and require preapproval for purchases of other surveillance tools. Across the bay, the cities of Oakland and Berkeley followed with their own bans. The California State Senate then passed a moratorium on the use of facial recognition with police body cameras. With wins mounting, privacy groups pushed the campaign to other states as well as to Congress, which launched a series of hearings where law enforcement agencies fought to fend off a federal ban.

To Daron Wyatt, a veteran police officer in Anaheim, California, there was no question about the value of facial recognition. In June 2019, a month after San Francisco passed its ban, Behind the Badge, a policing website funded by law enforcement agencies, told the story of an Anaheim PD staffer who had put a police sketch of a rape suspect photographed from a local TV news report through the department's facial recognition system, which led to an arrest the next day. Wyatt told us facial recognition had revolutionized the department. He recalled going through security camera footage by hand in a murder investigation he had conducted in 2012. "It took months of working on it, five to six days a week, ten hours a day," he said. "Whereas with this, it could be a matter of twenty minutes."

Anaheim PD, like the NYPD, only used facial recognition after the fact to match crime scene images with mugshots, Wyatt said. "We're not out there capturing video of somebody who's walking down the street minding their own business and trying to see if they have a warrant," he said. At the same time, he couldn't help but imagine how much more powerful the system would be if it had access to more faces, like in the DMV database, or if it could be used on the streets in real time. "This is not a policy of the Anaheim Police Department. It hasn't even been talked about," he said. "But, for example, we have the largest convention center on the West Coast. Could it be preventative to be able to [run real-time scans] and see if you have somebody who's on a watchlist somewhere in the facility? I mean, I can see an application for it."

Responses like Wyatt's were one reason some privacy activists and lawyers pushed for bans on facial recognition systems despite their usefulness in helping police track down bad guys. They argued the logic of mission creep meant that police were liable to help the technology wriggle out of any cage that lawmakers tried to erect around it.

Law enforcement agencies have attempted to self-regulate to avoid losing access to the systems altogether. In March 2020, the NYPD issued its first public guidelines for the Facial Identification Section. Announcing the policy, new police commissioner Dermot Shea said it drew clear lines marking what was permissible and "strikes the right balance between public safety and privacy." The rules made it explicit that search results had to be reviewed by a detective's peers and supervisor, but otherwise they largely repeated internal guidelines that had been in place for years. Later that year, in response to a freedom-of-information lawsuit by Albert Fox Cahn, the NYPD disclosed that its total number of FIS searches had risen to more than 22,000 since 2017, with more than half conducted in 2019 alone.

Recently, victims of the technology began to speak out. In September 2020, a Detroit man sued police after a facial recognition search led to a false arrest for larceny that led him to lose his job. Three months later, a Paterson, New Jersey, resident sued both police and prosecutors after he was falsely arrested for shoplifting and trying to hit an officer with his car because of a bad facial recognition match. Then, in 2021, the Detroit Police Department was sued again by Robert Williams, a resident who was falsely arrested in front of his daughters over a watch theft.

Williams discovered during a jailhouse interrogation that facial recognition had been used to identify him: his police interrogators flipped over a sheet bearing search results alongside the words "investigative lead only." According to his legal complaint, Williams pointed to the words on the sheet as he protested that the blurry image from the watch store surveillance camera looked nothing like him. The officers conceded that, in person, he didn't resemble the person in the surveillance image. "I guess the computer got it wrong," one of the officers said.

Reporting on the Williams case a year later, CBS's *60 Minutes* discovered that Michigan State Police had run the facial recognition search on the watch store's surveillance camera still, ending up with 243 possible matches. Williams's photo ranked ninth. Detroit Police couldn't explain why he was the one they had chosen to pursue.

Three years after Jackson took on the T.J. Maxx case, Williams and the other two men who filed lawsuits represented the sum total of known facial recognition misidentifications in the United States. "I have to emphasize that this is tip-of-the-iceberg-type stuff because most people are never going to know that facial recognition was used,"

Williams's lawyer, ACLU Michigan senior staff attorney Philip Mayor, told us. While police continued to insist that facial recognition's benefits outweighed the risks when used only as a lead in a larger investigation, Mayor argued that the technology exacerbated a demonstrated tendency among police, once they have a suspect, to ignore evidence that points in another direction.

"Any of us who have ever turned in the wrong direction because Google Maps told us to, even though we knew we were doing the wrong thing, shouldn't need an explanation that there's a tendency to trust the computer," he said. "Mistakes in the technology cause mistakes in the investigation."

Three years after the T.J. Maxx case, Jackson didn't feel the landscape had changed in any meaningful way. There was one minor sign of progress: occasionally, defense attorneys now managed to get their hands on the candidate list, which showed all the photos a facial recognition system identified as possible matches. But getting even that small glimpse into the workings of the machine often required getting the courts on board. "Candidate lists that 'absolutely don't exist' magically appear when a judge mentions the word 'subpoena,'" she said. Jackson and many other lawyers who had been forced to contend with police surveillance were skeptical that courts could solve the problem. Ultimately, Jackson believed, it would come down to lawmakers.

Throughout the latter half of the Trump administration, the spread of facial recognition and other new forms of digital surveillance was, along with suspicion of China, one of the only issues capable of bridging the bipartisan divide in Washington. Nearly everyone on Capitol Hill agreed that China was a threat to American interests, and nearly everyone agreed that the new age of surveillance was a threat to democratic values. That unity virtually ensured that some sort of action would eventually be taken to rein in AI tracking tools, though, as we'll document later, the unexpected transformation of Capitol Hill into a battle zone in the waning days of the Trump White House would complicate the debate.

PART IV

THE CHINA SOLUTION

10

PRIVACY REDEFINED

The site, launched in 2015, had all the design charm of Internet 1.0–era YouTube—a simple grid of video thumbnails, titles written in text below, laid out against a plain white background with a search bar at the top. But its bland appearance belied a unique body of content as disturbing as it was fascinating.

Each thumbnail led to a livestreaming video feed. The feeds came from every major city across China and offered peeks into a stunning variety of spaces: bars, restaurants, convenience stores, parking garages, hotel lobbies, and lingerie shops. One showed women doing downward dog in a Beijing yoga studio. Another showed customers awkwardly eyeing the wares in a wig shop in Xi'an. Yet another, located in the industrial city of Shijiazhuang, broadcast twenty-four hours a day of fluffy cud-chewing from a suburban alpaca farm. Several appeared to be streaming from inside people's homes, capturing them as they tossed in their sleep or sat motionless in front of the TV.

Water Droplet Livestream was named after a cheap brand of web-connected home security cameras sold by Qihoo 360, a Chinese internet security company that had recently expanded into consumer devices. The white plastic cameras were narrow at the bottom and widened, like an upside-down drop of water, into a sphere at the top that housed a wide-angle lens. Qihoo had set up the website so that owners could view live feeds from their cameras remotely. The feeds could be password-protected to keep them private, but thousands of them had been left unprotected, leaving them open for anyone on the internet to watch.

Around the same time Water Droplet Livestream came online, the Chinese artist Xu Bing was on the verge of giving up on a long-contemplated effort to weave a feature film from surveillance footage. A legend in the Chinese art world, celebrated for his ability to work in virtually any medium, Xu had become intrigued by the natural way people appeared on camera when they didn't know they were being filmed. He liked the idea of using the unvarnished reality captured by surveillance to spin a fictional story. But after months of trying to amass footage, he decided it would be impossible to gather enough and dropped the project.

In early 2016, one of Xu's assistants sent him a link to the Water Droplet Livestream. Xu couldn't believe what he was seeing. It was as if Qihoo had tapped his brain and decided to build him a real-world movie studio. Searching around, he found other copycat sites doing the same thing. He and a team of three assistants went out and bought twenty computers, setting them up in a room in his studio. They worked around the clock downloading, watching, clipping, and categorizing footage. After a year, they had logged more than 7,000 hours of video. Another year and six scripts later, they edited everything down into an eighty-one-minute film, which they titled *Dragonfly Eyes*.

Xu later recalled to us how making the film had given him a lot of time to contemplate privacy. In particular, he pointed to his experience securing permission from the dozens of people whose images appeared on screen.

The artist and his assistants spent a total of a year traversing the country, from Guangdong to Xinjiang, asking people to sign release forms allowing for the use of their likenesses. At the start, Xu fretted that people would feel violated and refuse to sign. Instead, nearly everyone granted permission.

Conversations with the people he met persuaded him that concern with privacy as a right in China was the province of the wealthy and well-educated. Residents in other parts of the country were too concerned with making ends meet to afford that luxury. Moreover, the proliferation of cameras, not just in public but in people's homes and pockets, had made the act of watching and being watched a regular part of life. "For people on the lower rungs, surveillance, streaming video, it's just a part of how they interact with the world," he said.

It was an observation that made sense in a country that was even more extremely online than the United States, with close to a billion internet users producing images of themselves and consuming images of others around the clock. It helped explain how the Chinese authorities had been able to install millions of cameras on street corners and in public squares without pushback. Yet a few months later, Water Droplet Livestream found itself at the center of a social media storm driven by outrage over its privacy violations. Soon after, the site disappeared.

◉

Privacy's role in the Communist Party's approach to handling personal information is one of the most surprising facets of the state surveillance story. The Chinese word for "privacy"—which combines the character 隐 (pronounced *yin* in Mandarin), for "concealed" or "secret," with 私 (*si*), meaning "personal" or "selfish"—didn't appear in popular Chinese dictionaries until the 1990s. Especially in the early decades of the post-Mao era, when the muscle memory of collectivist thinking was still strong, the term often carried negative connotations, suggesting a secret that an individual was trying to hide. When the Party first embraced the new era of surveillance, the concept of privacy as a right to be protected had currency mostly among the country's elite, many of them Western-educated. But then, as global attention began to zero in toward the end of the 2010s on the dangers lurking in the internet giants' troves of personal data, it began to catch on more widely. Soon it would grow popular enough to catch the Party's attention and force a response.

In his seminal book on privacy, George Washington University

Law School professor Daniel Solove described it as a "concept in disarray." The principal reason, Solove wrote, is that "nobody can articulate what it means." One of the earliest efforts to articulate privacy in a legal context, for example, came from future Supreme Court justice Louis Brandeis and a Boston lawyer named Samuel Warren, who in 1890 defined it as "the right to be left alone." But that leaves out a long list of other rights also jostling for space under privacy's tent, like protection against searches, the freedom to speak anonymously, and control over personal information.

Historically, changes in the concept of privacy have often been driven by advances in surveillance technology. When Brandeis and Warren wrote their defense of the right to be left alone, it was in part a response to the recent invention by Eastman Kodak of cheap, portable snap cameras that both men feared would magnify journalists' ability to document others' private affairs. "The press is overstepping in every direction the obvious bounds of propriety and of decency," Warren and Brandeis wrote.

More than a century later, the advent of the internet, online advertising, and social media prompted Solove to argue that the list of concerns covered by privacy should be expanded to include aggregation of public data. "When analyzed, aggregated information can reveal new facts about a person that she did not expect would be known about her when the original, isolated data was collected," he wrote. Aggregation was not new, of course, but technology had made it much more powerful—and potentially damaging.

In China, such aggregation would lead to an unexpected backlash that threatened to undermine the Communist Party's surveillance rollout just as it was gaining momentum. Yet Chinese leaders would prove quick to grasp the mutability of privacy and deft at redirecting it to serve their own aims.

◉

Privacy's elasticity as a concept made it an ideal topic for Xu Bing. A recipient of a MacArthur Foundation "genius" grant, he had built his extraordinary career on exploring metamorphosis and misdirection.

In one well-known work, he had arranged hundreds of thousands of cigarettes to resemble a tiger-skin rug. For another, he used dust from post-9/11 lower Manhattan to outline a stanza from a Zen Buddhist poem about emptiness.

By the time of our first visit to his studio in 2017, Xu had spent two years peering into people's lives through Water Droplet Livestream and a handful of copycat sites. Trying to explain the experience, Xu, who moved to the United States in 1990 and eventually became an American citizen before returning to China full-time in 2008, reached for a Hollywood analogue. "Have you ever seen *The Truman Show*?" he asked.

The 1998 science fiction film starring Jim Carrey, about a man who is adopted and raised by an entertainment company inside a simulated world crawling with cameras, was an underground hit in China in the early 2000s, disseminated around the country on black-market video compact discs. Two decades later, it owned a rating of 9.3 (out of 10) on Douban, China's equivalent of Rotten Tomatoes, with close to a million 5-star reviews. Tech companies had created a version of *The Truman Show* on a society-wide scale, Xu said. "The world has become a gigantic film studio. Surveillance cameras everywhere, live-streaming twenty-four hours a day," he said. "The performances of the people in the feeds are incomparable—more convincing than you could get from any actor."

Xu and his team of writers decided to build their own film around a conventional love story that would be easy to follow, to compensate for the complexity of the footage they were cutting together. Actors voice the stories of the two main protagonists: Ke Fan, a technician on a dairy farm, and Qing Ting, a woman who leaves her life at a Buddhist monastery to work at the same farm. Ke Fan finds himself growing enamored of Qing Ting (her name is a homonym for "dragonfly," an insect with compound eyes made up of thousands of lenses each) after spying on her through the farm's security cameras. The two embark on a dramatic romance that ends with him landing in jail. When he gets out, Ke Fan learns that Qing Ting had plastic surgery and ran off to become an internet chat room star. Heartbroken, he goes on a desperate search to find her, tracing a trail of camera footage she's left behind.

For months after *Dragonfly Eyes* debuted at the Locarno Film Festival in August 2017, the surveillance streaming websites continued to operate. New feeds popped up every week, and with them came new viewers. Then, in December, a young writer named Chen Feifei dropped a post on the public section of WeChat addressed to the CEO of Qihoo 360, the company that ran the Water Droplet Livestream site. It was titled "Stop Staring at Us."

Chen's post started out polite, addressing Qihoo CEO Zhou Hongyi as "uncle" and praising the company's cybersecurity products, but quickly pivoted into a biting takedown of the platform's "dazzling lineup" of privacy-eviscerating content. Her post contained a screenshot taken from a Waterdrop feed of a Beijing fitness studio where a woman was doing yoga poses on a pink mat. Chen wrote that she had gone to the studio and showed the feed to the woman, who "flew into a spitting rage."

Another screenshot showed a young woman sitting cozily in a restaurant with an older man. Chen wrote that she was in the restaurant when she saw users posting comments on the video feed, suggesting the woman might be the man's mistress. She showed the feed to the couple, who called over the manager. The manager begged forgiveness, saying he had viewed the livestreaming as a way to advertise how busy the restaurant was.

In a separate post, Chen recalled visiting a dance studio for young kids whose parents weren't aware their children's sessions were being broadcast online. She also reported seeing another feed that showed a six-year-old girl walking around half naked. "Uncle," Chen wrote in an appeal to Zhou, "are you really going to do nothing about this?"

Chen's post went viral and triggered a flood of media coverage. Zhou fought back at first, accusing rival companies of hiring Chen to defame his products, but Chen insisted she wrote it of her own volition. Qihoo said it had encouraged all camera owners to seek permission from customers before making livestreams public, but with the controversy still smoldering a week later, it decided to shut down the platform. In a statement, the company said it regretted that the combination of surveillance and livestreaming in one product had caused "misunder-standing by the public."

Over the next few months, the other platforms died their own, quieter deaths. As Xu Bing was taking *Dragonfly Eyes* to other film festivals, the country-sized movie studio he used to produce it was shuttered.

The explosion of digital surveillance elevated privacy in Chinese minds the same way Kodak cameras had for Americans in the late 1800s. The following year, in 2018, another controversy erupted after Robin Li, the CEO of Baidu, observed at an invitation-only gathering of tech executives and officials in Beijing that Chinese people were "more open" about sharing personal information. "If they are able to trade privacy for convenience, for safety, for efficiency, in a lot of cases they're willing to do that," he said, describing that lax attitude as an advantage for Chinese tech companies. Debate about Li's comments raged across the Chinese internet the next day.

While some defended the CEO, just as many were infuriated, calling Li "despicable" and "underhanded." After the company reiterated assurances that it protects user data, internet users noted that Baidu had been sued earlier in the year by a consumer group that said the company had been illegally collecting user data, including messages and contact lists.

The Qihoo and Baidu incidents crystallized diffuse but long-simmering frustrations inside China. For years, the country had been home to an unrestrained black market for personal information, much of it seemingly pilfered from government and corporate databases. In May 2016, a Chinese human rights activist tried to bring attention to the problem by publishing the ID card numbers, birthdays, and home addresses for Alibaba founder Jack Ma and Tencent founder Pony Ma on Twitter. In an interview, he said he had purchased the information through brokers on Tencent's messaging service QQ for the equivalent of less than a hundred dollars. "You don't need great hacking skills to break into anything," he said. "All you need to do is spend a little cash." Some internet users referred to living in such an environment as "running naked."

By 2020, more than 60 percent of Chinese people believed facial recognition technology in China was being abused, according to a survey by a newspaper based in the southern city of Guangzhou. Roughly a third of the 20,000 people surveyed reported privacy and property losses because of the leak and abuse of their facial data. That was a reversal from a smaller survey the previous year, conducted by a Beijing-based group, that found between 60 and 70 percent of Chinese people thought the use of facial recognition made life safer and more convenient.

If the flowering of privacy awareness in China was unexpected, so was the Communist Party's response. Though they censored some discussions, Chinese leaders didn't crack down the way they typically did with previous civic trends that threatened their agenda. Instead, they appeared to offer tacit support.

Each time a privacy controversy erupted, Party-controlled media piled on. When Robin Li stirred up social media with his comments about Chinese users' willingness to give up data, state broadcaster China Central Television (CCTV) weighed in with a scathing commentary. "Algorithms and big data are flowing like mercury into every field," it observed, arguing that user privacy had been obliterated with news apps and online stores tracking what everyone read or bought. "Are the data magnates going to suck out every last drop of consumers' surplus value?"

Even facial recognition technology started to come under fire, at least in some circumstances. In late 2020, a Hangzhou resident successfully sued the city's zoo for requiring that pass holders provide a biometric scan of their faces—a result reported widely in state media. The following March, during a widely watched annual show for Consumer Rights Day, CCTV named and shamed American bathroom product maker Kohler and German automaker BMW for installing surveillance cameras in showrooms that allegedly collected visitors' facial data without their consent.

With facial recognition technology coming under continued fire, government agencies began taking action. In late 2020, Hangzhou drafted rules to ban residential compounds from requiring face scans to access shared areas. The following summer, China's highest court issued a judicial interpretation that made clear that facial information was considered personal information. Hotels, shopping malls, and other businesses needed to get consent before using facial recognition, the court said, and use it only in limited ways. "The calls for strengthening protection of facial information are increasing," the court's vice president noted in a press conference announcing the rules.

◉

What was going on? The Party, for all its power, still had to respond to changes in public opinion. It was also growing concerned about its relationship to the country's tech giants. The first part of its response came through legislation. Chinese lawmakers and legal scholars started kicking around the idea of a national privacy law in 2003, though it languished for years amid a lack of interest among top leaders. The effort suddenly accelerated. By the time Xi Jinping was wrapping up his second five-year term in 2022, the country had not one but several laws that dealt with data collection and security.

The biggest was a sprawling law on the protection of personal information, which passed in the fall of 2021. It was modeled on the world's strictest digital privacy legislation, the European Union's General Data Protection Regulation. The GDPR was vehemently opposed by Silicon Valley when it was approved in 2016 because of the threat it posed to mass data collection. It required internet companies to get explicit consent to collect data, collect only as much as needed, limit the amount of time personal information is stored, and allow users to access, correct, and delete that information at will.

China's version contained all those same provisions, but it differed from Europe's legal regime in one vital respect: it placed few limits on data the state could access. The Chinese law required state agencies to notify individuals when they collected data and imposed limits on the sharing and use of data, but it made exceptions for data necessary to the agency's work, to respond to emergencies, "or to take other action in the public interest." It also contained consent and transparency exemptions in situations where secrecy was necessary, a category that in China covered a vast territory. The law allowed citizens to sue government agencies for mishandling their personal data, but in a country where the ruling party controlled the courts, that was not a meaningful restraint.

"At the end of the day, the law will not change the political dynamic in China," said Jamie Horsley, an expert in Chinese law at Yale Law School. "They want to establish these guardrails, make sure officials behave reasonably and effectively, and have the support of the people in doing so. But when it comes to national security issues, it's status quo."

Prior to the privacy law, Chinese authorities had already imposed a host of rules that ensured the internet giants would share information with the Party. Laws on counterterrorism and cybersecurity instruct companies to actively assist police, including by handing over user data, in any situation that could potentially "harm national security"—a deliberately vague term the authorities applied both to the buying of bomb components on e-commerce sites and to criticism of the government that goes viral on social media. A new data security law, also passed in 2021, classified consumer data according to its importance to state interests, threatening heavy fines and criminal penalties for anyone who compromised "core" data or disclosed other data that compromised China's national security, sovereignty, or development.

Confronted with demands for privacy protection, China's leaders took a novel approach. They co-opted and redefined the very notion of privacy: no longer an abstract individual right, instead it was now welded to the collective concept of national security, and in turn to the security of the Party itself.

The strategy was not cost-free for Chinese leaders. Limiting the amount of data that companies could collect ultimately limited the amount of data the government could access. Still, the benefits of tighter controls outweighed the costs, explained Samantha Hoffman, the American security analyst. "The way that private companies hold data is actually currently incredibly insecure," she said. "That puts individuals at risk in the privacy sense, but it also puts the state at risk." The privacy law, she continued, was "solving real economic problems, solving real technical problems, and solving real governance problems, all the while exerting more control in the end."

One cybersecurity researcher had demonstrated the security risks for the Party in striking fashion in February 2019. The researcher, Victor Gevers, ran a nonprofit that aimed to help organizations better protect their data. One way the group did this was by scanning the internet for unprotected databases. During one scan that month, Gevers discovered an unprotected Chinese-language database that belonged to SenseNets, the facial recognition and crowd-analysis joint venture set up by industry giants SenseTime and NetPosa.

According to screenshots Gevers shared publicly, the SenseNets database contained detailed records—names, addresses, ID card numbers, photographs, birth dates, and employer details—for more than 2.5 million people, ranging in age from ninety-five years all the way down to just nine days. Almost all of them lived in Xinjiang. Later, Gevers dug deeper and found that the data included millions of GPS coordinates tracking the movements of each of the people over the previous twenty-four hours, with location tags including "internet cafe" and "mosque."

He also discovered the company's developers had published code on the popular repository site GitHub that contained their email addresses, credentials, and passwords, making it easy for anyone to take control of the company's cameras. Instructions for operating the system also appeared on GitHub. "But even with that confidential information publicly exposed there is no technical knowledge needed to control these cameras," he wrote. SenseNets quietly secured the database. With inside details of the Party's surveillance in Xinjiang—one of the country's most secretive security projects—on display for the world to see, Chinese regulators were notably silent.

Besides improving security, throwing its support behind privacy also gave the Party an important weapon in constraining the power of the country's internet giants. The Party worked closely with the likes of Alibaba and Tencent, but tensions had grown. The companies often acted with impunity, shrugging off regulators to pursue new lines of business, such as lending, that officials considered risky. More importantly, the companies' swelling stores of data gave them far better insight into what was happening in many areas of society and the economy than the Party had—a power imbalance that didn't sit well inside the leadership compound in Beijing.

Even after the showdown over credit data in 2018 (discussed in Chapter 5), the companies were also still resistant to sharing their data in ways the authorities preferred, which heightened the anxiety. Chinese police and state security agents could request data on individuals and small groups, but the companies pushed back against the mass access needed for the type of sweeping analysis and social modeling the Party wanted to do.

Conflict spilled out into the open in November 2020, as Ant Financial was preparing to list in the United States in what was expected to be the largest initial public offering in history. Investors had already committed to buying $34 billion of the company's shares. But with days to go, Xi Jinping shocked everyone by ordering Ant to cancel the IPO. The cancellation was in part a response to a recent speech Jack Ma had given in which he had been dismissive of regulators, but there was another motivation: not long after, Chinese regulators began pressuring the company to share its troves of consumer credit data. Later, in a further message to Jack Ma to fall in line, they slapped Alibaba with a record $2.8 billion fine for "abusing its market dominance."

The assault on Ant and Alibaba was just the first move in a sweeping crackdown on China's tech sector. Using a combination of antitrust and privacy rules, the Party asserted its dominance over the country's most powerful companies. A year after the Covid-19 pandemic slowed global commerce to a crawl, China's economy was in a fragile state. That didn't stop Xi Jinping from making his move. Ride-hailing, delivery, and social media giants—all big drivers of consumption and employment—came under burning scrutiny over their business practices, including how they handled user data. The rectification shaved hundreds of billions of dollars off the value of Chinese tech stocks as investors panicked, but leaders in Beijing didn't blink. By the end of 2021, there was zero doubt left about who ultimately controlled the country's data.

◉

By the time the government passed the privacy law, Xu Bing had taken *Dragonfly Eyes* to more than forty international art and film festivals, where it had pulled in several awards, including a nod from the International Federation of Film Critics at Locarno. He tried and failed to secure a license from censors to show the film in Chinese theaters, but he still managed to show it in Chinese museums and art galleries.

Speaking about the shuttering of Water Droplet Livestream and the other surveillance sites so soon after the film was finished, Xu marveled at his team's good fortune. "It turns out there was a three-year window in which a film like this could have been made, and we happened to seize the opportunity," he told us in a call over WeChat in the summer of 2021.

Like many in China, Xu wasn't certain how to understand the sudden explosion of interest in privacy. Some of it, he believed, could be attributed to the influence of Western ideas, which affected China despite the Party's best censorship efforts. But he didn't expect Chinese people to turn around and rebel en masse against data collection.

Part of it was practical. "If you're not willing to have your data collected, you basically can't live," he said. "People have asked me at screenings, 'Is there a place that we can find where we're not subject to data collection?' I've thought about it and there really isn't, unless you're willing to bury yourself in a tank somewhere deep enough in the ground to escape mobile signals."

Another part of it was socioeconomic. He still believed that privacy was a concern mostly among the well-educated. "There's a difference in how higher-tier and lower-tier cities see privacy," he said. "There are a lot of third- and fourth-tier cities in China. A lot." The privacy debate may sound like it had grown nationwide, but that was because the first-tier China had more influence on social media debate. It wasn't that lower-tier China didn't understand or value privacy but that economic pressures focused its attention in other places.

Even if privacy consciousness did spread nationwide, Xu said, he believed it would look different from anything in the West. The continuing influence of collectivist ideas in China would produce a different notion of privacy, he argued. He pointed to public group activities like dancing and singing—something he rarely saw during his years in the United States but that are a daily feature of virtually every park in every city in China. "Americans just don't go for that kind of thing," he said. "There's inevitably a cultural element to how people understand privacy.'"

If Xu is right, and if the recent past is a guide, one way the Chinese notion of privacy might evolve differently is in its relationship to authority. In the United States, and in the West in general, the state often looms in the background of debates around the protection of privacy as the principal villain, and there's a celebrated tradition of asserting a right to privacy, like a verbal middle finger, in the face of probing questions from government goons. The state looms over almost everything in China, but Chinese discussions of privacy seldom target the government directly. Whether out of resignation, acquiescence, or agreement, most Chinese don't deny the government's claim to their personal data, even as some rage against privacy violations committed by others. Given the malleability of privacy, that could always change. For the moment, however, the Party has found a way to make China's version of privacy compatible with surveillance.

11

THE PANOPTICON AND POTEMKIN AI

One of the ideas that's critical to unlocking the operations of China's surveillance state was born on an estate in Krichev, in what is now eastern Belarus, in 1784. That year, the owner of the estate, a Russian governor named Grigory Potemkin, hired an inventive British mechanical engineer by the name of Samuel Bentham to help him manage his workshops and shipyards. With Catherine the Great planning a tour of the region, Potemkin gave Bentham an unlimited budget along with orders to make the estate appear to be a model of productivity.

As he worked to conjure Potemkin's fantasy of prosperity, Bentham developed an architectural concept for improving the management of workshops that itself relied on deception. It consisted of a circular building arranged around a station in the center called the Inspector's Lodge that gave workers the sense of being constantly monitored. In a fateful episode of fraternal intellectual property theft, Samuel's brother Jeremy, a social theorist, later appropriated the idea to design a new type of circular prison with hidden surveillance corridors that allowed three guards to monitor six floors of prisoners. He called it the Panopticon.

In the study of surveillance, no metaphor occupies a loftier position than Jeremy Bentham's ring-shaped prison. The image of the panopticon was central to Zamyatin's writing of *We* and the filmed version of Orwell's *1984*. It has been used to frame critiques of everything from urban planning to mass media to worker exploitation. It also helps explain how the Chinese surveillance state manages to be effective despite being in significant measure aspirational and in some instances illusory.

The word "panopticon" derives from the Greek word *panoptes*, meaning "all-seeing." In fact, the prison's guards didn't—couldn't—see everything happening on the two floors each was assigned to watch. But that was part of the design. "The inmate must never know whether he is being looked at any one moment; but he must be sure that he may always be so," explained Michel Foucault, the French philosopher who famously adopted Bentham's design as a way to explain the roles discipline and punishment play in the maintenance of social order. This constant sense of scrutiny was, in Foucault's mind, a form of "soul training" that could mold behavior with remarkable efficiency.

China's network of digital sensors is itself often described as "all-seeing." Without a doubt it sees more than any state surveillance network that has come before. And yet, it's riddled with blind spots. The overwhelming majority of Chinese people can still find refuge from the Party's prying eyes inside their own homes, even accounting for those who briefly broadcast their personal surveillance feeds on Water Droplet Livestream. Broad stretches of public space likewise fall outside of the government's field of vision, whether because of neglect, indifference, or broken cameras. Gaps exist in Chinese cyberspace as well, a result of missing or corrupt data and jumbled, incompatible databases.

If one corner of China comes close to justifying the "all-seeing" label, it's Xinjiang, where security forces have cultivated a tried-and-true ability to peer into every aspect of Uyghurs' lives—including, the Communist Party claims, their futures. But the Party falls short of omniscience even there, as we discovered on our reporting trips in 2017 and 2018. Like a ship capsized in shallow water, the region harbored pockets of air that offered escape from the suffocation of state scrutiny, even if only for a moment or two. Personal cars, remote stretches of desert, and crowded markets all offered one degree or another of space for snatches of candid conversation and exchanges of information that the authorities would rather not happen. Perpetually tracking 15 million members of a minority group spread over a vast area turned out to be difficult, even with the best surveillance systems China could muster.

In Xinjiang, at least, the surveillance systems are functional. In other parts of China, where security forces are tasked with keeping track of a much larger population over an even more expansive landscape, that is not a given. On several occasions, we read breathless stories in state-run media about stunning feats of surveillance only to discover, after traveling to the scene of the triumph, that the details had been embellished or fabricated entirely.

The disappointments were not a surprise. They were a familiar consequence of China's political system. In the Mao years, the Chinese leaders had funneled precious resources into literal Potemkin villages, like the community of Dazhai in the dusty inland province of Shanxi, meant to embody the intent, if not the actual reality, of policies dreamed up in Beijing. In the reform era, the Communist Party embraced more bottom-up policymaking but never fully relinquished its fondness for central planning. Accordingly, the safest path to a promotion for any official was to respond (or appear to respond) with extreme zeal to dictates from Beijing. When the order of the day was GDP growth at all costs, local governments fell over themselves to erect hastily planned bridges and residential towers—some of which themselves later fell over or apart. When Xi Jinping gave the orders to embrace big data and AI to improve how China was run, it was inevitable that lower-level officials would jump into digital surveillance with the same fake-it-till-you-make-it enthusiasm.

When it came to digital surveillance, Chinese officials already had a model to follow in Silicon Valley. Algorithmic sleight of hand is rampant among American tech companies, many of which won their first injections of venture capital by spinning grand visions around technologies that at the time were barely more than notional. Technology researcher Jathan Sadowski coined the term "Potemkin AI," after Catherine the Great's infamous flatterer, to describe the products of this chicanery.

He cites the example of M, a short-lived virtual assistant introduced by Facebook in 2015, that was astoundingly superior to easily stumped competitors like Apple's Siri, but which turned out to rely on an army of humans to step in when the AI failed. Where Potemkin erected elaborate facades, Sadowski writes, Silicon Valley marketers deploy technological buzzwords "as though they were a magician's incantations: *Smart! Intelligent! Automated! Cognitive computing! Deep learning! Abracadabra! Alakazam!*" Enchanted audiences were none the wiser.

In a certain sense, the digitization of state surveillance was an ideal endeavor for China's leaders. Beijing's social engineers could drum up elaborate plans to fine-tune the Party's control over the country using cutting-edge techniques with little fear of failure. That's because the surveillance state was a propaganda exercise as much as an infrastructure project—one that had fakery built in as a feature. The prisoners only had to believe that they were being watched.

This dynamic is important for understanding the entirety of China's surveillance state. But it is particularly useful in helping untangle the confusion that surrounds one of the few Chinese surveillance programs that enjoys widespread recognition in the West.

In the fall of 2015, the American Civil Liberties Union published a blog post that warned of a nightmarish development unfolding in the world's most populous country. "China appears to be leveraging all the tools of the information age—electronic purchasing data, social networks, algorithmic sorting—to construct the ultimate tool of social control," the post said. The tool was called the Social Credit System. Unlike the American credit system, with its exclusive focus on financial information, the post said, the Chinese system calculated a person's score based in part on political compliance, as well as hobbies, lifestyle, and the behavior of friends.

A torrent of foreign media coverage followed, with headlines around the world marveling at the arrival of a new Orwellian development few had seen coming. Much of that early reporting would later turn out to be mistaken, but in ways that ultimately proved illuminating.

The roots of the Social Credit System trace back to an effort China's government undertook in the early 2000s to emulate the consumer credit systems of Western countries. The undertaking was driven by China's then-premier, Zhu Rongji, who grew interested in credit systems, according to state media lore, after receiving a letter from a distraught entrepreneur whose educational toy company in Shenzhen had been driven into the ground by counterfeiters. The toymaker reportedly wrote the letter after visiting the United States, telling Zhu that building American-style regimes to protect intellectual property and rate creditworthiness "would have incalculable value in turning enterprise into an engine of economic growth." Zhu promptly gathered a group of experts and dispatched them to countries around the globe to study the world's credit systems.

One of the people Zhu tapped to lead the project in its early days was Lin Junyue, an American-educated expert in credit systems at the Chinese Academy of Social Sciences. With Zhu's blessing, Lin flew to the United States to meet with financial credit-rating companies in California, Maryland, and New York. He came back feeling overwhelmed. "The United States took 150 years to build up its credit system," he recalled to us. "We were supposed to come up with a plan to do the same thing in a fraction of the time."

Judging an individual or organization's financial creditworthiness is an example of one of the oldest functions of data collection: dividing society into groups according to what each deserves. Surveillance scholars call it "sorting." In capitalist countries, owners of capital have a strong incentive to find ways to sort would-be borrowers according to their ability to repay debts. In the 1950s, specialized credit-rating agencies in the United States trawled newspapers for "lifestyle" information to include in individual credit files, including drinking habits and sexual orientation, and helped revive what had been a long-dormant privacy movement. The invention of the FICO score by Fair Isaac Corporation in the late 1980s elevated financial sorting to new heights of efficiency, introducing Americans to the unsettling notion of having their financial integrity reduced to a three-digit number.

If Lin found the notion of trying to duplicate the American system daunting, his task would soon become even harder. In October 2011, a year before Xi Jinping was scheduled to take power, senior Communist Party officials met in Beijing to consider the country's direction. The verdict was not encouraging. After decades of unbridled growth, Chinese society was dripping with cynicism and dismissive of the government. A few years earlier, batches of baby formula tainted with the industrial chemical melamine killed six infants and sickened as many as 300,000 more. Memories were also fresh of the catastrophic high-speed train crash that summer in Wenzhou that led to accusations of a government cover-up and became a metaphor for the country's headlong pursuit of development no matter the human cost.

Faced with this constellation of moral and political crises, Party leaders decided to expand the scope of the social credit system. The new goal, according to the official readout from the meeting, was "the establishment and perfection of a credit system covering the entirety of society."

The Party still wanted a financial credit system that would unlock economic growth, according to Lin, but to that it had added a much grander ambition: to rebuild a moral structure that had collapsed in the post-Mao era. "China doesn't have churches to enforce morality. You can't rely just on education. If all you do is lecture people, saying 'This is how you should do it,' or 'This way is immoral,' you're not going to get good results," he said. Using a mechanism like social credit that offers real-world rewards and real-world punishments "makes the moral construction process a little more efficient." It was a solution taken from the business world to manage a society in which making money had become the last unifying pursuit.

Under Mao, the Communist Party had compelled people in urban areas to behave correctly by compiling secret dossiers on every individual. Known as *dang'an*, the files contained records of each person's family background, education level, political activities, job history, and personal achievements and failings. In the pre-reform era, when the state doled out housing and jobs, the *dang'an* had a terrifying power to determine a person's path through life. (A prominent Tibetan poet once recalled thinking of her own file as "like an invisible monster stalking you.") As the economy opened up in the post-Mao era and most Chinese people stopped relying on the government to feed and shelter them, the *dang'an* system lost its power. With social credit, the Party was looking to reboot it.

China's cabinet, the State Council, unveiled its blueprint for building the Social Credit System on June 14, 2014. Like most Chinese government plans, it was wildly dense. But to those willing to spend hours hacking through its thickets of officialese, it revealed a vision that was breathtaking in its ambition, and unlike anything any government had tried before.

The document began with a surprising burst of candor about the dearth of sincerity in China's economy and society, warning that a failure to address it could mean dire consequences for China's future. In order to provide broad incentives to act in good faith, the plan said, the Social Credit System would need to touch on every area of business. It offered a dizzying list: exports, exhibitions, health care, culture, education, sports, scientific research and stock trading, criminal prosecution and legal defense, pollution control, public security, intellectual property protection, tourism, media, insurance sales, even veterinary medicine. The aim, according to the plan, was to "allow the trustworthy to roam everywhere while making it hard for the discredited to take a single step."

In order to do this, the government would need to collect, organize, and analyze unheard-of quantities of data. Here too the plan was ambitious, calling for the creation of a network to "cover all information subjects, all credit information categories and all regions nationwide," with the basic infrastructure to be in place by 2020.

After the first burst of Western media coverage, Chinese state media fed the flames. Throughout 2016 and 2017, Party-controlled newspapers in cities around the country published articles about lamentable trends in society, from bad driving to violating birth restrictions, in each instance threatening offenders with black marks on their social credit records. In Hangzhou, subway authorities warned of negative credit consequences for fare evaders. Reporting in 2016 about construction of the Social Credit System, China Radio International, the country's official state-run radio broadcaster, published a photo on its website of an electronic billboard in the inland city of Taiyuan that displayed the photos and personal information of people with bad credit records.

For his part, Lin Junyue pitched the Social Credit System as a tech-driven alternative to China's beleaguered legal system. The courts were slow and onerous, he said, which discouraged people from using them. "With the Social Credit System it's there every day at every moment, it's in every corner of every business and household, recording data," he told us in 2016. "If you do well, it rewards you. And if you're doing something bad, maybe not to the point of breaking the law, you get a warning about your problems. . . . It's a great service."

As researchers and reporters dug deeper, however, social credit turned out to be something less than the pinnacle of algorithmic control that the early coverage suggested it was. The ACLU and several outlets turned out to have mistakenly conflated it with Sesame Credit, the purely commercial, AI-driven system that Jack Ma's Ant Financial had created to score users based on their behavior on Alibaba's e-commerce platforms. Despite intimations by local media and speculation by outside experts, the government's system didn't attempt to create a unified national score for all citizens. Local efforts to implement it stumbled over legal and technological barriers, and questions surfaced about whether it was algorithmic at all. Our own efforts to look under the hood of social credit taught us about both the limits of the Party's social engineering prowess and its skill at using propaganda to mask the clunkiness of some of its machinery.

◉

Our initial effort to understand the Social Credit System took us in the late spring of 2016 to a cluttered office in downtown Hangzhou that belonged to a legal scholar by the name of Zhuang Daohe. We had traveled to Hangzhou as part of a tour of cities in eastern China that were touting their efforts to roll out social credit. We wanted to see if people in those cities were being punished with bad credit ratings for political activity, as some reporting suggested.

A devout Christian, Zhuang participated in the 1989 pro-democracy movement as a college student and had maintained an interest in human rights throughout his career, most of which he had spent teaching law at Hangzhou University. He was among a group of activists whose signature appeared on Charter 08, an explosive manifesto that called for an independent legal system, freedom of association, and a multiparty political system. The government had refused to give him a license to practice law, but he still maintained a side job helping clients as a legal "advisor." We figured if anyone knew local malcontents with bad credit records, it would be him.

Zhuang answered the door wearing a red USB device in the shape of a cross on a chain around his neck. He was thickset and gregarious with a shock of black hair combed back from a high forehead that gave him a Mao-ish look. He had never heard of social credit, he said, but on hearing us describe it, he retreated to a corner of the office and began rummaging around in a file drawer. Minutes later, he returned with a stack of photocopied legal documents, which he laid down on a conference table. "I don't know if this is what you're looking for," Zhuang said. "But it seems related."

The documents described the case of a local travel service operator who had been placed on a list of "trust breakers" deemed to have defaulted on court judgments. According to Zhuang, the travel service operator and his wife were embroiled in a dispute with the owner of a small retail space they had rented in a mixed-use building years earlier. The couple had sublet the space to a friend, who in turn sublet it to a man from out of town who used it to open a noodle shop. Bombarded by complaints from residents about the noise and smell from the shop, the landlord sued the travel agent for breaking the terms of the lease. The travel agent agreed to give up the space and pay the remainder of the rent on the lease, but the noodle-maker refused to leave. Months later, the travel agent learned he had been put on a blacklist for having defaulted on a court judgment.

The blacklist system was established in 2013 by China's highest court as a way to help lower courts enforce rulings. In addition to having their names listed on the court website, people who ignored court orders could have their assets frozen and be prevented from taking out loans. Over time, the list of penalties expanded to include bans on air and high-speed train travel as well as stays in luxury hotels.

Blacklists would turn out to provide a critical, if flawed, solution to a central problem for the Social Credit System: how to measure and punish bad behavior in a way that is defensible. With financial credit systems, the equation is relatively simple because everything—behavior, rewards, and punishments—is defined in terms of numbers. If the numbers show you have a poor track record of paying loans back on time, then your credit score goes down and the amount you have to pay in interest to borrow money goes up. Calculations get much messier when the behavior and the punishments leave the realm of math. An official with the social credit office in the city of Wenzhou, south of Hangzhou, bragged about a system they had built to let anyone check whether a potential business partner had financial red flags, but they had set aside trying to track other types of behavior or develop a scoring system. "It's way too complicated. Very risky," he said.

The risk was legal. No one wanted to go out on a limb and create a rating system to punish bad behavior without a law specifically authorizing it, the Wenzhou official said. In 2010, Suining County in Jiangsu province had experimented with assigning letter grades to residents based on a 1,000-point scale, offering high scorers perks like better job opportunities while subjecting those on the low end to added scrutiny in applying for social welfare and business licenses. The scheme attracted biting criticism from the public and state media and was quickly scrapped. Data scientists and legal experts who advised the government on social credit raised doubts about scores, which they warned would be a nightmare to calculate fairly, even with the new technology and data the Party had available.

The blacklists, which were intended to punish violations of existing laws and regulations, offered an alternative for molding behavior that already had a basis in law and was thus easier to implement than a scoring system that might invite public criticism. Under the social credit plan, other branches of government were encouraged to copy the courts. The Ministry of Ecology and Environment set up its own blacklist for polluting companies. The Cyberspace Administration started one for people who posted information online that violated "social morality, business ethics, honesty, and integrity." Airline passengers who abused flight attendants or tried to open the emergency doors—not an uncommon occurrence in China—ended up on the airline regulator's no-fly list.

The lists were linked together in a system of "unified rewards and punishments" that copied names from one list to the others. This meant someone who stirred things up online wouldn't just have their internet access limited by the cyberspace authorities but might also be banned from taking out a mortgage by the banking regulator. Shame was a feature of the system as well. In some cities, mobile operators fixed it so that anyone calling a blacklisted person would hear a warning that they were about to talk to someone untrustworthy.

Blacklists were also applied extensively in business, an area where the social credit system was arguably most successful. Companies in China, like elsewhere, are subject to an expansive list of rules and regulations of varying severity that are intended to govern their behavior. The threat of blacklisting turned out to be effective in scaring businesses into respecting rules they had previously ignored, or not even bothered to read in the first place.

The results with individuals were murkier. Because they were rooted in the legal system, blacklists didn't offer the nimble feedback that Lin Junyue had envisioned. As Zhuang's clients discovered, the blacklisting process could also be capricious. In 2015, the travel agent tried to book a flight to Guangzhou and was denied. He was also banned from buying high-speed train tickets and wasn't allowed to accompany one of his tour groups on a boat cruise. "This guy runs a tour business. Now he can't go on a plane or take a high-speed train. How absurd is that?" Zhuang said. It emerged that his client had landed on the blacklist because the landlord had complained to the court that, in addition to paying the remaining rent, the travel agent was obligated to evict the noodle-maker from the space the couple had sublet. Zhuang argued that eviction was the landlord's responsibility. His appeals fell on deaf ears.

A few months after our visit, Hangzhou hosted the Group of 20 Summit, an annual gathering of the leaders of the world's largest economies.

As a security measure, police cleared out nonresidents doing business in the city, including the noodle maker. The travel agent suddenly found his name removed from the blacklist, though not before being blocked from flying to see his daughter's college graduation in the United States.

◉

In a twist, Zhuang was himself caught up in the vagaries of China's social credit rollout a few years later. His experience highlighted two of the Social Credit System's other great flaws: fractured systems for storing data, and opaque operations that were difficult to challenge.

In 2019, a local company specializing in hydraulic construction hammers, Hangzhou Mingyang Steel Machine Co., told Zhuang it wanted to bring him on as a legal supervisor. Zhuang had been advising the company on legal matters for years, but his lack of a law license meant he couldn't defend them in court. As a supervisor, he could at least be present in court as the company's legal representative.

Zhuang agreed to the arrangement, but when Mingyang went to the website of the local market regulator to register him in his new role, a warning window popped up: "Zhuang Daohe has a credit problem!" After calling the regulator, Mingyang learned that Zhuang had been placed on a blacklist banning him from serving as a legal representative because he had earlier served as the representative of a local company that had been stripped of its business license in 2011.

Zhuang had no idea what company the regulators were referring to. A person he spoke to at the regulator's office couldn't find a record of the company's name, and also couldn't explain why he was still on the list eight years after the alleged offense despite a three-year limit on individual listings.

Hoping to find out how his credit record had been sullied, Zhuang filed open-government information requests with multiple branches of the market regulator's office. All of them confirmed that he was on the blacklist, but none knew the name of the company that had ostensibly lost its business license. At one point, an official called Zhuang to ask whether he knew what the company was called.

Zhuang's predicament highlighted a problem that afflicted much of

China's bureaucracy. The Communist Party might control vast amounts of information about China's society and economy, but local officials often seemed to be cut off from it. A big part of the issue was architectural: most of the government's data was scattered among thousands of government agencies whose officials and computer systems didn't always play well with each other—a phenomenon engineers refer to as "data islands."

One of the first priorities of the social credit plan had been to solve this problem. The central and local governments set out to connect the islands and siphon their data into a single credit-specific platform. In theory, the local police, courts, tax bureaus, citizen affairs offices, health and family planning bureaus, and other agencies would submit records on local residents to the master database. Those records would then be entered into each citizen's social credit file, which would be accessible to officials who needed to see them, such as those in the Hangzhou market regulator's office. But five years after the plan was released, a year before the national social credit platform was supposed to be in place, even the most basic information could still be impossible to access.

A frustrated Zhuang decided to sue the regulator, demanding both an admission that his blacklisting was a fabrication and an apology. A few days later, the regulator's district-level office sent a letter saying it had applied to have his credit record wiped clean. Days later, Zhuang was able to apply in person to join Mingyang as a supervisor. Officials from the city-level office visited him with a fruit basket to apologize, begging him to drop his lawsuit, which he agreed to do. He never discovered how his name had ended up on the blacklist.

◉

Social credit is hardly the only corner of China's surveillance state that appears more impressive than it actually is.

In 2017, *The Wall Street Journal* sent reporters to Fengqiao, a township in Zhejiang province that had been named a pilot zone for Safe Zhejiang, an app residents could use to report local problems to provincial authorities in exchange for rewards like coupons at local stores. Fengqiao was chosen for the pilot due to its political history. The township had achieved fame in the 1960s after Mao praised local officials for mobilizing residents to root out and "rehabilitate" local landlords and other class enemies. As a provincial official in 2003, Xi Jinping had expressed admiration for the "Fengqiao experience." After Xi was anointed China's leader, the government tried to recreate the "Fengqiao experience" in digital form.

Despite months of glowing media coverage, the *Journal*'s reporters discovered that almost no one in the township had heard of Safe Zhejiang. At least some of the app's anonymity appeared to be the result of bureaucratic sabotage. A local Party secretary in a village on the outskirts of Fengqiao revealed that he had told villagers not to use it, but instead to report problems to him directly so that he could decide which ones to send along to higher-ups. At the end of every year, provincial authorities judge village officials on the number of problems they're able to solve, the Party secretary, Wang Haijun, explained. "If we report problems almost every day," he said, "we won't reach the required standard."

We found a similar situation in the summer of 2019, when we paid a visit to Jinxiu, a cluster of residential units built in bucolic surroundings an hour's drive from downtown Hangzhou. Local media had described the development as a paragon of "smart policing," where facial recognition systems had helped track down more than a dozen missing children and elderly residents in the space of a year. Stories of AI being used to help find lost or stolen children were a staple of Chinese technology journalism at the time. Though China's one-child policy was relaxed in 2015, fears around child abductions hadn't subsided. Writing about technology that was capable of tracking down lost sons and daughters, sometimes decades after they went missing, was a surefire way to drive rivers of traffic to a news site.

We arrived at Jinxiu to find a formidable-looking surveillance system guarding the main gate. Entering or leaving meant walking past multiple cameras and a line of face-scanning security consoles. But inside, not a single resident we interviewed could recall hearing about the cameras being used to track down a missing person. People working the desks at Jinxiu's residential committee said one staff member had once pretended to be a mother whose lost child was discovered through facial recognition. "But that was just an act that we used to film a promotional video," the manager said. The video played on a big screen inside the estate's dedicated police station. When we visited the police station in charge of Jinxiu's district to ask about the local media reports, a senior officer insisted the articles were true but declined to elaborate.

There appeared to be more substance to the Social Credit System than either of the projects in Fengqiao and Jinxiu. A year after the State Council's 2020 deadline to set up a basic social credit infrastructure, data from the Chinese central bank showed that the system had grown to cover 1.1 billion individuals and over 60 million enterprises and organizations. Its effects in regulating the behavior of business were concrete enough to have spawned a cottage industry of social credit advisors who offered to help companies get off the blacklists of various regulatory agencies.

The system's impact on individuals, however, was less clear. In 2019, the government announced that it had blocked the country's untrustworthy from purchasing plane and high-speed rail tickets more than 30 million times, and that pressure from being blacklisted had led more than 4 million people to "proactively" fulfill their legal obligations. But data for more recent years is scattered and difficult to parse. An assessment published by government researchers at the end of 2020 complained that local efforts to build social credit systems were disjointed and inconsistent, with some using letter grades to judge individual behavior, others using numbers, and still others ignoring ratings altogether. Regions varied in how they incentivized or punished bad behavior, the researchers noted, and even in how they judged whether behavior was bad or not. "Building a successful social credit system isn't something you can do overnight," they concluded wearily.

Party-controlled media offered a much less equivocal vision. Though they sometimes acknowledged flaws in the system, official newspapers and TV stations for the most part continued to produce a steady stream of social credit propaganda, running story after story on new bad behaviors that had supposedly come under the social credit umbrella. By 2021, the list had come to include, among other things, running red lights, evading subway fares, exceeding birth limits, defrauding social welfare systems, cheating on tests, plagiarizing academic work, failing to send children to school, backing out of joining the military, involvement in sports doping, refusing to leave the hospital when released, taking someone's seat on the high-speed train, and being insufficiently filial. Taken together, the stories offered a fascinating glimpse into the types of problems the Communist Party saw as most bedeviling Chinese society. They also revealed a system committed to delivering the impression, if not the reality, of omnipotence.

Lin Junyue reinforced that message in an interview that aired as part of a French documentary on surveillance in 2020. Describing the Social Credit System as a fait accompli, he professed a desire to export it to capitalist countries. "I think France should quickly adopt our Social Credit System to fix its social movements," he said, referring to the populist Yellow Vest protests that roiled Paris and other French cities through 2018 and 2019. "If you'd had the Social Credit System, the Yellow Vests would have never emerged. You'd have detected it before they acted. You could have foreseen it and prevented those events."

Whether or not the Social Credit System eventually cuts its way through the knot of technological, bureaucratic, and legal obstacles to achieve the immense powers Lin ascribes to it ultimately may not matter. More important to the Party is the ability to persuade people that it already has. If it can do that, then social credit will function as the apotheosis of Foucault's soul-training mind trick. Divorced from the physical limitations of video cameras, smartphone scanners, or prison architecture, it will be something much more powerful: an *idea* of surveillance that looms in the back of people's minds no matter where they go, compelling them to behave as if they were all the while being watched and judged.

By the time of Lin's interview, it was difficult to say whether the Party would succeed in constructing a panopticon out of social credit. One survey conducted in 2018 suggested that most Chinese people were aware of Ant Financial's Sesame Credit but not the government system. The same survey found that among those few who did know about the government system, most approved of it. The government's social credit propaganda push didn't begin in earnest until the following year. Unfortunately, there has been little reliable survey data since to indicate how deeply, or not, social credit has embedded itself in the minds of average Chinese citizens.

The steady beat of propaganda in 2020 indicated that the Party was determined to keep trying, though soon Chinese state media would find themselves preoccupied by another event with profound implications for the surveillance state.

12

CONTAGION

On the day the team of public health experts converged on Wuhan to investigate reports of a deadly new strain of coronavirus spreading among residents there, Vivian Xu left the city heading east at 120 miles per hour.

The first of the phone calls came two weeks later.

By then, Vivian was visiting her mother in a suburb outside the port city of Wenzhou, 530 miles east of Wuhan. The Lunar New Year holiday was about to wrap up. The night before, she and her mother had curled up on the couch and binge-watched a Taiwanese romantic comedy series. The call set her smartphone jangling at 9:00 A.M., only a few hours after the twenty-seven-year-old had finally gone to sleep. The numbers on the screen were blurry without her contact lenses in, but, squinting, she could see it was coming from a Wenzhou landline.

The man on the other end of the line was polite but persistent. He asked where she was, how long she had been in town, and how long she planned to stay. Then he asked whether she had recently been to Wuhan.

This last question gave Vivian pause. How did he know where she had been? Still half awake, she mumbled a yes.

A cascade of questions followed: When did she go there? When did she leave? How was she feeling? Did she have a fever? A cough?

Eventually, she shook off enough sleep to ask who the man was. He said he worked for the subdistrict office in charge of her mother's neighborhood. His manager had given him a list of names to call and a list of questions to ask. He had no idea what it was for. At the end of the call, the man—he never gave his name—told Vivian to isolate herself at her mother's place.

Trapped in the twentieth-floor apartment, Vivian was soon bombarded by more calls. First the health authorities in Wencheng, then police from Hangzhou, where she worked as a production assistant at a livestreaming company. Then others, at least once a day, sometimes twice, for six days in a row, all asking the same questions.

Vivian rarely dealt with officials in her job producing videos for the internet. She had tried to be polite. But one day, after a second call from officials in Xuekou, a tiny town southwest of Wenzhou that she hadn't visited for years, irritation overcame fear. She demanded to know why they were calling and how they'd found her.

"It's probably because you passed through here and the mobile company sent us an alert," the official said.

The comment unsettled Vivian. The mobile company? She started thinking about her recent travels. As was the case for many Chinese people, the weeks leading up to Lunar New Year had been a blur. Vivian's boss at the livestreaming company had first asked her to go to Wuhan in late December to shoot footage of a local calligraphy hobbyist. The short-video trend had blown up in China, and demand was sky high for even the most obscure content. She had shuffled back and forth to the city twice before wrapping up work and traveling to see her mom.

On the way to Wuhan for her first trip, Vivian had seen news on her phone about a cluster of mysterious pneumonia cases connected to a wet market in the city. State media reports at the time said there was no evidence of it spreading between people, so she had decided to press on.

When she had arrived at the station, she had found the city humming along as if nothing was wrong.

A manufacturing and transportation hub of 11 million people, Wuhan sprawled out on either side of the Yangtze River in central China. Foreign news reports compared it to Chicago. Around China it was known mostly for the sesame-drenched "hot-dry" noodles that residents slurped for breakfast with invigorating spoonfuls of pickled mustard greens. Locals told Vivian the virus wasn't spreading between people and said she'd be fine as long as she avoided the market. Satisfied, she spent a few days filming the calligrapher, then came back a couple of weeks later to get some shots she had missed the first time. When she boarded the high-speed train back to Hangzhou on January 18, she was just as unsuspecting as everyone else of what was about to unfold.

As the train sliced through a ruffled sheet of low mountains into the flatness of central Anhui province, Vivian had curled up in her seat in the second-class section with her new iPhone. She used it to pass the time, chatting with friends and getting lost in the perpetual scroll of on-line video—an occupational hazard. Silently, her carrier, China Mobile, tracked her movements.

Throughout the journey, as it had during her time in the city, the iPhone sent radio waves carrying the unique signature of her SIM card bouncing off passing cellphone towers. With each new connection between her phone and a tower, the network compared the relative strength of the signals to generate data about her location. Packaging it with additional location information from the GPS receiver in the phone, China Mobile shipped that data to a computer server that was simultaneously capturing the real-time movements of hundreds of millions of other users. The data helped retailers target ads at people nearby and allowed authorities to send text alerts about local emergencies, but to most users, including Vivian, the process was invisible.

The towers traced her entire journey home. They were still tracking her location two days later in Hangzhou, when the head of the expert team in Wuhan announced on state television that the pathogen at the center of the pneumonia cluster, a coronavirus similar to the one that had caused the SARS outbreak almost two decades earlier, was spreading between people. The towers were also recording her whereabouts another two days later, halfway between Hangzhou and Wenzhou, when she heard that officials were sealing off Wuhan.

News of the lockdown exploded across the country. Never before had any government attempted to quarantine a city of that size in an effort to stop a disease from spreading. The decision came with the death toll having just hit seventeen. While the lockdown might solve one problem, it had created another: Convinced that the situation was worse than local authorities let on, hordes of people rushed to leave the city before police cut off the exits at 10:00 A.M. the following morning. Once out, many of them mingled with the hundreds of millions of other Chinese people traveling to their hometowns for the holiday—the perfect scenario for a public health catastrophe.

The years that China's government had spent building out its digital surveillance systems made it better equipped than any other to head off a crisis of this magnitude. Unfettered access to SIM card location data through state-run carriers and rules requiring every SIM card to be linked to the user's government ID meant the government could uncover the location of any mobile user in the country at any time. Quickly, China Mobile and the other carriers started to compile reports on users who had been in Wuhan, tracked where they went, and sent names to local governments. Matching that information with data sifted from airlines, the national rail operator, and tourist agencies, they were able to further narrow their target lists.

In practice, the process was at times haphazard and often redundant, hence the incessant calls to Vivian's phone. We found out from her friends that Vivian had been in Wuhan, and first reached her by phone not long after she had returned to Wencheng. After the call from Xuekou, she told us, she couldn't shake the curiosity. How many local government officials knew where she had been?

She expressed her discomfort to her friends but found little sympathy. "I was in a pretty unique situation then, having been one of the few who had come back from Wuhan. So I told them about my discomfort in a joking manner." But they didn't understand. Vivian had spent a year studying abroad in Spain, during which she had taken a greater interest in Western views on speech and privacy, which tended to place more value on the rights of the individual. That made her "an outlier," she said. "Most of my friends have a collectivist mindset." The contrast led to an argument later when she saw one friend spreading around in mobile chat messaging groups the names of a family of six who had broken quarantine rules, to shame them and pass judgment. Vivian suggested to the friend that the local government may have been at fault for not explaining the rules clearly enough. "I thought it was bad form and started arguing against revealing their names, but no one in my group seemed to understand my point of view," she said. Their counterargument: "When we are facing this sort of unique emergency, why are you talking about personal privacy?"

Vivian eventually started to ask that question of herself. At the time of our first conversation, in the spring of 2020, the death toll was climbing toward 2,000. More lockdowns were being announced. The country—and the rest of the world—was on the verge of disaster. Maybe, she thought, this wasn't the time to make a fuss.

In *Discipline and Punish: The Birth of the Prison*, the work that introduced the panopticon as a metaphor for modern surveillance, Michel Foucault prefaced his introduction of Jeremy Bentham's circular prison with a grisly traipse through the landscape of seventeenth-century European plague quarantines. He described how each street in a stricken town was overseen by an official, who locked each family inside its house from the outside and periodically ordered them to appear before a window to be counted. Militia guarded the gates and sentinels prowled the neighborhoods. Anyone who flouted the rules, whether resident or official, did so on penalty of death.

Foucault took particular interest in the management of information during quarantines. Lists were made of the name, sex, and age of each inhabitant, and notes were kept of every death, illness, or irregularity, he wrote. The incessant observation, recording, and supervision represented the height of society's power to impose discipline: "It lays down for each individual his place, his body, his disease and his death, his well-being, by means of an omnipresent and omniscient power," the philosopher wrote. "Against the plague, which is a mixture, discipline brings into play its power, which is one of analysis." Bentham's prison design, he believed, was the same notion rendered in architecture.

In China itself, the arrival of the novel coronavirus that eventually came to be known as Covid-19 provided the greatest test yet of the Party's surveillance state. A pandemic was, in many respects, just the sort of crisis the country's new surveillance machinery was built to defeat. The initial results illuminated important limits to algorithmic social control—among them, the cover-up of a contagious disease and the inability to prevent it from spreading. But as the pandemic unfolded, experience would fill the Party, and many Chinese people, with even greater confidence in the value of mass digital tracking.

For democracies, the contagion forced difficult choices about how aggressively to adopt technological tools in protecting their populations. Some smaller democratic countries, several of which had been scarred seventeen years earlier by outbreaks of SARS, leaned more in China's direction, imposing hard quarantines and deploying digital systems to track violators.

Like the 9/11 attacks, Covid-19 would prove to be a catalytic event. It forced a global reconsideration of the trade-off between privacy and freedom, on one hand, and security and personal safety, on the other. In the past, many governments had focused on national security as a reason to justify widespread data collection and use. Now, the rationale for deploying such technologies was a public health one. The borderless and indiscriminate nature of the pandemic meant it spared no one. Questions flowing from the state exploitation of surveillance were no longer the faintly perceived concern of a faraway foreign country or of minority populations in distant-seeming urban neighborhoods. They had bearing on every household.

◉

By February 2020, Vivian Xu started to see evidence that the digital surveillance mechanisms that had tracked her down were being overwhelmed. The virus was running rampant in Wenzhou, with cases creeping up toward 500—the largest number outside of Hubei province, where Wuhan was located. Wencheng and several other parts of Wenzhou had been ordered locked down, with residents issued paper permits that allowed them outside only for essential activities like grocery shopping. Unlike Chinese New Years of the past, when residents flooded into local shopping malls, karaoke parlors, and online gaming cafes, the city was now a ghost town.

With the virus spreading around the country, the Party had reached back into its Mao-era playbook and deployed thousands of neighborhood watchdogs. While in Mao's day they had been deployed to carry out Communist Party mandates, resolve disputes, and maintain grassroots social order, now they would go door-to-door checking on residents, taking temperatures, and enforcing lockdowns. Control measures refined in Xinjiang made an appearance too: cities began shutting off small side streets and side entrances of apartment complexes, funneling residents through main roads and gates, making it easier for the neighborhood monitors to keep track of movements. At some villages around Wencheng, village leaders rolled logs across road entrances to prevent anyone from leaving or entering. Volunteers and village officials—contactless thermometers in hand—would staff the new checkpoints, questioning each person who came by and verifying their movement permits. At its height, the quarantine covered at least twenty provinces and regions. *The Wall Street Journal* conservatively estimated that China's government had at one time or another confined more than 500 million mostly healthy people to their homes in January and February 2020.

As awe-inspiring and effective as China's mass mobilization was, the fact that the Communist Party had to resurrect tactics from the twentieth century raised questions about whether its twenty-first-century data-driven model of social control was ready for prime time. In theory, the system not only should have tracked the infected quickly enough to limit the spread of the disease outside Wuhan but also should have been able to recognize the threat early enough that it never left Wuhan in the first place.

Some of the system's failures were technological: location-tracking systems were overly reliant on cameras and not well integrated enough across regions to quickly follow a virus that left no visible tracks for its cameras to catch. Where "ideological viruses" like those the Party was worried about in Xinjiang took time to spread, this actual virus was so infectious it moved from group to group before data could be gathered and analyzed. Vivian's experience was a good example. It had taken the authorities almost two weeks to find her in Wencheng. Had she been infected, she could have passed the virus on to dozens or even hundreds of others in that time.

Politics and human weakness also played critical roles. Evidence of this appeared as Vivian was still making her way home to see her mother in late January, when the newspaper *Beijing Youth Daily* published an interview with a young ophthalmologist in Wuhan by the name of Li Wenliang. In the interview, Li said he recalled seeing reports of an unusual cluster of pneumonia linked to a Wuhan animal market in late December. After he posted a message to former classmates in a WeChat group warning them about the development, he told the paper, he was interrogated by Party disciplinary officials and hospital management, who forced him to write a statement criticizing himself for spreading rumors. Li later contracted the virus while treating a patient—clear evidence of human-to-human transmission, which local health authorities were reluctant to admit at the time—and died from the infection on February 7. News of his death exploded online, sparking waves of outrage and demands that authorities formally apologize for their treatment of the doctor.

The local government's silencing of Li and others who tried to sound the alarm about the new virus turned out to be part of an effort by local officials to keep the virus from interfering with politics. The new pathogen had begun to spread just as Wuhan's top leaders were preparing for the country's annual legislative gathering in Beijing. One advisor to the Wuhan government told *The Wall Street Journal* that the virus hadn't been included on the agenda in city policy meetings even as some officials were privately raising concerns about the response. "Everyone was blindly optimistic," the advisor said. The priority, he said, was to present a picture of stability.

That revelation and the effort to silence Li pointed to a crucial flaw in the Party's techno-totalitarian feedback loop. In Xi Jinping's hard-line China, local officials afraid of Beijing's wrath often try to bury neg-ative news in the hope that it will stay unnoticed long enough for them to move on to another job. In that crucial early period, when Wuhan could have used the country's new digital tools to corral and eradicate a major threat to the country as the Party envisioned, the realities of Party politics incentivized officials to sit on their hands.

Despite the setback, the Party didn't give up on digital surveil-lance as a solution to the crisis. The second effort proved more suc-cessful. As Wencheng and other towns prepared to gradually reopen in mid-February 2020, authorities worked with Alibaba, Tencent, and state-owned enterprises to introduce smartphone-compatible health passports. Hangzhou, where Vivian hoped to return soon, was in Feb-ruary 2020 one of the first cities to mandate that citizens download health QR codes before securing approval to resume work.

Early versions of the health codes required users to self-report their physical condition—choosing from options such as a dry cough, fever, or asymptomatic—and asked where they had traveled in the last four-teen days. The system would then crunch the data to assess the health risk of the user and churn out a red, yellow, or green QR code. Red codes meant a user might show symptoms or might be a possible carrier and should isolate themselves for two weeks. Yellow codes indicated possible contact with an infected person and a quarantine of seven days. A green code gave the user a clean bill of health and allowed them unrestricted access to subways, retail stores, offices, and restaurants. Residents were required to flash their QR codes at entrances to subway stations, at road checkpoints, and in malls. The code wasn't technically compulsory, but it was impossible to do anything outside the house without one. Later, a nationwide version was rolled out, with the system using data from the three state-run mobile carriers to scan the user's travel history over the last fourteen days, giving governments an idea of that person's exposure to virus hotspots.

Vivian returned to Hangzhou on March 5, downloading the health code app before she set off. Her code was green. Soon her misgivings about the surveillance began to fade. Having to flash the app multiple times a day as she went about the city was irritating, but it was also reassuring, she told us. The thought of all the days she had spent in Wuhan with no one doing anything about the contagion was unnerving. "The strict checks make me feel safer," she said. Many others in Hangzhou also appeared to accept the health codes as the price of safety.

Perhaps encouraged by the acquiescence, Hangzhou took the next step. Three months after introducing the health code system, the city announced a proposal for a permanent version. The new, enhanced codes would sort residents into different colors and assign them a health score depending on their medical records, physical examination results, and lifestyle habits such as smoking and alcohol consumption. It was a textbook example of surveillance creep.

The nearby city of Taizhou went even further, introducing a system that ranked the political "health" of local Communist Party members. Green codes indicated someone who was dutiful and personified Party values, while yellow and red codes could lead to admonishment and possibly even expulsion. Local media told the story of a village Party official, Xu Xujiao, who had been given a yellow code after it was discovered that some funds meant for the local elderly association had been misused. After the incident, he sought to redeem himself by turning in an "exemplary performance" in fighting Covid-19, and his code soon turned to green.

The expansions of the health code system did not all go over well. The Hangzhou plan, in particular, encountered fierce resistance on social media. In a poll on the Twitter-like Weibo platform, 86 percent of the roughly 7,000 votes were opposed to the proposal. The result was hardly scientific, but it was reinforced by a flood of angry comments. One user of a Quora-like question-and-answer platform speculated that employers might one day use the code to deny employment to people whose health might not stand up to the rigors of China's overtime work culture. This was a rare instance in which government surveillance became the target of public rage and ridicule.

Nevertheless, the pandemic proved a boon to the Chinese surveillance industry. Sales of "fever-detecting" cameras exploded despite studies suggesting they were wildly unreliable. Facial recognition companies began producing products that could scan crowds to quickly identify people not wearing masks. They also marketed algorithms they said could identify people even if they were wearing face masks—a dubious claim, but also an enticing one to police departments as mask mandates spread.

A drone company in southern China, Shenzhen Smart Drone UAV Co., started offering the use of its high-end temperature-detecting drones to local police. The company's deputy general manager, Kellen Tse, told us that the drones were typically used to spot forest fires. Now, police were flying them over crowds to check for people running fevers. Tse conceded that the drones didn't always work as well as hoped. "Every technology has to start somewhere. You'll never succeed if you don't try," he said.

Thanks to a combination of surveillance and disease control strategies—including liberal use of localized lockdowns and mass testing—new Covid-19 cases in China fell from more than 15,000 per day at their height in early February 2020 to less than 100 per day in March. By the end of April, Wuhan was declared free of cases.

◉

Roughly seven months after the lockdown of Wuhan dominated news feeds around the world, the city again became the subject of global headlines. This time it was because of a pool party.

On the weekend of August 15, 2020, the Wuhan Maya Beach Water Park hosted an electronic music festival, offering female visitors half-price tickets. Thousands showed up. People in the United States and Europe, suffering the effects of weeks of social distancing and battered by debates over the moral obligation to wear face masks, stared slack-jawed at the resulting images: photos and video of DJs playing to crowds of scantily clad Chinese people rubbing shoulders as they bobbed together on inflatable rubber donuts, their maskless faces an undulating tapestry of carefree smiles. The sheer density of partygoers would have been noteworthy in any circumstance. Coming from the former epicenter of the pandemic, the scene was a slap in the face to anyone living in a Western democracy, nearly all of which had failed catastrophically in confronting the pandemic up to that point. Projections that China would be one of the only major economies in the world to grow that year added extra sting.

Xi Jinping was likely also celebrating inside the Communist Party's secretive compound in Beijing. When the pandemic broke out, pundits described Covid-19 as Xi's Chernobyl—a disaster and a cover-up that would set in motion the Party's fall from grace. Instead, it not only burnished his reputation but also bolstered popular support inside China for the surveillance state. In a study published in the journal *Surveillance and Society*, a University of California, San Diego scholar named Liu Chuncheng documented how public support for pandemic surveillance in China evolved over time. Surveying social media and conducting interviews with three dozen people inside China—a number he admitted was small—Liu tentatively concluded that negative coverage of China's initial Covid-19 response in the Western media eventually produced a "reverse psychological effect" that led people to rally around the government. As the infectious disease began to ravage Western nations and China steamrolled ahead with its recovery, Liu found, a second wave of popular support rose around the belief that democracy was fundamentally flawed and couldn't cope with public health crises.

Xi reflected that confidence as 2020 drew to a close. In a speech that November at the Group of 20 Summit (held online that year), Xi pushed for a system that would allow international travel to begin again so that the global economy could begin to recover. His solution would have sounded familiar to anyone from Hangzhou. "China has proposed a global mechanism on the mutual recognition of health certificates based on nucleic acid test results in the form of internationally accepted QR codes," he said. At the time, China said it had recorded fewer than 87,000 total confirmed Covid-19 cases with just over 4,600 deaths. The United States, in the grip of a new surge, was on the cusp of 12 million cases and a quarter million deaths.

While the Trump administration spewed rage-filled statements that suggested the pandemic was impossible to control and accused the Communist Party of deliberately starting it to crash the American economy, other democracies were quick to enlist the latest digital wizardry in their efforts to contain the virus. Some accessed the smartphone data of virus patients and posted details of their travels online. South Korea scoured credit card data to hunt down possible patients. In Israel, the government passed an emergency decree allowing its intelligence agency, Shin Bet, to use its powers of surveillance for coronavirus control. Authorities monitored the cellphone signals of confirmed patients and asked those in close contact with them in the past two weeks to isolate themselves. Once news of these methods got out, the questions came thick and fast: Was it okay to subject ordinary people to the levels of electronic scrutiny usually reserved for violent criminals? Should governments be publicizing the details of people's movements?

As the infection numbers and death tolls in Europe and the United States continued to soar grimly upward, some of the most zealous defenders of civil liberties began to soften their opposition to digital intrusions. Adam Schwartz, a senior lawyer for the Electronic Frontier Foundation, a nonprofit known for its fierce opposition to surveillance, said that with the pandemic "some temporary adjustment of our digital liberties may be necessary." In Western Australia, lawmakers approved a bill allowing the state to install electronic monitoring devices in people's homes to monitor those under quarantine. The health minister in privacy-obsessed Germany tried, albeit unsuccessfully, to insert a location-tracking clause into a Covid-19-related amendment to the country's law on fighting infectious disease.

Bruno Maçães, a senior fellow at the conservative Hudson Institute and former Europe minister from Portugal, argued that the outbreak would force the world to rethink privacy. "So far the Western counterpandemic effort has been stunningly primitive," Maçães wrote in an essay for *Foreign Policy*, lamenting that health authorities in Western countries were still often tracing the close contacts of suspected patients by hand. "Privacy hawks may disagree, but a surveillance system can be a way to leave people alone," he wrote. "Properly designed, it consists of a kind of security perimeter—mostly virtual—within which life can go on undisturbed." Big data and predictive algorithms were already in wide use in the fight against crime and terrorism, he noted.

In the face of an attack more deadly than any a terrorist could hope to pull off, Maçães argued, applying those same tools to health was inevitable.

More and more democracies came to agree, and their first move was typically to embrace digital contact-tracing apps. These mobile applications aimed to quickly narrow down individuals who had come into contact with infected patients, allowing health authorities to take measures to stamp out the transmission chain before it expanded out of control. Centralized digital-tracing apps, like those used in Singapore, were the most effective. They tapped data from a variety of sources and funneled it to a single server, where it could be easily and quickly analyzed. But privacy advocates in the United States and Europe hated that model, which they said put too much personal data in the hands of the government with too few safeguards around how it could be used. The alternative was to use decentralized apps that relied on Bluetooth technology and anonymous key codes to determine proximity to infected people during the key contagious period and to inform users of their exposure risk, without the storage and collection of data in a single large government database. Among the highest-profile initiatives was a rare joint effort by Apple and Google that aimed to keep information on personal devices about who people come into contact with rather than sending it to a server.

Still, these apps ended up being challenging to execute. They required a large percentage of the population to download them in order to be effective. Most countries failed to achieve high enough adoption rates either because of privacy fears or because residents didn't see the need for it. After initially making the apps voluntary, some nations began to mandate that citizens use them or carry around Bluetooth tokens that performed similar tasks.

One of the most illuminating democratic efforts to balance privacy and security unfolded just off China's southeastern coast, on an island that the Communist Party claimed as part of China despite never having controlled it.

Taiwan split from China in 1949 at the conclusion of the country's civil war. As Mao prepared to announce the founding of the People's

Republic of China in Beijing, the remnants of the defeated Kuomintang, or Nationalist Party, fled to Taiwan, with plans to regroup. Though the Kuomintang claimed to continue to represent the Republic of China, it never succeeded in its promise to retake the mainland. Eventually, most countries, including the United States, switched diplomatic recognition to Beijing, leaving Taiwan to develop into a de facto independent country with a vibrant democracy but little international influence.

Taiwan had extensive experience dealing with China, including during the SARS outbreak, when Chinese officials deliberately stifled the flow of information to neighboring countries. SARS had killed nearly 200 on the island. So when news of the novel coronavirus seeped out of China in December 2019, officials in the capital, Taipei, moved quickly. By early 2020, they had effectively closed their borders to China. They ordered strict quarantines for those who arrived, rationed masks, and made mask-wearing mandatory early on. They also were among the first in the world to institute a digital contact-tracing system.

While both countries rushed to set up surveillance to fight the spread of the virus, Taiwan's approach was otherwise the polar opposite of China's. Where the Party collected vast quantities of personal information, Taiwan collected as little as it could, initially asking businesses and property managers to gather emails and mobile numbers from visitors so authorities could get in touch if needed. Where China kept all of the information it gathered in a central database with no timeline for when it would be removed, Taiwan initially left the data in the hands of those who collected it and demanded it be destroyed after four weeks. For privacy-obsessed patrons of hostess bars (nightclubs where men pay for the company of women, often through the purchase of high-priced drinks), Taiwan allowed the use of anonymous, encrypted ProtonMail accounts as a contact method.

To enforce quarantines, the island also tried to balance privacy with the need to track people's whereabouts. Several countries, including South Korea, developed apps that tracked the location of people in quarantine using smartphone GPS and prompted them to periodically enter body temperature and other health information. Taiwan rejected that

option, fearful that any hastily developed app would inevitably be riddled with bugs that could leak sensitive personal data. Instead, it tracked
people by triangulating the location of their devices—a method that was
less precise but more secure—and had health workers call daily to check
on their health status. "Taiwan serves as an example that you can think
beyond the forced dilemma, between public health on one side, and human rights, privacy, and democratic institutions on the other," Audrey
Tang, the nation's digital minister, said in an online panel hosted by the
National Bureau of Asian Research in August 2020. The data backed her
up: By the end of the year, as the United States was creeping toward 20
million cases, Taiwan, a nation of about 24 million, had chalked up fewer
than 1,000 and gone 253 days without registering a single local infection.

Watching Western nations finally embrace surveillance only to
seemingly fail at it reinforced for many in China a sense of the West as
hypocritical and their own system as superior. China's perceived success at dealing with Covid-19 also fueled yet another wave of nationalistic support inside the country, Liu Chuncheng discovered. Liu noted
that a large number of Chinese commentators seemed not to grasp
that the Western systems had been voluntary, but such nuances were
never going to survive the crucible of social media chest-thumping. On
December 10, 2020, with bodies continuing to pile up in the United
States, a post by the US embassy in Beijing commemorating World
Human Rights Day drew waves of snark. "Where are the human rights
of 300,000 Americans [who died from Covid-19]?" read one comment.
In a matter of hours, it attracted more than 2,000 likes.

In the eyes of another scholar, Huang Yanzhong, a senior fellow for
global health at the Council on Foreign Relations and a Seton Hall University professor, the novel coronavirus was a rousing victory for China.
Huang, who has not been shy about calling China out for some of its
past failings, said that the nation was able to succeed because it utilized
harsh, centralized, and restrictive measures, many of which would be
impossible to implement in Western democracies. This allowed China to
bring the disease under control by April 2020, and the country has since
managed to sustain a very low level of infection, he added. "If success is

measured in terms of ability to break the domestic transmission chain, China is indisputably a success story," he wrote in an opinion piece in the *China Leadership Monitor* in June 2021.

◉

As February 2021 rolled around, Vivian Xu spent her Chinese New Year in a very different fashion than she had twelve months earlier, when she'd been forced to quarantine after the Wuhan outbreak. As the holiday approached, she packed up her luggage and headed to the Hangzhou rail station, ready to hop on a high-speed train back to Wenzhou to see her mother and extended family. Despite a government propaganda campaign asking Chinese to avoid long-distance travel, the train station was teeming with travelers—just as it is every Lunar New Year holiday. This time, travelers had to flash a green QR health code to a staffer at the entrance of the train station before being allowed in. As she approached the start of the line to enter the station, Vivian scrambled to pull out her mobile phone from her jacket and open up the app. "Sometimes you just completely forget about showing them the code, because things are so normal, almost back to how it was pre-Covid," she later told us.

Following government regulations, Vivian wore her mask while on the train, but otherwise she left it in her bag. Other signs of the pandemic had also gradually begun to disappear. The fever detectors installed at the entrance to her office building in early 2020 were gone by the fall. The ubiquitous bottles of hand sanitizer and boxes of tissues placed in elevators vanished without her noticing. In early 2021, when Vivian's office was looking to sign up volunteers to take China's coronavirus vaccine, barely anyone signed up. The pandemic felt over. Vivian told us she barely gave a thought to the risk that she might contract the virus. "The government reacts so strongly when there is just one suspected patient," she said. "I'm confident they have things under control and the people around me are Covid free."

Back in Wencheng for the seven-day public holiday, things felt so normal that Vivian almost forgot about her experience the previous year. On the first day of the New Year, a day traditionally set aside for visiting older relatives, Vivian and her mom headed to her grandfather's apartment for lunch. Her extended family were all present: close to a dozen aunts, uncles, cousins, and their spouses. They all gathered around the table for lunch, filling the air with excited chatter as they shared a feast of fried sweet-potato vermicelli tossed with mixed vegetables, dumplings, and local specialties like braised duck's tongue. Two days later, Vivian and nine other relatives packed themselves into two cars and took a day trip to a national park in Taishun County about sixty miles away. The park was a second-rate destination, peppered with tacky human-made attractions, but on that day it was heaving with visitors.

More than 256 million Chinese took holiday trips over the Lunar New Year festival in 2021, Xinhua reported after the holiday. This was despite restrictions limiting cross-province travel. Reflecting on the holiday, Vivian echoed the sentiments of many Chinese. "Objectively speaking, China had the best Covid containment response in the world," she told us. Many of the moves China had taken heat for—the lockdowns and forced quarantines—turned out to be right in retrospect, she said. "Covid containment just happens to be perfectly suited for authoritarian governments."

That observation notably omitted Taiwan, which battled a brief flare-up of community spread in the spring of 2021 but ended the year with fewer than 17,000 infections and 900 deaths—lower numbers per capita than anywhere besides China. It was unlikely that Vivian had heard of Taiwan's success, however, as Chinese state media studiously avoided covering it.

Inside China, the government's continued success in keeping the virus at bay killed off any fledgling pushback to excessive government data collection. Like Vivian, many found it hard to argue about intrusions in the name of public health. The technology's success demonstrated to the Chinese Communist Party and local governments that surveillance on such a scale and in an emergency was feasible and effective.

The impact outside China was arguably larger. Where Chinese people had been acclimating to the creeping expansion of the Party's surveillance state over a period of years, the pandemic forced populations elsewhere to confront the power of state surveillance suddenly and under the gravest of circumstances. Nor were the effects limited to the virus itself. Lockdowns and stay-at-home orders forced people around the globe to move their lives almost entirely online, where they were even more vulnerable to digital snooping. Those who used to see pervasive surveillance as a distant concern for people living under autocratic regimes oceans away now found it affecting every aspect of their lives, from health to work to their children's education.

13

NEW ORDER?

If the Global War on Terror seeded the field of digital state surveillance, then the pandemic was the Miracle-Gro that fed its explosion. Any hope of ripping it out by the roots that might have persisted during the post-9/11 era has been eradicated post-Covid-19.

In this new world, China's surveillance state embodies the awesome power of data harvesting and artificial intelligence to simplify, and occasionally save, human lives. It also presents an unprecedented challenge to the notion of free will and to the individual liberties that animate democracy. By launching a new era of social control, the Communist Party has wrapped its hand firmly around the steering wheel of history. Where we go from here is difficult to predict.

China's own path appears clear, at least for the moment. By early 2022, as we were wrapping up this book, Xi Jinping and the Party had never been more dominant or in control. New laws regarding data security, privacy, and antitrust had cemented the Party's hold on the country's vast reserves of data. A sweeping crackdown on internet industry practices sent a clear signal to China's powerful tech companies about who was in charge. Meanwhile, China was steaming ahead with trillion-dollar plans to build even more infrastructure for industries that would help refine the digital feedback loops the Party needed to manage problems at home: data centers, artificial intelligence research labs, mobile communication towers, and semiconductors.

The Party was also giving space to start-ups to experiment with even more extreme and questionable forms of surveillance—including some forms of digital phrenology that felt destined to lead to dark ends. Among the most disquieting of those was emotion recognition. Despite plentiful research showing that facial expressions aren't universal and can't be reliably used to judge emotional states, several companies were attempting to do just that, some claiming accuracy rates as high as 80 percent. The companies had partnered with Chinese public security bureaus, using police interrogation footage to train algorithms to detect micro-expressions that could ostensibly be used to identify "dangerous people" and "high-risk groups" without prior criminal histories. At least one company touted its interrogation tech for use in schools, where it could allegedly help teachers identify different categories of students, such as the "falsely earnest type" who "attentively listens to lectures [but has] bad grades."

Incentivized by the surveillance frenzy in Xinjiang, China's biggest AI start-ups were rushing to perfect their ability to conduct race-based digital profiling. Police used their systems to scan crowds for Uyghurs in Hangzhou, Wenzhou, and the city of Sanmenxia, near a famous dam on the Yellow River. The Ministry of Public Security included a demand for the ability to recognize ethnicity in the technical requirements for any facial recognition system a police department purchased. As Samantha Hoffman pointed out to us, there was a risk that Chinese security giants like Hikvision and Dahua could normalize race-focused surveillance in other countries by exporting these systems around the world.

Already, growing numbers of governments were following the Party's lead in using digital surveillance to solve social and political challenges. In 2020, India, the world's largest democracy, deployed facial recognition systems developed by a local start-up to identify protesters marching against a new citizenship law in its capital city, New Delhi. Singapore, one of Asia's wealthiest countries and a regional partner of the United States, announced that it aimed to install more than 200,000 police cameras as soon as 2030 despite low crime rates and a total land area smaller than New York City. And when insurrectionists stormed the US Capitol in early 2021, American law enforcement agencies were quick to deploy an entire suite of surveillance tools in response.

The China Solution had proven that it could challenge and undermine the liberal democratic order. Even if other countries failed to replicate China's system perfectly, the technology gave authoritarian leaders around the globe new tools to quash dissent and entrench themselves.

China's embrace of the digitally engineered society comes with potential costs. The Communist Party wants China to evolve into a leader in global tech innovation. But in reducing choice and intensifying control, the state is eliminating the friction, uncertainty, and freedom that are vital to creativity. Many of the country's top young scientists and engineers go abroad to study. Despite the government's investment of hundreds of millions of dollars in salaries, bonuses, and research grants to lure them back to China, studies show that most still prefer to continue to work and live abroad if they can. Short of closing the country's borders, it's hard to see how the Party can stem the outflow of talent. Meanwhile, its tightening grip on China's technology industry has led many of its most brilliant entrepreneurs, including Jack Ma, to step back from their corporate roles—removing from view the role models who have driven much of the country's recent business success.

Despite these setbacks, the Party is brimming with confidence in its ability to disrupt and rearrange the global order. That certainty spilled across the front page of *The People's Daily* one day in late September in an editorial that exulted in the spectacle of the Communist Party's one-hundredth-anniversary celebrations in Tiananmen Square months earlier. "The world today is undergoing profound changes unseen in a century," it proclaimed. "One of the most striking features of these changes is the irreversible trend that the East is rising and the West is declining." China's leaders believe they have arrived at a new form of human civilization—one based on a strong state with surveillance at its core—that is more efficient, stable, and responsive than democracy. They also sense that the time is ripe to sell its virtues.

How should democracies respond? The last time democratic governments banded together to oppose the Communist Party on a matter of principle was in the aftermath of the Tiananmen Square massacre in 1989, when the United States suspended military visits and arms sales and several countries in Europe froze diplomatic relations. That coalition began to fray almost as soon as it was formed, undermined by the allure of the Chinese market. It was replaced by the long era of engagement, sustained for decades by the notion that market forces, commerce, and exposure to Western culture would lead to a liberalized, possibly democratic China—a dream that now seems, if not dead, then in a comatose state on the ricketiest of life-support systems.

Under the Trump administration, the United States adopted a new policy of direct confrontation. In 2019, the White House began adding Chinese companies involved in state surveillance to the Commerce Department's Entity List, which allowed the United States to cut off supplies of advanced American-designed chips, like the GPUs needed to run high-end facial recognition systems, that China wasn't capable of replicating. The State Department followed by slapping sanctions on senior officials in Xinjiang, including Party boss Chen Quanguo, that banned them from entering the United States or using the American financial system. Washington also sanctioned the Bingtuan, the paramilitary organization that runs much of Xinjiang's economy.

Under the Biden administration, the United States has stepped up the pressure further by leading a return to something resembling the post-Tiananmen moment. In 2021, the United States organized a coalition that included Canada, the United Kingdom, and the European Union in imposing additional, coordinated sanctions on Bingtuan and Xinjiang officials—the first time that Britain or Europe had imposed sanctions on China in twenty-two years.

The sanctions on Chinese surveillance companies had their intended effect. Huawei suffered double-digit drops in revenue through 2020 and 2021, due mostly to the effect of American sanctions and efforts by Washington to persuade allies not to buy the company's 5G mobile internet equipment. Public pressure also persuaded Huawei to backtrack on a patent it had filed alongside the Chinese Academy of Sciences for a facial recognition algorithm capable of identifying Uyghurs. Some companies were able to exploit loopholes in order to continue accessing American technology, and China's immense domestic market kept them supplied with customers, but torrid growth became a thing of the past. In the winter of 2021, SenseTime announced that it was planning a $770 million initial public offering in Hong Kong, with Chinese state-owned companies and investment funds buying up 60 percent of shares—a precipitous step down from the multi-billion-dollar New York listing that many had expected the company to pursue before the sanctions. A few days later, the Treasury Department added the company to an investment blacklist for entities the United States said were supporting Chinese military development, banning Americans from buying its shares. SenseTime promptly postponed the IPO, which later went ahead with American investors excluded.

The impact in Xinjiang was more difficult to determine. In 2019, Adrian Zenz, the German data scientist whose scouring of government documents underpinned much of the reporting out of Xinjiang, revised his estimate of the scope of Xinjiang's "reeducation" campaign from 2017. Based on testimonies gathered by a nonprofit group in Kazakhstan, media reports of emptied streets and bazaars in Muslim districts, and the continued expansion of the camps, Zenz said he believed as many as 1.5 million people—roughly one out of every six adult Turkic Muslims— had been detained in one of the facilities at one point or another.

The camps were being kept full by the continued expansion of Chen Quanguo's web of surveillance. Security gates, most equipped with facial recognition, had been installed in virtually every public venue: at the entrances to bazaars and banks, mosques, hotels, tourist sites, bus stations, train stations, fancy malls, and cut-rate department stores. The police purchased drones, also loaded with facial recognition technology, to track people in remote areas outside the reach of regular cameras.

Toward the end of 2019, a few months after the United States imposed its first round of sanctions, Chen Quanguo began releasing camp detainees. Life on the streets of Xinjiang's cities began to regain some semblance of normalcy, with fewer police patrols and less razor wire. Near the end of 2021, Chen was replaced as Party boss, possibly ahead of promotion to a more powerful post in Beijing in 2022. But fundamentally, little has changed. Mosques remain closed or closely watched, and calls to prayer stay silenced. Uyghurs and other Turkic minorities still live inside a web of inescapable surveillance, afraid they could be dragged away at any time. Though some camps have been closed, many of the remaining facilities have been expanded or converted into prisons. Calculating the floor space of roughly 350 prisons and internment camps in Xinjiang based on satellite images and Chinese prison construction standards, Buzzfeed News concluded in 2021 that the region maintained the capacity to detain at least a million people at any given time—seven times higher than the criminal detention capacity of the United States.

These mixed results have inevitably raised questions about whether the United States and like-minded countries need to adjust their response. The limits on technology sales to Chinese surveillance companies have undoubtedly hurt American companies. That is arguably a worthwhile sacrifice, except that so far the restrictions have done little to slow the rollout of the Chinese surveillance state or the global spread of Chinese surveillance systems. They have also encouraged China to develop advanced core technologies of its own, which in the long run will allow it to shut out foreign technology entirely and turn its system into a true black box. It's far from clear, in other words, that the benefits of the status quo justify the costs.

Theoretically, China's surveillance state could collapse on its own. The writer Wang Lixiong, who earlier compared the plight of the Uyghurs to that of the Palestinians, explored the possibility of such an implosion in *The Ceremony*, a dystopian novel he published in Taiwan in 2017. In the book, a near-future Chinese surveillance state is toppled when the head of the national security agency, fearing he will be scapegoated for allowing an underling to perpetuate a fake flu epidemic for political gain, assassinates a Xi-like leader with a swarm of bee-shaped miniature drones. Leaders in techno-totalitarian states are vulnerable because they are forced to rely on tools and systems they don't understand, Wang explained when discussing the novel with another Chinese writer. Regular people may be unable or unwilling to rebel, but the bureaucrats who know how to control the technology are in a position to cause immense damage. "To topple the autocratic machine from within, sometimes all that is needed is command over a single nodal point," he said.

For anyone tempted to simply wait things out, however, it pays to note that past predictions of Communist Party collapse have fared poorly. Wang's prognosis may be more insightful than most, but it is also in many ways more speculative. Whether such a scenario would even be good for China, or for the rest of the world, is also an open question. As Wang himself observes, a robust and democratic China is hardly guaranteed to rise from the wreckage of a suddenly collapsed surveillance state. Chances are just as high that a new autocratic regime would rise in its place, or that the country would fracture and fall into a long period of internal conflict with dire implications for the global economy.

If democracies want to do more to constrain the Chinese surveillance state, one path suggested by human rights activists and some lawmakers in Washington is to close loopholes in export restrictions and tailor them so they more precisely target activities like censorship and surveillance. This would increase the pain for American companies that supply technology to China, but it would also make sure that any sacrifice is purposeful.

Another route is to be more strategic about fighting Beijing's efforts to export the China Solution by offering democratic alternatives. As scholars of Chinese surveillance have argued, doing that requires first understanding why individual governments are attracted to China's surveillance systems. "Many countries see these platforms as providing a real potential solution to important problems facing their populations," writes Sheena Greitens, one of the political scientists who has mapped China's surveillance exports. Some countries turn to Chinese technology for help in fighting crime. Others use it to better control traffic or to suppress political opposition. If the United States and other advanced democracies want to counter the Communist Party's influence, they have to find the nuance to address those different problems.

Before democracies can sell the world alternatives, though, they need to decide for themselves what they believe. As documented by scholars in the United States and elsewhere, including China, the rise of tech-driven authoritarianism has coincided with a moment of weakness, confusion, and paralysis among countries that are supposed to best embody the benefits of democratic government. Increasingly in China, the United States is referred to by the phrase *dengtaguo* (灯塔国), or "beacon nation," a satirical jab at its fading status as a beacon of freedom and good governance. Post-Brexit Britain has experienced a similar reputational slide. One of the greatest failures of wealthy democracies, particularly those in the West, is deciding how to reconcile the use of surveillance technologies with individual values like privacy, choice, and free speech that are vital to the functioning of democratic societies.

In her 2020 book *Twilight of Democracy*, historian Anne Applebaum cites research that suggests a significant number of people in every society harbor an "authoritarian predisposition" that is repelled by diversity and disorder. "Authoritarianism appeals, simply, to people who cannot tolerate complexity," she wrote. Applebaum was concerned with intellectuals who erode democracies by advancing views of the world rooted in deceptive simplicity, but surveillance technology offers much the same thing: the promise of a predictable life in which messy questions are streamlined and choices are limited or even eliminated.

Both the allure of algorithmic simplicity and the complexity of the challenge it poses to democracies became evident in the opening weeks of 2021, as the United States struggled to respond to the January 6 insurrection. The images were difficult to process: more than 10,000 people, who had been fed viral lies about election fraud on Facebook and Twitter, marching on Capitol Hill to stop Congress from certifying Joe Biden's victory over Donald Trump in the previous November's presidential election. The American public was pummeled by a string of firsts: The first breach of the Capitol building since British troops set fire to Washington during the War of 1812. The first-ever appearance inside the Capitol of a Confederate battle flag. The first time a sitting president incited a mob of supporters to overturn a lawful vote, resulting in injuries to police officers and calls for the vice president to be hanged.

Within days of the attack, police departments in Alabama and Florida turned to Clearview AI's facial recognition system to identify rioters and send possible matches to the FBI. Hoan Ton-That, Clearview AI's CEO, bragged to *The New York Times* that search volume jumped 26 percent immediately after the attack. Charging documents would later show the FBI also relied on an arsenal of other surveillance tools, including license plate readers and cellphone data, to track down suspected rioters.

The attack on the Capitol demonstrated how fraught the conversation around state surveillance could be. The use of facial recognition to identify participants in a political protest is a clear violation of free speech. But what happens if that protest crosses the line into an assault on the very heart of democracy? Where does the line get drawn?

Clearview AI's legal team seized the opportunity to claim victory for the technology in the defense of democratic institutions in the Opinion section of *The Wall Street Journal*. "Facial-recognition technology is here to stay," they wrote. "China demonstrates its dangers, but its use after the Capitol insurrection shows its promise." In a twist, they also evoked free speech in criticizing local laws that sought to restrict biometrics, saying the Constitution guaranteed the right to create and disseminate information like face prints.

The following day, a nationalist Chinese state-owned tabloid unleashed an English-language editorial skewering the West's double standards. "Despite its frequent defamation against China's use of technology in protecting public security, the US authority did not mind screening its own citizens with Clearview AI after the riot," it read, making note of the American sanctions on Chinese AI companies. "It forms a sharp contrast to US politicians who have been relentlessly attacking Chinese AI firms by accusing them of violating human rights and infringing on privacy."

The Chinese editorial was an exercise in top-level trolling, but it also laid bare a painful reality. Two decades after passing the Patriot Act and eight years after Edward Snowden's exposure of the NSA, American society hadn't developed the antibodies against digital surveillance that many thought, or at least hoped, it would.

Where people living in authoritarian countries can only register their opposition with small acts of protest, if at all, Americans and other citizens of advanced democracies have vastly more power to choose how to respond to the spread of state surveillance—a power they have to use wisely.

A faith in the intrinsic value of technological innovation runs deep in the American psyche. With algorithmic surveillance, innovation has produced a technology that is extremely valuable but also fundamentally undemocratic. Fed mass quantities of personal data, artificial intelligence offers predictions but not explanations, and nudges people to surrender to its conclusions. The black box of the algorithm, like the inner sanctum of the autocrat's palace, brooks no scrutiny. "We need not and cannot know how the correlations were derived, or what causal explanations might explain them," write technology scholars Mark Andrejevic and Kelly Gates. "We must simply accept that data science knows best." As Andrejevic and Gates observe, algorithmic authoritarianism is also self-perpetuating. The more data that companies and governments collect, the greater the range of future risks a society can imagine anticipating. And the more risks a society imagines, the more data it needs to preempt them.

Like all authoritarian forces, state surveillance functions as a radical reinforcer of the status quo—a consequence of algorithms that inevitably reflect the biases of the present day. As a result, wealthy members of the racial majority will almost always experience state surveillance as a source of security and convenience, having no incentive to imagine its side effects on marginal members of society until, whether by choice or circumstance, they find themselves living on the margins.

As the oppressive potential lurking inside digital surveillance technology has grown more apparent, momentum has grown to simply ban it. Robert Williams, the Detroit man who was arrested in front of his daughters after being misidentified by facial recognition in 2020, offered a powerful argument in favor of a ban during a House Judiciary

Committee hearing in July 2021. "Even if this technology does become accurate (at the expense of people like me), I don't want my daughters' faces to be part of some government database," he wrote in a statement. "I don't want cops showing up at their door because they were recorded at a protest the government didn't like. I don't want this technology automating and worsening the racist policies they could be protesting." The same sentiment can, and has, been applied by members of the far right to protests against Black Lives Matter.

Particularly in the case of facial recognition, the impulse to banish feels both natural and reasonable. A face print is many orders of magnitude more personal than a fingerprint, and exponentially more effective as a tool for tracking people in places where they should be able to enjoy the freedom of anonymity. Few government agencies anywhere have demonstrated the kind of restraint required not to abuse technology that powerful.

Still, prohibition works as a solution only in specific circumstances, not as a general approach. A blanket ban on government use of surveillance technologies isn't politically or practically feasible. Digital tracking is already built into the machinery of every modern state. Even if it were a possibility, a full ban would be as shortsighted in ignoring the benefits of the technology as China has been in ignoring its costs.

In the search for a middle ground between the unrestrained surveillance of Beijing and the digital straitjacket imposed in places like Berkeley, one of the most cogent solutions can be found in the formula that sits at the heart of Europe's privacy law. Rooted in international human rights law, it argues that digital surveillance should only be used when necessary, and then only to the degree necessary to achieve the goal. In practical terms, this means police departments would need to demonstrate reasonable suspicion of a crime and prove that they had exhausted other, less invasive means of tracking the suspect before being granted permission to use advanced surveillance.

Paired with necessity, the principle of proportionality offers perspective in thinking about when the risks of employing digital surveillance are justified. The use of facial recognition systems to track a murder suspect makes sense. Solving a sock theft at T.J. Maxx? Not so much. Similar safeguards would apply to government departments pursuing other aims, whether it's optimizing health care or detecting tax cheats: use surveillance only when it's needed, and only to the extent it's needed.

Whatever approach democracies choose, they will ultimately need to start with transparency. Digital surveillance prefers to work out of sight, in the shadows. Minimizing its harms means dragging it into the light. "This is Civics 101," Kevin Haggerty, a sociologist at the University of Alberta who studies surveillance in policing, told us in the early days of our work on this book. "You can introduce whatever structure you want, but if you don't have a vibrant tradition of independent journalism, civic engagement, they mean nothing."

Exposure, of course, only gets us so far. Even with the reality of state surveillance laid out on the dissection table under the glare of surgical lights, we still have to wrestle with difficult choices. A system of face-tracking cameras to find abducted children or an app to track carriers of the next pandemic virus may seem justified in themselves, but what happens when you factor in the potential for surveillance creep? How else might such systems be used by people in power once everyone else has stopped paying attention?

There are no easy answers, but understanding and accepting that—finding a way to embrace complexity and inconvenience—is ultimately the best antidote to the Communist Party's vision of a society ruled by numbers.

EXILE

Tahir, Marhaba, and the girls spent their first night in the United States at an Extended Stay America hotel in Fairfax, Virginia. The next morning, Aséna woke up and made her way to the dining area for breakfast. Buzzing with excitement, she said "good morning" to everyone she passed in the hallway. To her delight, every single person said "good morning" back to her. After eating, and a few more exchanges of morning salutations, she wandered onto the grass outside the hotel and took selfies in front of an upright stone slab with the words "Stay America" written on them and posted the best one on her WeChat feed. Almost immediately, the comments came flowing in.

"You went to the United States?" one teacher asked.

Aséna typed out her reply: "Yes, I'm staying in America!"

As more likes and comments from friends and relatives poured in, she went online to check out Google and Facebook for the first time. Soon it dawned on her: she could search for anything she wanted. She entered "Xi Jinping" and was shocked to find page after page of people openly cursing the Chinese leader and the Communist Party. She had heard growing up about the freedom and vastness of the internet outside the Great Firewall, but to actually experience it was something else. Instantly the borders of her world exploded.

While his daughters seemed to slide into their new American lives with ease, Tahir struggled. Almost from the moment they arrived in August 2017, and throughout the fall, he suffered nightmares. In some, he was being chased by police through the streets of Urumqi. In others, Marhaba and the girls had gone back to visit relatives and had their passports confiscated again. Each morning, he would wake up with his heart in his throat, look around the room, and remember where he was.

He tried to keep himself up—to keep himself in the United States—by watching movies on TV, but eventually exhaustion would carry him back to Xinjiang. The lack of sleep turned him into a zombie in English class, his mind and body separated by thousands of miles.

Eventually, his subconscious caught up with him. He started to have new dreams of himself eating meals with Uyghurs he'd met in Virginia and Washington, DC. Sometimes friends from Urumqi would make cameos. Tahir was finally able to enjoy his nights. By then, though, events in Xinjiang had begun to haunt his days.

When Tahir, Marhaba, and the girls arrived in the United States, they had a limited sense of what was unfolding in Xinjiang. China's state-controlled media had obscured everything behind an impenetrable barrier of anti-extremist slogans and political jargon, which forced them to piece together a picture from scraps of information gathered from conversations with others and observations from the streets. In Fairfax, a Washington suburb with a large Uyghur community, they had access for the first time to uncensored news. What they saw filled in the dim outline of their understanding with dark, unsettling color.

A couple of weeks after the family arrived, Western news organizations and human rights groups issued the first wave of reports about the new network of "political education" centers in Xinjiang, corroborating the whispers that Tahir and Marhaba had heard in Urumqi. Other reports surfaced of Xinjiang police using facial and voice recognition systems to create "three-dimensional" biometric portraits of individuals—a revelation that helped explain their strange experience in the police basement. Still other reports described the creation of classification systems for Uyghurs based on behavior and personal background, confirming Tahir's suspicions about the data collection form.

That October, a friend asked Tahir to help him edit a video. A cousin of Tahir's used to handle editing and other technical tasks in Tahir's studio in Urumqi. Without thinking, Tahir called him to ask for tips on how to use the editing software. There was no answer. Tahir tried two more times before giving up. Days later, they learned from a relative that the cousin had been taken away "to study." The relative wondered whether it was Tahir's phone calls that caused it. Tahir was flooded with guilt. The thing they feared the most had come to pass, and over something as mundane as video editing. Why had he called? Immediately, Tahir and Marhaba cut off contact with their relatives.

It hadn't occurred to Tahir to become an activist. For more than two years, he had been preoccupied with the struggle to get his family to safety. Once they landed in Virginia, he was just as consumed with getting them settled in the United States and sorting out the practicalities of exile: a place to live, transportation, school for the children, language lessons for him, banking and budgets, sources for halal food, materials for the asylum application. His own experience in a labor camp decades earlier had persuaded him that the best way to fight the Communist Party's influence in Xinjiang was indirectly, through the nurturing of Uyghur culture. But the more that emerged about what was happening in Xinjiang, the more compelled he would feel to confront the Party head-on, the way he had as a student in Beijing. It was a trajectory that many other Uyghurs in exile around the globe would also eventually follow.

Tahir's first step back onto the more confrontational path came near the end of October 2017, when we contacted him through a Uyghur rights activist to ask if he would allow us to interview him about his escape for *The Wall Street Journal*. He agreed to talk to us but wavered on whether to let the newspaper quote him by name. Tahir knew that attaching his name to the story would lend it more credibility. But he also knew it would make things worse for people back home.

Tahir and Marhaba talked over whether to go on the record,

weighing their relatives' freedom against the chance to draw more attention to what was happening. The idea of choosing to do something, yet again, that would make things worse for their families was almost physically painful. But reports coming out of Xinjiang were so incredible that many had dismissed them as fake news. To counteract that, it was important to be as transparent as possible. After days of back and forth, they decided Tahir should go public.

After Tahir had talked to us but before the story was published, the family heard that Marhaba's brother and one of Tahir's brothers had both been taken away. The news was wrenching. In a dark way, though, it was also liberating—proof that their relatives would suffer regardless of whether Tahir and Marhaba chose to speak.

The story was published in the *Journal* on December 19, 2017. Days later, Tahir received word that his missing brother had been sent to a camp and that two female relatives had been called in by police and interrogated, though they had been allowed to leave. *The Globe and Mail* and *Financial Times* called him for interviews. The next summer, a video interview he did to go along with *The Wall Street Journal* story was featured in a segment about Xinjiang on comedian John Oliver's *Last Week Tonight*.

Around the same time as the *Last Week Tonight* episode, Tahir got a call from the State Department inviting him to speak at a three-day summit in Washington, DC, chaired by then–vice president Mike Pence, on religious freedom. He hesitated at first. He didn't consider himself particularly religious. But it was another opportunity to draw attention to the Uyghurs' plight. When the day of the summit arrived, he put on a new dark blue suit and traveled to Washington. "There are unprecedented restrictions on the religious lives of Uyghurs," he testified with help from an interpreter. "The government has confiscated and burned religious books and demolished mosques." A new flurry of headlines followed.

Tahir hoped that other Uyghurs would follow his example and talk publicly about what was happening in Xinjiang. Few did, at least at first. Of the reasons they gave for their reluctance, the most common was uncertainty. Unlike Tahir, most Uyghurs abroad had left Xinjiang before the new campaign had started and didn't have firsthand knowledge of what was unfolding there. Instead, they relied on relatives back home to keep them informed. Those communication channels were gradually disappearing, creating an informational void that the Chinese government was starting to weaponize against them.

Like anyone with family living in China, Uyghurs abroad communicated with their relatives back home through WeChat. A few overseas Uyghurs noticed family members going inexplicably silent on the app in early 2017, just as Chen Quanguo was starting to round people up. Toward the end of the year, as foreign media began to uncover the extent of the campaign Chen had unleashed, more Uyghurs in Xinjiang went quiet. Some even wrote to relatives abroad with messages begging to not be contacted. By the next year, the silence had grown thunderous.

Around the same time as they lost touch with relatives, exiled Uyghurs began getting messages from unknown people in Xinjiang claiming to be police or local government officials. The strangers wanted to know what was happening in Uyghur communities in other countries. They offered enticements to those who were willing to report on the activities of their fellow exiles and threats to those who weren't. Cousin in a camp? Maybe he would get let out early. Sister still roaming free despite being caught listening to Turkish music? She might find herself being sent off for reeducation. The strangers used a similar blend of carrots and sticks in demanding that Uyghurs abroad stay silent about what little they knew.

Eventually, the Party's spell broke. Whether from outrage or because they felt they had nothing left to lose, or some combination of the two, exiled Uyghurs began speaking to the press. The more they spoke, the more other exiles joined them in speaking. Soon, foreign news sites were filled with stories of Uyghur families torn apart by the Party's assimilation campaign. Western governments, slow at first to believe reports out of Xinjiang, began to ask questions.

In August 2018, a year after Tahir and his family escaped, Hu Lianhe, the counterterrorism expert sent to help implement the Party's new ethnic policy in Xinjiang, admitted to the existence of the camps during a panel on racial discrimination at the United Nations offices in Geneva. Hu denied as "completely untrue" the widely cited estimate that as many as a million people had been detained in them. He also denied press accounts of mass brainwashing. Instead he characterized the camps as vocational schools designed to help "criminals involved only in minor offenses" become productive members of society. Still, it was a stunning admission after months of denials—a small but important victory.

◉

Over the following months, Uyghur exiles, scholars, and journalists debated whether Xi Jinping would be able to achieve his ultimate aim in Xinjiang. Could he actually succeed in reengineering Uyghur identity? Some argued that brainwashing on a mass scale was impossible, even for an organization as powerful as the Party. Forcing people to learn Mandarin, disparage Islam, and proclaim their gratitude to Xi wouldn't yield the sort of loyalty the Party expected, argued Adrian Zenz, reflecting a popular view. Zenz, an evangelical Christian, observed that belief does not change through brute force: "If anything it will just make Uyghurs more resentful of the Party." Tahir was among the pessimists. The Party might never fully succeed in making Uyghurs Chinese, he thought, but there was no telling what damage it could do simply by trying.

The Party's assault on Uyghur knowledge and tradition was unrelenting. A who's who of Uyghur scholars and artists—keepers of the culture whom Tahir previously worked and dined with—had disappeared into the camps. Rahile Dawut, a renowned professor of Uyghur folklore, went missing on her way to a conference in Beijing at the end of 2017. Musician Abdurehim Heyit, a master of the two-stringed *dutar* and referred to by some as Xinjiang's equivalent of Bob Dylan, was also detained in 2017; rumors of his death prompted outrage in the Turkish-speaking world until Chinese state media produced a hostage-style video of an emaciated Heyit proclaiming he was in good health. The head of Xinjiang University, a geographer and Communist Party member named Tashpolat Tiyip, was handed a death sentence with a two-year reprieve for inciting separatism following a secret trial, at least according to his relatives. Meanwhile, police had cleared bookstores of Uyghur-language books, even those previously approved by censors, that the Party saw as doing too much to promote a separate Uyghur identity.

At the same time, in Urumqi and elsewhere, the government had begun to create a Disneyfied version of Uyghur culture that it marketed as safe for consumption by Han Chinese tourists. Government bulldozers reduced mosques and Uyghur cemeteries to rubble and razed Uyghur migrant settlements that the Party claimed were breeding grounds for separatists. Construction crews transformed Erdaoqiao, a neighborhood in Urumqi's Tianshan District that used to form the heart of Uyghur commerce, into an ersatz version of itself where heavily made-up Uyghur children in traditional clothing danced onstage and souvenir shops sold bottle openers with handles in the shape of *nan*.

With so much of Uyghur culture swept away, locked up, or sanitized, Tahir felt the burden of trying to keep alive what remained. At the same time, though, he was struggling with his own sense of self. America was a paradise, but he felt lost within it. With next to no English, he struggled to find work his entire first year in Virginia—a poet whose language limitations made him unemployable. After he had learned enough to get around, he used some of the family's dwindling savings to buy a hybrid Honda Accord and started working as a Lyft driver. On his first day he made $56. Friendly riders would occasionally ask him where he was from and he would try to explain what was happening in Xinjiang. He struggled to get the words out, but once in a while he succeeded. A few customers had offered him money after hearing his story. He found it awkward but moving.

The daily struggle of adjusting to a new country and culture, along with his increasing involvement in advocating the Uyghur cause, pulled Tahir away from the work that had defined him. He struggled to write. Shooting film was impossible—he had no camera, no crew, no way to navigate the complicated logistics. Gone were the *olturush* gatherings where he sat at the center of conversations that excavated the depths of Uyghur history and tradition. Now he was just another struggling immigrant hunched behind the wheel of a car, giving rides to strangers.

The sense of dislocation—of being stuck between two distant places, between a wounded past and an uncertain future—permeated the family's house. They lived in one-half of a duplex, pale gray with white trim, in a neighborhood of Fairfax known for its good schools. A "Wipe Your Paws" doormat greeted visitors at the door, though they didn't have a dog. Above the mantel in the living room hung a series of framed items: a rumpled copy of the United States Constitution, a map of Xinjiang, family photos, and posters for old poetry readings Tahir had done. On a nearby wall was a triptych of photos from the State Department religious freedom event that showed Tahir posing with Vice President Mike Pence, Secretary of State Mike Pompeo, and Nikki Haley, then the US ambassador to the United Nations.

More evidence of their divided lives graced the kitchen, where Marhaba waged a valiant battle with equipment ill suited to cook food that would keep them connected to the lives they had left behind. A shelf in one corner served as an impromptu graveyard for scorched American pans and woks that hadn't been able to stand up to the rigors of Uyghur cooking. Marhaba had better luck with the convection oven, which she had coaxed into baking a decent nan, though it was still not the same as nan from the tandoor ovens back in Urumqi.

In February 2019, the family's world was jolted once again when Marhaba discovered she was pregnant. With all the disruption in their lives, Tahir and Marhaba hadn't planned on having another child. The news thrust Tahir into a more frantic search for a job, ideally one that would provide health insurance. He found part-time work editing studio interviews and occasionally going on shoots around Washington for Radio Free Asia, a US-funded news organization with services in several languages, including Uyghur. By September, he was working there full-time, but as a contractor with no benefits.

This latest struggle had taken Tahir still further away from himself. One day not long after starting the full-time position at Radio Free Asia, he found himself sitting alone with his eldest daughter, Aséna, who had adjusted much faster to the conditions of their new life. During a pause in conversation, she looked at him. Then, with the casual brass of an American teenager, she offered an observation that sliced into him like a knife: "You've become a philistine."

◉

That fall, Tahir and Aséna climbed into the family Honda and drove southeast on Highway 50 toward Fairfax proper to attend a gathering of the local Uyghur community. At the office park next to the National Rifle Association's National Firearms Museum, Tahir and Aséna filed into a room packed with a few hundred other people. The rest of the venue was taken up by circular tables, each one draped in a bright blue tablecloth and set with paper plates of dried fruit.

The atmosphere was festive, but the mood was uncertain. Earlier in the year, it had become clear that the Party's "educational" efforts in Xinjiang weren't focused solely on adults. Xi Jinping and Chen Quanguo were also going after Uyghur children, taking sons and daughters of camp detainees and placing them in boarding schools where they were subjected to a similar curriculum as their parents. One Uyghur living in Turkey, who hadn't been able to contact his four-year-old son and three-year-old daughter since his wife was detained years earlier, stumbled across images of his son in a propaganda video answering a teacher's questions in Mandarin. Researchers later uncovered a policy document posted on the website of the Ministry of Education showing that nearly half a million children—40 percent of the region's pre-college students—were enrolled in boarding schools. It called for further expansion of boarding schools so that education officials could "to the greatest extent possible break the influence on children of the religious atmosphere at home." The current generation of Uyghurs might be able to resist the brainwashing, but children were impressionable. Suddenly the Party's assimilation plans began to seem more plausible.

Meanwhile, the government in Beijing had launched a bold propaganda campaign to cast its policies in Xinjiang as worthy of emulation rather than condemnation. In a 16,000-character white paper given the Orwellian title "Xinjiang's Counter-terror and De-radicalization Struggle and the Protection of Human Rights," China's State Council

Information Office argued that the "preemptive" measures authorities installed in Xinjiang had made interaction and communication between ethnic groups "more intimate." An accompanying Xinhua story aligned the campaign in Xinjiang with the global war on terror. In an echo of Nazi Germany in the early days of the Holocaust, the Chinese government had also invited media from friendly countries to visit select camps on tightly controlled tours. Uyghur detainees, under the watch of authorities, gave interviews praising the education they had received. Allowed to join one of the tours, a Reuters reporter wrote of being taken into a classroom where Uyghur students were made to stand up and greet their visitors with a rendition of "If You're Happy and You Know It, Clap Your Hands."

But amid the parade of grotesqueries, there were signs of hope. The United States had just begun to slap sanctions on Chinese companies involved in surveillance inside Xinjiang, a milestone in Western government support for the Uyghur cause. Though no one was quite sure why, a trickle of Uyghur detainees had begun to be let out of the camps. And news coverage of the Party's campaign in Xinjiang, which many had expected to tail off, was going strong.

The night's speakers chose to emphasize the positive, marveling at how the Uyghur cause had emerged from secrecy and obscurity. Sporting a *doppa*, the Uyghurs' traditional four-cornered cap, one elderly exile leader took the microphone in a spirit of exuberant defiance. "Our gathering here is a rebuke to the Communist Party. Whoever imagined we would have this much support?"

Tahir offered a robust burst of applause, though both he and Aséna struggled through the rest of the event. It was heartening to see so many Uyghurs gathered in one place, celebrating with a lightness and joy impossible in China. But the other speeches and musical performances, many of them clumsily earnest efforts put forth by second-generation Uyghurs born in the United States, only served to remind them that they were a long way away from Xinjiang and, in all likelihood, would never be able to go back.

Less than a month later, on December 3, 2019, the US House of Representatives voted 407–1 in favor of the Uyghur Human Rights Policy Act, which paved the way for American sanctions on officials involved in the Xinjiang crackdown. The vote came after a similar bill had passed through the Senate by unanimous consent. Within days, Xinjiang's top Uyghur official, governor Shohrat Zakir, appeared at a press briefing in Beijing where he made an extraordinary claim. All of the people sent to the camps (he continued to call them vocational training centers) had "graduated," he said, adding: "With the help of the government, stable employment has been achieved and their quality of life has been improved." The facilities would continue to operate, he said, but participants in the training would be "free to come and go."

Zakir was exaggerating. Large numbers of Uyghurs remained in the camps and were not free to leave. But an increasing number of exiles had indeed begun to receive word of long-detained relatives being let out. Encouraged by the Chinese government's softening tone, and desperate to see family members, a few overseas Uyghurs took the risk of flying back to Xinjiang for short visits.

One of the people who braved the journey home was a woman named Madina. She had left Xinjiang for Germany in 2016 to study for a master's degree. She had heard through relatives that her mother was gravely ill, stricken by a medical condition that left her unable to walk and barely able to speak. She flew to Kashgar in December 2019, and was taken for interrogation by police for three hours before she was allowed to continue on to her parents' home. She was asked to hand over her cellphone and its password, and the police fumbled through the contents of her phone. Madina had heard about such checks from other friends who had earlier traveled home and was well prepared—she had bought a cheap burner phone for a hundred euros before departing. Once out, Madina hailed a taxi to bring her home, and what she saw on the streets during the forty-minute drive rattled her. As her driver navigated the streets of the city, Madina immediately noticed how few people were out on the sidewalk; the parks, typically filled with crowds singing, dancing, and eating, were empty.

"I asked my taxi driver why there were so few people on the street," she recalled to us. "'Is it because it is Monday?' He said, 'All the people are studying at university,' which was a reference to the camps."

Back home, she saw her nephew, who had been recently released from a camp. He had been taken away in 2017 after police discovered his wife had studied religious materials four years earlier while a college student. He was in his mid-twenties when Madina left for Germany. She remembered him as a happy kid who liked to crack jokes. But now he sat around the house in silence, avoiding interaction with others. Madina's sister didn't want to discuss what her son had gone through. "It's better not to talk about these things. It's horrible," she said. The family had heard that the nephew's wife was scheduled to be let out the following year. They didn't know why she was being held longer.

Since their escape in 2017, five of Tahir and Marhaba's relatives had been sent to the camps. All of them were let out near the end of 2019. In pictures, Marhaba's and Tahir's brothers evoked Allied soldiers in Japanese POW camps or Jews rescued from Auschwitz, pale and gaunt. Marhaba cried for three days after seeing the images. All five of them were under constant surveillance. Tahir had heard stories from friends whose relatives had died shortly after coming out of the camps, had returned with strange diseases, or had suffered psychotic breaks. He didn't know how his brother or the other four were faring. Their only family member still willing to make contact always said the same thing: "They're good." Tahir figured that meant none of them had developed serious problems, and for that he was thankful.

Zakir's "graduation" announcement seemed to signal the start of a new phase of the campaign in Xinjiang. As 2020 unfolded, the police presence on the streets subsided and some of the camps closed down. In a field behind one shuttered camp in Kashgar, piles of bunk beds were left to rust in the open air, some of them bearing red stickers that read "Recognize your mistakes, admit your mistakes, repent." Life returned to markets and public squares. Some Uyghur exiles, hearing about the changes from relatives, took it as a sign that foreign pressure was working.

But other changes were less encouraging. Of the camps that weren't shut down, many were being converted into formal detention centers or prisons. And of the detainees who weren't released, large numbers were being found guilty of national-security-related crimes and handed double-digit prison sentences without their relatives ever receiving notice of a trial. Even those who were released were far from free: besides subjecting the "graduates" to surveillance, officials often compelled them to take low-paying jobs in factories, sometimes in cities or towns far from their families, or else risk being sent back into detention.

At the same time, a disturbing picture began to emerge around the government's treatment of Uyghur women. Previously, ethnic Kazakh women had crossed the border into Kazakhstan with chilling accounts of their experiences in the camps. They talked about having their heads shaved and being crammed together with dozens of other women in a single cell crawling with cameras and microphones, about being forced to sleep under bright lights and banned from covering their eyes, and about being shocked with electric batons if they spent too much time in the bathroom. Later, Uyghur women came out of the camps with stories of sexual assault and gang rape. Several reported being given injections or forced to take pills that stopped their menstrual cycles.

The women also revealed that family planning officials in Xinjiang had begun strictly imposing birth limits in Uyghur communities—even as they desperately encouraged Han Chinese women to have more children to counter the aging of the country's population elsewhere. Having three or more children was a common reason for Uyghur women to be sent to the camps, where many were forced to have intrauterine devices inserted to prevent them getting pregnant. Officials used the same engineering language they applied in surveillance to describe the tightening birth restrictions, casting them as part of a "population optimization" strategy. Comparing population projections from before the crackdown to new projections under an "optimized" scenario, Adrian Zenz estimated the new policies could reduce the number of Uyghur births by between 2.6 and 4.5 million by 2040.

Combined with the policy of shipping Uyghur children off to boarding schools, the implication was clear: the Party was hanging its assimilation strategy on the next generation of Uyghurs, who would not only be educated to be Chinese but also be fewer in number.

These discoveries stirred strong reactions outside Xinjiang. Both

Mike Pompeo and his successor as secretary of state under the Biden administration, Antony Blinken, accused the Party of carrying out genocide. Canada's House of Commons and the British Parliament voted to designate the campaign as genocide as well. Others stopped short of endorsing that label, though nearly every Western country condemned the situation in Xinjiang as an atrocity.

In June of 2021, at the request of World Uyghur Congress, a panel of human rights lawyers and scholars based in London set out to conduct an independent investigation. Proclaiming respect for China and for differences in political systems, the Uyghur Tribunal, as the group came to call itself, limited itself only to considering clear breaches of international laws that China itself had endorsed. After more than a year of listening to testimony and examining evidence, including a leaked set of secret Communist Party documents that tied Xi Jinping directly to policy in Xinjiang, the panel found that the number of likely Uyghur births prevented by the Party's policies, in conjunction with efforts to forcibly assimilate the Uyghurs already born, was egregious enough to fit the definition of a genocide. "The Tribunal feels some unease about making findings of this crime on the basis of evidence that links the crime to the very highest political figure of a country. It would seem altogether more appropriate for such things to be dealt with by governments or international organizations," the panel wrote in its final judgment. "But governments have no courage to do such things; neither does the [United Nations] where a powerful state is involved." With no power of its own to sanction China, it concluded by urging the world's governments to contemplate why they had to more forcefully intervene.

◉

Tahir and Marhaba's son was born in November 2019. They decided to name him Tarim, after the Tarim River, which snakes through the center of Xinjiang. They chose the name so their son would always have a connection to the land where his parents had grown up and that had nurtured Uyghur culture. Marhaba held out hope that they would one day be able to take their son back to Xinjiang to visit his namesake.

Around the time Tarim was born, Tahir heard that a friend of his, the novelist Perhat Tursun, had been sentenced to sixteen years in prison on unknown charges—a sign that the Party wasn't done eliminating Uyghurs it saw as threatening. More recently, the government has gone on a rampage trying to refute the genocide allegations, dismissing them, in the words of China's foreign minister, as "a rumor with ulterior motives and a complete lie." Chinese officials also dismissed the sanctions, describing them as part of an effort to contain China's rise. Xi Jinping offered an unequivocal signal at a two-day conference on Xinjiang in the fall of 2020, when he proclaimed the Party's strategy for controlling the region "completely correct."

Meanwhile, the surveillance technologies and some of the techniques the Party had deployed in Xinjiang were spreading to other minority-dominated regions in remote parts of the country. Systems for monitoring mosques migrated to Gansu and Ningxia, northwestern regions home to large numbers of Hui, another Muslim minority culturally and politically closer to the Han Chinese. In heavily Tibetan areas of western Sichuan province, the government installed facial recognition systems and a total of more than 180 surveillance cameras inside seven Buddhist monasteries. Government procurement documents showed that they also used drones to map some monasteries and built databases to categorize monastery residents. The database used triangles to denote "patriots," stars for "special persons of interest," and circles for "regular persons of interest."

All of this made Tahir skeptical of Marhaba's dream that their son might one day see his homeland. "That will never happen as long as the Communist Party is in control," he told her. As he settled into that reality, he began to recover some of himself. He started writing more. In July 2021, Tahir published an account of his experiences and escape in *The Atlantic*. In it, he recalled the biometric data collection in the police basement, his friend Kamil's disappearance, and his landing in Boston weighed down by the realization that he would forever carry the guilt of having made it to safety while leaving so many loved ones behind. He concluded it with a poem that he wrote after his arrival, titled "Somewhere Else."

Besieged by these discolored words
within all these disordered moments
the target on my forehead
could not bring me to my knees
and also
night after night
one after another
I spoke the names of ants I've known

I thought of staying whole
by the road or somewhere else
Even
cliffs grow tired staring into the distance
But
in my thoughts I trimmed your ragged hair
with two fingers for scissors
I splashed your chest with a handful of water
to douse a distant forest fire

Of course
I too can only stare
for a moment into the distance

(Translated by Joshua L. Freeman)

Aséna, now nineteen years old, ruminated on her journey in a podcast interview with *The Atlantic* that accompanied her father's piece. For her first year and a half in the United States, she too felt consumed by guilt, she said. "It's a pretty dark thought, but I wished I could die in a way that [would let] everybody know what's going on in Xinjiang," she said. "If I could go back and die in a way that's beneficial for my people, I felt like this guiltiness would go away."

Those thoughts began to change when she learned her mother was pregnant, she said. At first she was opposed to the pregnancy, but when Tarim arrived, it forced the family to pull back from the brink. Everybody's energy went into raising the baby. "He basically saved us," she said. When Tarim was forty days old, the family invited Uyghur children over for *qiriq suyi*, a bathing ceremony in which participants pour water over a newborn with wooden spoons while expressing wishes for the child's future. Other children wished Tarim wealth and professional success. "When it's my turn," Aséna recalled, "I grabbed the spoon of water and poured it on him and said, 'I hope you become a free person.'"

As she contemplated the future for her brother, an American by birth, Aséna wrestled with the concept of freedom, and with the burden of battling the Communist Party's surveillance machinery for the future of Uyghur identity. She didn't know if it was fair to saddle Tarim with the weight of being a Uyghur. "I just want him to have a choice," she said. "But you can't escape it."

After escaping from Xinjiang, Tahir Hamut and his family settled in Virginia in 2017. Two years later, Tahir's wife, Marhaba, gave birth to a son, Tarim, pictured here in 2020 with his parents and sisters, Almila (2nd from right) and Asena (far right). *(Courtesy of Tahir Hamut)*

ACKNOWLEDGMENTS

We owe our deepest bow of respect and gratitude to those who were generous enough to tell us their stories, sometimes at risk to themselves or their loved ones. That begins with Tahir Hamut and his family, whose fateful decision to go on the record with their experiences in Xinjiang ultimately made this book possible, and whose patience and openness through hour after hour of interviews made it vastly richer. Immense thanks also to Bobi Wine, who took us inside his home and onto the battlefields of Ugandan politics; Vivian Xu, Qiu Liqun, and Xu Bing, who opened our eyes to the myriad ways Chinese people contend with surveillance; and Kaitlin Jackson, who helped us see how the same challenge is unfolding in the United States.

None of these words would have been written, much less assembled in coherent form, without the talent, insight, and support of Gillian Wong. She encouraged the book from its conception and midwifed it through a turbulent gestation with a perfect symphony of encouragement, cajoling, and interrogation. She was, simply put, amazing.

We owe immense thanks to our colleagues at *The Wall Street Journal*, whose journalistic skill and generosity are a constant source of wonder. Clément Bürge was a brilliant reporting partner on some of the toughest assignments that fed the book, as well as a continual source of storytelling inspiration. Joe Parkinson, in addition to letting us ride his investigative coattails, also served as an A-plus commiserator in trying to balance book writing with daily reporting. John Corrigan saw state surveillance for the huge story it was. Nicholas Bariyo, Eva Dou, Jeremy Page, Natasha Khan, Wenxin Fan, and Dan Strumpf broke new ground with early stories that helped form the foundation of this project. Charles Hutzler, Sofia McFarland, Neil Western, and Patrick Barta kept us pointed in the right direction. Matt Murray, in addition to giving the book his blessing, also wisely counseled us not to tie it too tightly to any given technology.

Our editor at St. Martin's, Tim Bartlett, was a pathfinder of surpassing grit, helping us hack our way out of more thickets than we care to count. We are particularly grateful for his Buddha-like patience as we navigated an expulsion from China and a surprise global pandemic. Immense thanks also to our agent, Gail Ross, a reassuring advocate and a vital source of belief and advice throughout.

Several others played outsized roles: Andreas Weigend, who at times almost seemed more enthusiastic about this undertaking than we were, was an inexhaustible source of ideas, expertise, and reassurance. Ian Johnson offered a steady stream of wisdom over Belgian beers in Beijing and Singapore. Bryan Salvatore helped us improve our prose and gave us a much-needed shot of confidence for the final push.

A massive thank-you to Tom Wright, who persuaded us to indulge our biggest ambitions, as well as to Richard McGregor, John Pomfret, Mei Fong, Dinny McMahon, and Jim McGregor, all of whom provided crucial advice and encouragement in the early stages of this project.

Researchers and fact-checkers are essential in any credible journalistic effort of such size. We had the good fortune to work with a topnotch team. Immense thanks to Rachel Zhang, Dave Yin, and many others who prefer not to be named.

We offer humble genuflections to Darren Byler, James Millward, and Sean Roberts for sharing their deep knowledge of Xinjiang; Zuoyue Wang and Mara Hvistendahl for their guidance on the story of Qian

Xuesen; Samantha Hoffman, Sheena Grietens, Steven Feldstein, Samm Sacks, Greg Walton, Peter Furhrman, and Charles Rollet for helping us navigate the confluence of technology and politics in China; Jeremy Daum for helping us separate fact from fantasy when it comes to the Social Credit System; Lokman Tsui, Clement Chen, Jamie Horsley, and Clarisse Girot for challenging us to think more deeply about Chinese notions of privacy; Susan Shirk, Helen Toner, and Jessica Chen Weiss for illuminating the geopolitics of state surveillance; Claire Garvie, Evan Selinger, Albert Fox Cahn, Nicole Ozer, and Jennifer Lynch for helping us grasp the implications of surveillance in an American context; and David Lyon, Kevin Haggerty, Mark Andrejevic, James Rule, and Oscar Gandy Jr. for helping us think more deeply about the role surveillance plays in societies more generally.

Profound thanks to New America for helping fund the research that went into this book and for inviting us into an extraordinary community of storytellers. Thanks also to *The Wall Street Journal*, not only for supporting the journalism that underpins the book but also for granting us the time to write it.

Finally, a deep nod of appreciation to those who took time to read early drafts of the manuscript and offer advice on ways to improve it: Matt Sheehan, Aaron Krenkel, John Delury, Jude Blanchette, Jessica Batke, Katina Michael, Ronald Kline, Keith Zhai, Felix Kapron, Daniel Tam-Claiborne, Val Chin, Steve Chin, and Kristi Kramer. Any remaining errors, whether of fact or interpretation, are ours and ours alone.

SELECTED BIBLIOGRAPHY

Applebaum, Anne. *Twilight of Democracy: The Seductive Allure of Authoritarianism.* New York: Knopf Doubleday Publishing Group, 2020.

Ball, K., K. D. Haggerty, and D. Lyon, eds. *Routledge Handbook of Surveillance Studies.* New York: Taylor and Francis, 2012.

Black, Edwin. *IBM and the Holocaust: The Strategic Alliance Between Nazi Germany and America's Most Powerful Corporation.* Washington, DC: Dialog Press, 2012.

Blanchette, Jude. *China's New Red Guards: The Return of Radicalism and the Rebirth of Mao Zedong.* New York: Oxford University Press, 2019.

Bovingdon, Gardner. *The Uyghurs: Strangers in Their Own Land.* New York: Columbia University Press, 2010.

Byler, Darren. *In the Camps: China's High-Tech Penal Colony.* New York: Columbia Global Reports, 2021.

Chang, Iris. *Thread of the Silkworm.* New York: Basic Books, 1995.

Davis, Bob, and Lingling Wei. *Superpower Showdown: How the Battle Between Trump and Xi Threatens a New Cold War.* New York: Harper Business, 2020.

Feldstein, Steven. *The Rise of Digital Repression: How Technology Is Reshaping Power, Politics and Resistance.* New York: Oxford University Press, 2021.

Foucault, Michel. *Discipline and Punish: The Birth of the Prison.* Trans. Alan Sheridan. New York: Vintage, 1977.

Frischmann, Brett, and Evan Selinger. *Re-engineering Humanity.* Cambridge: Cambridge University Press, 2018.

Funder, Anna. *Stasiland: Stories from Behind the Berlin Wall.* New York: Harper Perennial, 2002.

Griffiths, James. *The Great Firewall of China: How to Build and Control an Alternative Version of the Internet.* London: Zed Books, 2019.

Hoffman, Samantha R. "Programming China: The Communist Party's Autonomic Approach to Managing State Security." PhD thesis, University of Nottingham, 2017.

Hsien, H. S. (Qian Xuesen). *Engineering Cybernetics*. New York: McGraw-Hill, 1954.

Kline, Ronald R. *The Cybernetics Moment: Or Why We Call Our Age the Information Age.* Baltimore: Johns Hopkins University Press, 2015.

Kuhn, Philip A. *Soulstealers: The Chinese Sorcery Scare of 1768.* Cambridge, MA: Harvard University Press, 1990.

Lee, Kai-fu. *AI Superpowers: China, Silicon Valley and the New World Order.* Boston: Houghton Mifflin Harcourt, 2018.

MacKinnon, Rebecca. *Consent of the Networked: The Worldwide Struggle for Internet Freedom.* New York: Basic Books, 2012.

McGregor, Richard. *The Party: The Secret World of China's Communist Rulers.* New York: Allen Lane, 2010.

Millward, James. *Crossroads of Eurasia: A History of Xinjiang.* New York: Columbia University Press, 2009.

Minzner, Carl. *End of an Era: How China's Authoritarian Revival Is Undermining Its Rise.* New York: Oxford University Press, 2018.

O'Neil, Cathy. *Weapons of Math Destruction: How Big Data Increases Inequality and Threatens Democracy.* New York: Crown/Archetype, 2016.

Parenti, Christian. *The Soft Cage: Surveillance in America from Slavery to the War on Terror.* New York: Basic Books, 2003.

Reid, Richard. *A History of Modern Uganda.* New York: Cambridge University Press, 2017.

Rice, Andrew. *The Teeth May Smile but the Heart Does Not Forget: Murder and Memory in Uganda.* New York: Henry Holt, 2009.

Rid, Thomas. *Rise of the Machines: A Cybernetic History.* New York: W. W. Norton, 2016.

Roberts, Sean R. *The War on the Uyghurs: China's Internal Campaign Against a Muslim Minority.* Princeton: Princeton University Press, 2020.

Schell, Orville, and John Delury. *Wealth and Power: China's Long March to the Twenty-First Century.* New York: Random House, 2013.

Schoenhals, Michael. *Spying for the People: Mao's Secret Agents, 1949–1967.* Cambridge: Cambridge University Press, 2013.

Scott, James C. *Seeing Like a State: How Certain Schemes to Improve the Human Condition Have Failed.* New Haven: Yale University Press, 1998.

Solove, Daniel J. *Understanding Privacy.* Cambridge, MA: Harvard University Press, 2008.

Tse, Edward. *China's Disruptors: How Alibaba, Xiaomi, Tencent, and Other Companies Are Changing the Rules of Business.* New York: Portfolio, 2015.

Wang Lixiong. *Da Dian (The Ceremony).* Taipei: Locus Publishing, 2017.

Weigend, Andreas. *Data for the People: How to Make Our Post-Privacy Economy Work for You.* New York: Basic Books, 2017.

Wiener, Norbert. *Cybernetics: Or Control and Communication in the Animal and the Machine.* 2nd ed. Cambridge, MA: MIT Press, 1961.

Yang Jisheng. *Tombstone: The Great Chinese Famine, 1958–1962.* Trans. Stacy Mosher and Guo Jian. New York: Farrar, Straus and Giroux, 2012.

Zamyatin, Yevgeny. *We.* Trans. Natasha S. Randall. New York: Random House Publishing Group, 2006.

Zuboff, Shoshana. *The Age of Surveillance Capitalism: The Fight for a Human Future at the New Frontier of Power.* New York: Public Affairs, 2019.

NOTE ON SOURCES AND NAMES

This book was distilled from interviews with roughly 150 people in fourteen countries; hundreds of research reports, books, and Communist Party speeches; and thousands of pages of government and company documents, as well as on-the-ground reporting in China, Uganda, and the United States. Sources for direct quotes that did not come directly from our interviews are listed in the notes for each chapter.

Chinese people employ a variety of systems for rendering their names in the Latin alphabet. Mandarin-speaking residents of mainland China almost all use the pinyin Romanization system, with surnames listed first and two-syllable given names rendered as a single word, though many of those who have taken on English names will put their surnames last. We have chosen pinyin as a default unless an individual has expressed a personal preference otherwise. Qian Xuesen presents a unique challenge in that he spelled his name a number of different ways. Though he is often referred to as Tsien Hsue-Shen (or H. S. Tsien) in the United States, we decided to go with the pinyin spelling, as that is increasingly how his name appears in both Western and Chinese media reports.

Censorship has long presented a challenge to journalists and researchers writing about China. In recent years, the Party has grown even more aggressive and systematic in deleting source material that it perceives as potentially sensitive. As a result, some of the news reports, social media posts, and official documents that we relied on in writing this book no longer exist in digital form, or can only be accessed from a Chinese internet connection. Digital sources that have been deleted or are otherwise unavailable online are denoted as such in the notes.

In describing events that we didn't report ourselves, we relied on sources with a track record of credible news coverage in China and elsewhere. That list includes, but is not limited to, *The Wall Street Journal, The New York Times, The Washington Post,* the Associated Press, Reuters, Agence France-Presse, *The Economist,* the BBC, *The Financial Times, Caixin,* Buzzfeed News, The Intercept, the *South China Morning Post,* and *Sixth Tone.* In instances where we made use of others' exclusive reporting, we noted the source either in the text or in the notes.

NOTES

Introduction

6 **people and livestock:** Carlos Gómez Grajalez, "Great Moments in Statistics: Ancient Censuses," *Significance* (Royal Statistical Society), Dec. 2013, 21.

6 **description:** In the introduction to *Seeing Like a State: How Certain Schemes to Improve the Human Condition Have Failed* (New Haven: Yale University Press, 1998), James C. Scott describes research he conducted into efforts by states to force mobile groups like Gypsies to settle down. "The more I examined these efforts at sedentarization, the more I came to see them as a state's attempt to make a society legible. . . . The premodern state was, in many crucial respects, partially blind; it knew precious little about its subjects, their wealth, their landholdings and yields, their location, their very identity. It lacked anything like a detailed 'map' of its terrain and its people" (2).

8 **end to end:** In *Stasiland: Stories from Behind the Berlin Wall* (New York: Harper Perennial, 2002), Anna Funder writes: "In its forty years, 'the Firm' generated the equivalent of all records in German history since the middle ages. Laid out upright and end to end, the files the Stasi kept on their countrymen and women would form a line 180 kilometers long" (5). Funder notes that by the fall of the Berlin Wall, the Stasi had 97,000 employees and more than 173,000 informers.

9 **"social systems":** From "Xi Jinping: Wanquan youxinxin wei renlei dui genghao shehui zhidu de tansuo tigong zhongguo fang'an," Xinhua, July 1, 2016, https://www.thepaper.cn/newsDetail_forward_1492012.

9 **state control:** Sheena Chestnut Greitens, "Dealing with the Demand for China's Global Surveillance Exports," Global China: Assessing China's Growing Role in the World, Brookings Institution, Apr. 2020.

11 **the group found:** Freedom House, "Freedom in the World 2021," February 2021, https://freedomhouse.org/sites/default/files/2021–02/FIW2021_World_02252021_FINAL-web-upload.pdf.

1. "Critical Data"

For the portions of this chapter that deal with the history of Xinjiang and the Uyghurs, we drew on a variety of books and scholarly articles. We owe a heavy debt to three books in particular: James Millward's *Crossroads of Eurasia*, Gardner Bovingdon's *The Uyghurs,* and Sean Roberts's *The War on the Uyghurs.*

16 **clear, Russia:** The government hasn't to our knowledge officially published the full list. Tahir and Marhaba were presented with the list by a police officer in Xinjiang when being asked about their travel history. According to Tahir, that list included the following countries: Algeria, Afghanistan, Azerbaijan, Egypt, Pakistan, Kazakhstan, Kyrgyzstan, Kenya, Libya, South Sudan, Nigeria, Saudi Arabia, Somalia, Tajikistan, Turkey, Turkmenistan, Uzbekistan, Syria, Yemen, Iraq, Iran, Malaysia, Indonesia, Thailand, Russia, and the United Arab Emirates. The same twenty-six countries were described as "terror-related" on a data collection form circulating inside Xinjiang in 2017, a photo of which was provided to scholar Adrian Zenz by a local contact that same year.

17 **vague on details:** Often abbreviated in English using the acronym IJOP, the platform is referred to in Chinese as 一体化联合作战平台 (*yitihua lianhe zuozhan pingtai*). James Millward argues that a closer English translation is "integrated joint warfare platform," and we agree, but we've chosen to stick with the translation most commonly used elsewhere to avoid confusion.

19 **their own areas:** In *The Crossroads of Eurasia: A History of Xinjiang* (New York: Columbia University Press, 2009), James Millward writes that under the Qing, "local government in the southern oases remained in the hands of Muslim elites, and the imperial state did not in its first century of rule (1760–1864) interfere much in the Islamic legal system or religious matters" (97).

20 **called in:** In *The Uyghurs: Strangers in Their Own Land* (New York: Columbia University Press, 2010), Gardner Bovingdon writes that during the radical collectivization of the Great Leap Forward, "even ethnicity itself became an 'obstacle to progress,' and party leaders stepped up their attacks on Islam and other 'backward customs'" (Kindle version, location 1234).

20 **sent back:** "The Race Card," *The Economist,* Sept. 3, 2016.

21 **in Palestine:** Joanne Smith Finley, "The Wang Lixiong Prophecy: 'Palestinization' in Xinjiang and the Consequences of Chinese State Securitization of Religion," *Central Asian Survey* 38, no. 1 (2019): 81–101.

22 **the long term:** Dingding Chen and Ding Xuejie, "How Chinese Think About Terrorism," *The Diplomat,* Apr. 19, 2014.

23 **"Hurrying":** Tahir Hamut, "Unity Road," translated by Joshua L. Freeman, originally published in *Southern Review* 56, no. 1 (2020): 24–29.

27 **at least two:** News reports from the time present a muddied picture of what happened in Shaoguan. James Griffiths provides a good summary of what is now considered to be the most likely sequence of events in *The Great Firewall of China: How to Build and Control an Alternative Version of the Internet* (London: Zed Books, 2019).

27 **one street alone:** Gillian Wong, "After Violence, Western China Looks for Answers," Associated Press, July 12, 2009.

28 **bulletproof vests:** Adrian Zenz and James Leibold, "Xinjiang's Rapidly Evolving Security State," *China Brief* (Jamestown Foundation) 17, no. 4 (Mar. 14, 2017).

29 **"This neighborhood":** Tahir Hamut, "My Habitat," translated by Dilmurat Mutellip and Darren Byler, Apr. 21, 2015. Originally published by *Bonango Street.*

30 **their true purpose:** Details here come from Josh's reporting trips to Xinjiang in 2017 and 2018, during which he spent several hours detained in convenience police stations in Urumqi.

36 **she stopped replying:** The names of Kamil and his wife, Munire, have been changed to protect their identities.

2. Engineers of the Soul

See note under Chapter 1 for the list of books that we relied on in describing the history of the Uyghurs' tensions with Han Chinese and the Communist Party.

39 **for no reason:** Details of this scene are recounted in "Xinjiang shuji anfang weiwen gongzuo Baojing hou jingcha 54 miao ganddao xianchang," *Xinjiang Daily*, Feb. 21, 2017, https://news.sohu.com/20170222/n481360658.shtml.

40 **"tsunami-like proportions":** Quoted in "Xinjiang juxing fankong weiwen shishi dahui Wang Ning Chen Quanguo jianghua," Tianshan.net, Feb. 28, 2017, http://news .sina.com.cn/c/nd/2017–02–28/doc-ifyavvsk3799160.shtml.

41 **post-Mao era:** For Chen Quanguo's backstory, we drew heavily from Peter Martin, "The Architect of China's Muslim Camps Is a Rising Star Under Xi," Bloomberg News, Sept. 28, 2018, and on sources Martin listed in an accompanying Twitter thread: Peter Martin, @PeterMartin_PCM, "If one individual sums up the values gap between a rising China and the West, it may be Xinjiang Party boss, Chen Quanguo," Twitter, Sept. 27, 2018, 8:45 P.M., https://twitter.com/PeterMartin_PCM/status/1045474636522291200.

41 **twenty-five minutes:** Daniel S. Bennet, "Police Response Times to Calls for Service: Fragmentation, Community Characteristics, and Efficiency," Stanford University, Nov. 2018, https://www.hoplofobia.info/wp-content/uploads/2015/08/2018-Police-Response -Times-to-Calls-for-Service.pdf.

41 **him as saying:** "Xinjiang shuji anfang weiwen gongzuo Baojing."

43 **foreign imams online:** Darren Byler describes this phenomenon at length in "Ghost World," *Logic*, May 1, 2019.

44 **dealing with separatists:** Austin Ramzy and Chris Buckley, "'Absolutely No Mercy': Leaked Files Expose How China Organized Mass Detentions of Muslims," *The New York Times*, Nov. 16, 2019.

45 **"Uyghur population":** In *The War on the Uyghurs: China's Internal Campaign Against a Muslim Minority* (Princeton: Princeton University Press, 2020), Sean R. Roberts notes the steady increase in violence: "However, none of these developments suggested that there was any organized 'terrorist threat' within China's Uyghur population, let alone one that was connected to TIP or any other international jihadist group. Instead, almost all of the incidents appeared to have their own local peculiarities that informed their motivations and intentions" (163).

45 **"use the situation":** Xi Zhongxun, quoted in Joseph Torigian, "What Xi Jinping Learned—and Didn't Learn—from His Father About Xinjiang," *The Diplomat*, Nov. 16, 2019.

45 **"hesitation or wavering":** Ramzy and Buckley, "'Absolutely No Mercy.'"

46 **headscarves and veils:** Timothy Grose, "Beautifying Uyghur Bodies: Fashion, 'Modernity,' and State Power in the Tarim Basin," Contemporary China Centre blog, University of Westminster, Oct. 11, 2019.

46 **"back to China":** Gerry Shih, "Uighurs Fighting in Syria Take Aim at China," Associated Press, Dec. 23, 2017.

46 **fringe religious movements:** Adrian Zenz, "New Evidence for China's Political Re-education Campaign in Xinjiang," *China Brief* (Jamestown Foundation) 18, no. 10 (May 15, 2018).

47 **local party members:** Chun Han Wong, "China's Hard Edge: The Leader of Beijing's Muslim Crackdown Gains Influence," *The Wall Street Journal*, Apr. 7, 2019.

48 **easier monitoring:** Adrian Zenz and James Leibold, "Xinjiang's Rapidly Evolving Security State," *China Brief* (Jamestown Foundation) 17, no. 4 (Mar. 14, 2017).

49 **"chess board":** From "Jianjue guanche yi Xi Jinping tongzhi wei shuji de dang-zhongyang zhijiang fanglue jinjin weirao shehui wending he changzhijiu'an zong-mubiao tuijin gexiang gongzuo," *Xinjiang Daily*, Sept. 18, 2016, http://cpc.people .com.cn/n1/2016/0918/c117005–28721669.html.

49 **year and a half:** Wong, "China's Hard Edge."

51 **"would be recorded":** Darren Byler, "China's Government Has Ordered a Million Citizens to Occupy Uighur Homes. Here's What They Think They're Doing," China-File, The Asia Society, Oct. 24, 2018.

52 **behavior to police:** Shai Oster, "China Tries Its Hand at Precrime," Bloomberg News, Mar. 3, 2016.

52 **described to Bloomberg:** "China: Big Data Fuels Crackdown in Minority Region," Human Rights Watch, Feb. 26, 2018.

53 **software on smartphones:** "China's Algorithms of Repression: Reverse Engineering a Xinjiang Police Mass Surveillance App," Human Rights Watch, May 1, 2019.

53 **"or the Party":** "The China Cables," International Consortium of Investigative Journalists, Nov. 24, 2019.

53 **taken into custody:** Yael Grauer, "Revealed: Massive Chinese Police Database," *The Intercept*, Jan. 29, 2021.

53 **close to it:** Javier Parra-Arnau and Claude Castelluccia, "On the Cost-Effectiveness of Mass Surveillance," *IEEE Access* 6 (2018): 46538–46557.

55 **$100 million:** This figure is based on a 2018 estimate by researcher Adrian Zenz, cross-checked with budget data for sixty-five county-level government departments we culled from Xinjiang government websites and online documents that same year. Many of the original data sources are no longer available.

56 **family members inside:** Footage of this camp appears in a short documentary Josh made with *Wall Street Journal* video journalist Clément Bürge, "Life Inside China's Total Surveillance State," Dec. 21, 2017, https://www.youtube.com/watch?v=OQ5LnY21Hgc.

56 **custody buildings:** Jeremy Page, Eva Dou, and Josh Chin, "China's Uighur Camps Swell as Beijing Widens the Dragnet," *The Wall Street Journal*, Aug. 17, 2018; Shawn Zhang, "Satellite Imagery of Xinjiang 'Re-education Camp' No. 3," *Medium*, May 20, 2018.

57 **"standard firearms":** Ben Dooley, "Inside China's Internment Camps: Tear Gas, Tasers and Textbooks," Agence France-Presse, Oct. 25, 2018.

57 **"saying something wrong":** Nathan VanderKlippe, "'Everyone Was Silent, End-lessly Mute': Former Chinese Re-education Instructor Speaks Out," *The Globe and Mail*, Aug. 2, 2018.

58 **"rounded up":** Austin Ramzy and Chris Buckley, "'Absolutely No Mercy': Leaked Files Expose How China Organized Mass Detentions of Muslims," *The New York Times*, Nov. 16, 2019.

58 **Xinjiang's Muslim population:** Adrian Zenz, "'Thoroughly Reforming Them To-wards a Healthy Heart Attitude': China's Political Re-education Campaign in Xinjiang," *Central Asian Survey* 38, no. 1 (2019): 102–28.

58 **"attack on the Jews":** Jerome Cohen, "China Sends Uyghurs to Re-education Camps as a 'Preventive Measure,'" JeromeCohen.net, Mar. 27, 2018.

58 **in need of treatment:** "Xinjiang Political 'Re-education Camps' Treat Uyghurs 'Infected by Religious Extremism': CCP Youth League," Radio Free Asia, Aug. 8, 2018.

58 **reeducation facility:** Chris Buckley and Austin Ramzy, "China Is Detaining Muslims in Vast Numbers. The Goal: 'Transformation,'" *The New York Times*, Sept. 8, 2018.

59 **social unity:** James Leibold, "The Spectre of Insecurity: The CCP's Mass Internment Strategy in Xinjiang," *China Leadership Monitor*, Mar. 1, 2019.

59 **from the minorities:** Hu Angang and Hu Lianhe, "Di'erdai minzu zhengce: Cujin minzu jiaorongyiti he fanrongyiti," *Xinjiang Shifan Daxue Xuebao*, no. 5 (2011), http://www.shehui.pku.edu.cn/upload/editor/file/20180626/20180626195224_5647.pdf.

59 **"beneficial order":** James Leibold, "Hu the Uniter: Hu Lianhe and the Radical Turn in China's Xinjiang Policy," *China Brief* (Jamestown Foundation) 18, no. 16 (Oct. 10, 2018).

60 **"engineers of the human soul":** John Garnaut, "Engineers of the Soul: Ideology in Xi Jinping's China," transcript published by Sinocism.com, Jan. 17, 2019.

60 **"washing clean the brains":** Adrian Zenz, "'Wash Brains, Cleanse Hearts': Evidence from Chinese Government Documents About the Nature and Extent of Xinjiang's Extrajudicial Internment Campaign," *Journal of Political Risk*, Nov. 2019.

62 **or political activity:** Darren Byler, "Chinese Infrastructures of Population Management on the New Silk Road," in *Essays on the Rise of China and Its Implications*, ed. Abraham Denmark and Lucas Meyers (Washington, DC: Wilson Center, 2021), 7–34.

3. Man and Machine

In sketching the trajectory of Qian Xuesen's life, this chapter draws extensively from Iris Chang's *Thread of the Silkworm* and unpublished research into Qian's life conducted by Zuoyue Wang at California State Polytechnic University, Pomona. Thomas Rid's *The Rise of the Machines* and Ronald Kline's *The Cybernetics Moment* were valuable references for grasping the history and significance of cybernetics. Writings by the journalist Mara Hvistendahl and security analyst Samantha Hoffman were critical to understanding Qian's influence on the Communist Party and its systems of control.

71 **"ideology of machines":** Thomas Rid, *Rise of the Machines: A Cybernetic History* (New York: W. W. Norton, 2016), 6.

71 **"five divisions anywhere":** Quoted in Iris Chang, *Thread of the Silkworm* (New York: Basic Books, 1995), 200.

71 **"of this field":** Quoted in "Jet Propulsion Scientist Sailing to Red China: Dr. Hsue-Shen Tsien Ends Long, Honorable Career Here to Help People of Own Nation," *Los Angeles Times*, Sept. 18, 1955. A yellowed copy of the story is preserved behind plexiglas inside the Qian Xuesen Museum in Shanghai.

73 **without knowing it:** See Michael Schoenhals, *Spying for the People: Mao's Secret Agents, 1949–1967* (Cambridge: Cambridge University Press, 2013).

74 **"hoodwinking the state":** David Barsamian, "Amartya Sen," *The Progressive Magazine*, Sept. 29, 2011.

74 **top Party official:** Quoted in Yang Jisheng, *Tombstone: The Great Chinese Famine, 1958–1962*, translated by Stacy Mosher and Guo Jian (New York: Farrar, Straus and Giroux, 2012), 336.

75 **prone to chaos:** Norbert Wiener understood information as the polar opposite of entropy (or disorder). In *Cybernetics: Or Control and Communication in the Animal and the Machine*, 2nd ed. (Cambridge, MA: MIT Press, 1961), he wrote: "Just as the amount of information in a system is a measure of its organization, so the entropy is a measure of its disorganization; and the one is simply the negative of the other."

77 **a landmark text:** H. S. Tsien, *Engineering Cybernetics* (New York: McGraw-Hill, 1954), viii.

77 **"diseases of society":** See original introduction to the first edition of Norbert Wiener, *Cybernetics: Or Control and Communication in the Animal and the Machine* (New York: Wiley, 1948), 11.

78 **"work on time":** Quoted in Ida Hoos, "A Critical Review of Systems Analysis: The California Experience," Internal Working Paper No. 89, Social Sciences Project, University of California, Berkeley, Dec. 1968, 2.

78 **"pumping systems":** Hoos, "A Critical Review of Systems Analysis," 7.

78 **automatically self-correcting:** Quoted in Wang Feiyue, "Cong gongcheng kongzhi dao shehui guanli: Kongzhilun Cybernetics benyuan de geren renshi yu zhanwang," *Kongzhi Lilun yu Yingyong* 21, no. 12 (Dec. 2014), 1624.

79 **out of control:** An extensive account of Song's role in the creation of China's family-planning regime appears in Susan Greenhalgh, "Missile Science, Population Science: The Origins of China's One-Child Policy," *China Quarterly* 182 (June 2005).

80 **"flow of history"**: Song Jian, "Xitong gongcheng yu guanli tizhi de gaige," *People's Daily*, Sept. 13, 1984, cited in Samantha R. Hoffman, "Programming China: The Communist Party's Autonomic Approach to Managing State Security," PhD thesis, University of Nottingham, 2017.

81 **"disorder, chaos, and collapse"**: Qian Xuesen, "Shehui zhuyi wenmin de xietiao fazhan xuyao shehui zhuyi zhengzhi wenmin jianshe," *Zhengzhixue Yanjiu*, no. 5 (1989), 3.

81 **the Milky Way**: Qian Xuesen, "Yige kexue xin lingyu—Kaifang de fuzaju xitong yiqi fangfa lun," *Ziran Zazhi*, no. 1 (1990), 526.

82 **then-president Jiang Zemin**: See Pang Yuanzheng, "Yige yingxiangle jidai zhongyang lingdao jiti de zhongyao sixiang—lun Qian Xuesen shehui xitong gongcheng sixiang yiqi lilun gongxian," *Liaoning Xueyuan Xuebao*, no. 1 (2014).

83 **on the Uyghurs**: See Greg Walton, *China's Golden Shield: Corporations and the Development of Surveillance Technology in the People's Republic of China* (Montreal: Rights & Democracy, 2001).

83 **"very original idea"**: From "Hu Jintao kanwang kexuejia Qian Xuesen Wu Wenjun jishi," Xinhua, Jan. 19, 2008.

84 **"the new god"**: Mara Hvistendahl, "A Revered Rocket Scientist Set in Motion China's Mass Surveillance of Its Citizens," *Science*, Mar. 12, 2018.

4. The China Dream

88 **"in modern times"**: Full text in translation available from the *China Copyright and Media* blog: https://chinacopyrightandmedia.wordpress.com/2012/11/29/speech-at-the-road-to-rejuvenation/.

89 **to extinguish them:** Full text in translation available from the Asia Society's China File: http://www.chinafile.com/document-9-chinafile-translation.

89 **"as could be":** Jude Blanchette, *China's New Red Guards* (New York: Oxford University Press, 2019), Kindle Location 3138.

90 **"advanced technology":** Chris Buckley and Paul Mozur, "What Keeps Xi Jinping Awake at Night," *The New York Times*, May 11, 2018.

91 **"Jello to the wall":** The Jello line was the work of Clinton administration speech writer Paul Orzulak, who told us he had come up with it after hearing administration officials talk about how hard it was to "nail China down" on anything. When Orzulak tried it out in the draft of a speech for Clinton's national security advisor, Sandy Berger, another White House speechwriter scribbled his admiration in the margins: "[ZING!!!! Bravo!]." The decision was made to save it for Clinton's speech. See Clinton Presidential Records, National Security Council collection, OA/Box no. 4022, Clinton Presidential Library.

91 **"but losing the war":** Loretta Chao and Jason Dean, "China Is Losing a War over Internet," *The Wall Street Journal*, Dec. 31, 2009.

92 **"controls the initiative":** Quoted in "Guojia dashuju zhanlue—Xi Jinping yu 'Shisanwu' shisi da zhanlue," Xinhua, Nov. 12, 2015, http://www.xinhuanet.com/politics/2015–11/12/c_128422782.htm.

92 **"safe and efficient":** Full translation of China's AI development plan is available from New America: https://www.newamerica.org/cybersecurity-initiative/digichina/blog/full-translation-chinas-new-generation-artificial-intelligence-development-plan-2017/.

93 **$2.1 billion:** Jessica Batke and Marieke Ohlberg, "State of Surveillance," ChinaFile, Asia Society, Oct. 30, 2020.

93 **would largely achieve:** From "Guanyu jiaqiang gonggong anquan shipin jiankong jianshe lianwang yingyong gongzuo de ruogan yijian," National Development and Reform Commission, 2015 (No. 996). Original deleted online, available here: https://web.archive.org/web/20160616221428/https://www.ndrc.gov.cn/zcfb/zcfbtz/201505/t20150513_691578.html.

94 **"prevent risks":** Remarks delivered during an internal Politburo meeting on

big data strategy in Dec. 2017. "Xi Jinping: Shishi guojia dashuju zhanlue jiakuai jianshe shuzi zhongguo," Xinhua, Dec. 9, 2017, http://www.xinhuanet.com/2017–12 /09/c_1122084706.htm.

97 **paper in 2015:** Lü Zhiqing, "Dashuju shidai xia zhengfu zhili fanshi chonggou," *Jingji Yanjiu Cankao* no. 45 (2015) 45.

97 **mechanism of society:** Di Yun, "Zhongguo dashuju zhili moshi chuangxin ji qi fazhan lujing yanjiu," *Dianzi Zhengfu* no. 8 (2018).

97 **socialism's superiority:** Li Huaijie and Xia Hu, "Dashuju shidai gaoxiao sixiang zhengzhi jiaoyu moshi chuangxin tanjiu," *Sixiang Zhengzhi Yanjiu* no. 9 (2015).

98 **on Xi's shelf:** Christoph Scheuermann and Bernhard Zand, "Pedro Domingos on the Arms Race in Artificial Intelligence," *Der Spiegel*, Apr. 16, 2018.

99 **"leads the world":** "'Tian wang' wang shenme," *Renmin zhoukan*, no. 20 (2017) 20, https://web.archive.org/web/20200515220622/;http://paper.people.com.cn/rmzk/ht%20 ml/2017-11/20/content_1825998.htm.

100 **"20th-century totalitarians":** Francis Fukuyama, "What Kind of Regime Does China Have?" *The American Interest*, May 18, 2020.

5. Little Brothers

This chapter is the product of years of covering China's internet industry and speaking to dozens of staff and investors within and close to the sector. Chinese lawyers, who wish to remain unnamed, were especially helpful in explaining the nuances of content and data regulation.

102 **origami decorations:** Alibaba press release, Aug. 3, 2021, https://www.alibabagroup .com/en/news/press_pdf/p210803.pdf.

103 **"judge the future":** From "Ma Yun: Shuju shidai shi yuce weilai de shidai," CNR, Oct. 22, 2016, http://tech.cnr.cn/techgd/20161022/t20161022_523213660.shtml.

104 **"finally find suspects":** From "Ma Huateng gei 150 wan zhengfa ganjing shan-gle yitangke jiang ruhe yonghao heikeji," Sina, June 10, 2017, https://tech.sina.com.cn /roll/2017–06–11/doc-ifyfzhpq6540913.shtml.

104 **through mobile devices:** All data on Chinese internet users comes from the 2020 edition of the official "China Statistical Report on Internet Development," published in Feb. 2021 by the China Internet Network Information Center, http://www.cnnic.cn /hlwfzyj/hlwxzbg/hlwtjbg/202102/P020210203334633480104.pdf.

105 **with Chinese alternatives:** In 2013, a magazine published by the *People's Daily* warned in a cover story that the "eight guardian warriors" had "seamlessly infiltrated China." It illustrated the story with an image borrowed from the famous "He's Watching You" World War II–era American propaganda poster of a scowling Axis soldier. The full list included Cisco Systems, IBM, Google, Qualcomm, Intel, Apple, Oracle, and Microsoft. See Carlos Tejada, "Microsoft, the 'Guardian Warriors' and China's Cyber-security Fears," *The Wall Street Journal*, July 29, 2014.

107 **MasterCard that year:** "2020 nian zhifu tixi yunxin zongti qingkuang," Zhong-guo Renmin Yinhang [People's Bank of China], Mar. 24, 2021, http://www.pbc.gov .cn/goutongjiaoliu/113456/113469/4213347/2021032414491874847.pdf.

109 **"big and strong":** Full Chinese transcript published as "Xi Jinping zai wangxin gongzuo zuotanhui shang de jianghua quanwen fabiao," Xinhua, Apr. 24, 2015, http:// www.xinhuanet.com//politics/2016–04/25/c_1118731175.htm.

112 **fill the gap:** See Chuin-Wei Yap, "A Missing Piece in China's Economy: Consumer Credit Ratings," *The Wall Street Journal*, Sept. 24, 2017.

113 **the average gamer:** In February 2015, Sesame Credit's technology director, Li Yingyun, told *Caixin* magazine: "Someone who plays video games for 10 hours a day, for example, would be considered an idle person, and someone who frequently buys diapers would be considered as probably a parent, who on balance is more likely to

have a sense of responsibility." The original interview is no longer available online but is quoted by Celia Hatton in "China's 'Social Credit': Beijing Sets Up Huge System," BBC News, Oct. 26, 2015, https://www.bbc.com/news/world-asia-china-34592186.

6. Datatopia

114 **"celestial regions":** Quoted in Shen Hong, "An English Missionary's Contribution to the Historical Memories of Hangzhou: A Study of Arthur Evans Moule's Writings and Photographs," in *Creative Spaces: Seeking the Dynamics of Change in China*, ed. D. Gimpel, B. Nielsen, and P. Bailey (Copenhagen: Nordic Institute of Asian Studies Press, 2012).

116 **"smart cities":** From "Xinxing zhihui chengshi jianshe qidai gengduo de 'zhibian,'" *Keji Ribao*, May 24, 2021, https://tech.chinadaily.com.cn/a/202105/24/WS60ac554fa3101e7ce97516b4.html.

122 **"avoid misunderstandings":** Te-Ping Chen and Li Jie, "Chinese Urban Enforcer Hopes Google Glass Will Prevent Violence," *The Wall Street Journal*, Apr. 21, 2014, https://www.wsj.com/articles/BL-CJB-21714.

124 **"urban operations":** Wang's speech is quoted in "Hangzhou to Build 'City Brain' with Alibaba and Foxconn," *People's Daily Online*, Oct. 13, 2016, http://en.people.cn/n3/2016/1013/c90000–9126738.html.

126 **International Data Corporation:** Data from "Zhongguo zhihui chengshi jianshe zai yiqing wenkong xingshixia jixu baochi gaozhiliang fazhan," International Data Corporation, Dec. 22, 2020, https://www.idc.com/getdoc.jsp?containerId=prCHC47212520.

7. Digital Silk Road

For the portions of this chapter that deal with Uganda's history, culture, and politics, we drew heavily on Andrew Rice's excellent *The Teeth May Smile but the Heart Does Not Forget* and Richard Reid's *A History of Modern Uganda*.

132 **"corporate social responsibility":** From a Chinese Foreign Ministry press release on Sept. 21, 2015: "Zhu wuganda dashi Zhao Yali peitong Musaiweini zongtong chuxi Huawei juanzeng huodong," https://www.mfa.gov.cn/web/zwbd_673032/gzhd_673042/t1298492.shtml.

134 **rest of the country:** Joe Parkinson, Nicholas Bariyo, and Josh Chin, "Huawei Technicians Helped African Governments Spy on Political Opponents," *The Wall Street Journal*, Aug. 15, 2019.

134 **a decade later:** Jennifer Valentino-DeVries, Julia Angwin, and Steve Stecklow, "Document Trove Exposes Surveillance Methods," *The Wall Street Journal*, Nov. 19, 2011.

135 **across 45 countries:** Most of the data in this section comes from the Chinese state media or the companies' websites and marketing materials. Huawei's supplying of systems in Belgrade was reported by James Kynge, Valerie Hopkns, Helen Warrell, and Katherin Hille in "Since Then, Chinese Surveillance Systems Have Expanded Across the Globe with Breathtaking Speed," *The Financial Times*, June 8, 2021.

135 **worldwide by 2020:** Sheena Chestnut Greitens, "Dealing with Demand for China's Global Surveillance Exports," Global China: Assessing China's Growing Role in the World, Brookings Institution, Apr. 2020.

135 **$50 billion by 2025:** "Worldwide Video Surveillance Camera Forecast, 2020–2025," IDC, July 14, 2020, https://www.idc.com/getdoc.jsp?containerId=prUS46694720. And updated version (July 2021), https://www.idc.com/getdoc.jsp?containerId=US46354621.

136 **around the world:** Sheridan Prasso, "China's Digital Silk Road Is Looking More Like an Iron Curtain," *Bloomberg Businessweek*, Jan. 10, 2019.

137 **a resounding "maybe":** Nicholas Thompson and Ian Bremmer, "The AI Cold War Threatens Us All," *Wired*, Oct. 23, 2018.

137 **"change of guards":** Quoted in Andrew Rice, *The Teeth May Smile but the Heart Does Not Forget: Murder and Memory in Uganda* (New York: Henry Holt, 2009), 9.
138 **"Hotels are known":** Details of the "Fungua Macho" operation are laid out in "For My God and My President: State Surveillance in Uganda," Privacy International, October 2015.
139 **"where we are today":** The full Chinese text of Ren Zhiqiang's 2006 speech to Huawei staff in Sudan, Congo, and Benin is posted on the Huawei public online forum for employees, http://app.huawei.com/paper/newspaper/newsBookCateInfo.do?method=showDigestInfo&infoId=13436&sortId=8&search_result=1.
140 **"send their experts":** Steven Feldstein, *The Rise of Digital Repression: How Technology Is Reshaping Power, Politics and Resistance* (New York: Oxford University Press, 2021), 203.
149 **in phase two:** Museveni posted the photos of his visit to the surveillance center on Twitter. Yoweri Museveni (@KagutaMuseveni), "Commissioned the first phase of the National CCTV System at the Police Headquarters in Naguru, Kampala. Kampala Metropolitan alone has 83 monitoring centres, 522 operators under 50 commanders," Twitter, Nov. 29, 2019, https://twitter.com/KagutaMuseveni/status/1200120752114196481.
149 **an ominous headline:** Morris Kiruga, *The Africa Report*, Nov. 19, 2020.
149 **"are looking for":** Museveni posted video of the speech on his personal Twitter account. Yoweri Museveni (@KagutaMuseveni), "Uganda is stable and the NRM government will not allow those seeking to mess with this stability to get away with it," Twitter, Nov. 20, 2020, 1:51 A.M., https://twitter.com/KagutaMuseveni/status/1329678653534433285.
150 **her congressional testimony:** Jessica Chen Weiss, "A World Safe for Autocracy?" *Foreign Affairs*, July/August 2019, https://www.foreignaffairs.com/articles/china/2019-06-11/world-safe-autocracy.
151 **"few strings attached":** Steven Feldstein, *The Rise of Digital Repression: How Technology Is Reshaping Power, Politics and Resistance* (New York: Oxford University Press, 2021), 49.
152 **for his protection:** Quoted in "Uganda Opposition Leader Bobi Wine Says Military Enters Home," Associated Press, Jan. 16, 2021.
152 **the country's history:** Rodney Muhumuza, "Uganda Faces Pressure to End Bobi Wine's House Arrest," Associated Press, Jan. 22, 2021.
152 **"court of the people":** Rodney Muhumuza, "Uganda's Wine Withdraws Court Challenge to Election Results," Associated Press, Feb. 23, 2021.
152 **"own national conditions":** From "Wuganda zongtong Musaiweini huijian Yang Jiechi," Xinhua, Feb. 22, 2021, http://www.xinhuanet.com/2021-02/22/c_1127122518.htm.
153 **human rights abuses:** Sheena Chestnut Greitens and Edward Goldring, "Global Use of Chinese Surveillance Technology: Causes and Effects," paper prepared for ISA annual conference, Apr. 2021.

8. Partners in Pre-Crime

155 **yet to discover:** Intel, "Intel to Build 300mm Wafer Fabrication Facility in China," press release, Mar. 26, 2007.
155 **"be a rapprochement":** Paul Otellini interview, *Charlie Rose*, PBS, Feb. 26, 2010.
156 **"interesting going forward":** Jonathan Shieber, "Intel Bets on China's Growing Surveillance Industry with NetPosa," *Dow Jones Venturewire*, Nov. 1, 2010.
156 **research firm Omdia:** "Omdia: Coronavirus Threatens to Disrupt Global Video Surveillance Market," March 3, 2020, Securityinfowatch.com, https://www.securityinfowatch.com/video-surveillance/news/21127827/omdia-coronavirus-threatens-to-disrupt-global-video-surveillance-market.
157 **"safe city" industry:** China Security and Protection Industry Association, "2018 Namelist for the Companies with Excellent Industry Solutions for 'Safe Construction,'" Nov. 5, 2018, http://news.21csp.com.cn/special/PAJS2018/c727/201811/11374827.html.

159 **enthusiastically toward it:** Greg Walton, *China's Golden Shield: Corporations and the Development of Surveillance Technology in the People's Republic of China* (Montreal: Rights & Democracy, 2001).

160 **"and other hostiles":** Don Clark and Loretta Chao, "Cisco Faces Lawsuits, Criticism over Past China Activities," *The Wall Street Journal*, July 5, 2011.

161 **considered crimes:** Rebecca MacKinnon, *Consent of the Networked: The Worldwide Struggle for Internet Freedom* (New York: Basic Books, 2012).

163 **the company's website:** China Security and Protection Industry Association, "Zhuanfang Dongfang Wangli dongshizhang Liu Guang: zuo zhihui chengshi de jiagouzhe," Netposa.com, Nov. 17, 2011, https://www.netposa.com/2011/1117/News/614.html.

163 **prevent and deter crimes:** Intel Capital, "Investing in Global Innovation: Stories of Intel Capital's Impact on Portfolio Companies," slide deck (2013), 12, https://www .intel.com/content/dam/www/public/cn/zh/pdfs/intel-capital-storybook.pdf.

164 **China every year:** Liza Lin and Josh Chin, "U.S. Tech Companies Prop Up China's Vast Surveillance Network," *The Wall Street Journal*, Nov. 26, 2019.

165 **orders of magnitude:** Edwin Black, *IBM and the Holocaust: The Strategic Alliance Between Nazi Germany and America's Most Powerful Corporation* (Washington, DC: Dialog Press, 2012), 24, 25.

166 **"without skipping a note":** Ibid., 371.

166 **"once the smoke cleared":** Ibid., 375.

167 **other limited partners:** Ryan Mac, Rosalind Adams, and Megha Rajagopalan, "US Universities and Retirees Are Funding the Technology Behind China's Surveillance State," Buzzfeed News, May 30, 2019.

170 **"avenues of discovery":** "MIT and SenseTime Announce Effort to Advance Artificial Intelligence Research," MIT News, Feb. 28, 2018, https://news.mit.edu/2018 /mit-sensetime-announce-effort-advance-artificial-intelligence-research-0228# .WpaxVsyFBEE.facebook.

171 **human genetic records:** Wenxin Fan, Natasha Khan, and Liza Lin, "China Snares Innocent and Guilty Alike to Build World's Biggest DNA Database," *The Wall Street Journal*, Dec. 26, 2017.

172 **Uyghurs in Xinjiang:** Sui-Lee Wee, "China Uses DNA to Track Its People, with the Help of American Expertise," *The New York Times*, Feb. 21, 2019.

172 **"a police state":** Zahra Chaudhry, "'Hold Your Institution Accountable': The Uighur Crisis, Genetic Research, and Yale," *The Politic*, Feb. 10, 2020.

174 **Germany, or Japan:** Caroline S. Wagner, Lutz Bornmann, and Loet Leydesdorff, "Recent Developments in China-U.S. Cooperation in Science," *Minerva* 53 (2015): 199–214.

174 **"catch that automatically":** Chaudhry, "'Hold Your Institution Accountable.'"

9. Homeland Security

180 **on Chinese streets:** Clare Garvie and Laura M. Moy, "America Under Watch," Center on Privacy and Technology at Georgetown Law, May 16, 2019.

180 **scanned as well:** Davey Alba, "The US Government Will Be Scanning Your Face at 20 Top Airports, Documents Show," Buzzfeed News, Mar. 11, 2019.

180 **police in Minneapolis:** From a United States Government Accountability Office report, "Facial Recognition Technology: Federal Law Enforcement Agencies Should Better Assess Privacy and Other Risks" (GAO-21-518), June 3, 2021.

181 **went too far:** Polling data from David W. Moore, "Public Little Concerned About Patriot Act," Gallup, Sept. 9, 2003, https://news.gallup.com/poll/9205/public-little -concerned-about-patriot-act.aspx; Darren K. Carlson, "Liberty vs. Security: Public Mixed on Patriot Act," Gallup, July 19, 2005, https://news.gallup.com/poll/17392/liberty -vs-security-public-mixed-patriot-act.aspx.

181 **United States history:** Christian Parenti, *The Soft Cage: Surveillance in America from Slavery to the War on Terror* (New York: Basic Books, 2003), 76.

183 **230 million people:** From "Who's Behind ICE? The Tech and Data Companies Fueling Deportations," Mijente, Immigrant Defense Project, and the National Immigration Project of the National Lawyers Guild, Oct. 2018.

183 **total cost of $60:** Sahil Chinoy, "We Built an 'Unbelievable' (but Legal) Facial Recognition Machine," *The New York Times*, Apr. 16, 2019.

184 **United States or abroad:** From "New York City Police Department and Microsoft Partner to Bring Real-Time Crime Prevention and Counterterrorism Technology Solution to Global Law Enforcement Agencies," Microsoft News Center, Aug. 8, 2012.

184 **color of jacket:** New York's DAS is documented in great detail by Ángel Díaz in "New York City Police Department Surveillance Technology," Brennan Center for Justice, Oct. 7, 2019.

188 **"embedded in mathematics":** Cathy O'Neil, *Weapons of Math Destruction: How Big Data Increases Inequality and Threatens Democracy* (New York: Crown/Archetype, 2016), 21.

192 **"missing or distorted data":** James O'Neill, "How Facial Recognition Makes You Safer," *The New York Times,* June 9, 2019.

193 **the Hispanic community:** See June 21, 2018, open letter from Privacy International to Thomson Reuters CEO James Smith, https://www.documentcloud.org/documents/4546858-PI-Letter-TR-21–06.html.

194 **around the United States:** Drew Harwell, "Home-Security Cameras Have Become a Fruitful Resource for Law Enforcement—and a Fatal Risk," *The Washington Post,* Mar. 2, 2021.

194 **caught on camera:** Ibid.

194 **facial image database:** According to Government Accountability Office testimony in front of the House Committee on the Judiciary's Subcommittee on Crime, Terrorism, and Homeland Security in July 2021, the FBI's Next Generation Identification Interstate Photo System allows users to search a database of over 40 million photos. See https://docs.house.gov/meetings/JU/JU08/20210713/113906/HMTG-117-JU08-Wstate-GoodwinG-20210713.PDF.

197 **"safety and privacy":** From "NYPD Announces Facial Recognition Policy," New York Police Department, Mar. 13, 2020.

197 **in 2019 alone:** See "S.T.O.P. Condemns NYPD For 22K Facial Recognition Searches," Surveillance Technology Oversight Project, Oct. 23, 2020.

197 **chosen to pursue:** Anderson Cooper, "Police Using Facial Recognition Amidst Claims of Wrongful Arrests," *60 Minutes,* CBS, May 17, 2021.

10. Privacy Redefined

203 **until the 1990s:** See Yang Wang, Huichuan Xia, and Yun Huang, "Examining American and Chinese Internet Users' Contextual Privacy Preferences of Behavioral Advertising," Proceedings of the 19th ACM Conference on Computer-Supported Cooperative Work and Social Computing, Feb. 2016.

204 **articulate what it means:** Daniel J. Solove, *Understanding Privacy* (Cambridge, MA: Harvard University Press, 2008), 1.

204 **"The press is overstepping":** Louis Brandeis and Samuel Warren, "The Right to Privacy," *Harvard Law Review,* Dec. 15, 1890. In *Understanding Privacy* (Cambridge, MA: Harvard University Press, 2008), Daniel Solove writes: "The development of new technologies kept concern about privacy smoldering for centuries, but the profound proliferation of new information technologies during the twentieth century—especially the rise of the computer—made privacy erupt into a frontline issue around the world" (4).

204 **"data was collected":** Solove, *Understanding Privacy,* 118.

207 **Chinese tech companies:** As of this writing, video of Robin Li's comments is available on Tencent Video at https://v.qq.com/x/page/w0614r4qgvo.html.

207 **"spend a little cash":** Josh Chin, "Chinese Data Leaker Seeks to Expose Personal-Information Trade," *The Wall Street Journal,* May 13, 2016.

207 **"running naked"**: Li Yuan, "No Privacy: Chinese Feel They're 'Running Naked' Online," *The Wall Street Journal*, Mar. 10, 2017.

208 **city of Guangzhou:** "Many Think Facial Recognition Technologies Are Being Abused: Survey," *Global Times*, Oct. 19, 2020.

208 **safer and more convenient:** "Renlian shibie luodi changjing guancha baogao (2019)," Nandu Personal Information Protection Research Center, Dec. 5, 2019. Screenshots available here: http://www.cbdio.com/BigData/2020–01/07/content_6154002 .htm.

209 **announcing the rules:** Eva Dou, "China Built the World's Largest Facial Recognition System. Now, It's Getting Camera-Shy," *The Washington Post*, July 30, 2021.

211 **lived in Xinjiang:** Victor Gevers (@0xDUDE), "Inside China's 'thought transformation' camps by @TheJohnSudworth of the @BBCNews," Twitter, June 21, 2019, 6:58 A.M., https://twitter.com/0xDUDE/status/1142024106109558784.

211 **"internet cafe" and "mosque":** Zak Doffman, "Interview—Meet Victor Gevers, the Ethical Hacker Who Exposed 'BreedReady' and 'SenseNets,'" *Forbes*, Mar. 13, 2019.

212 **"consumer credit data":** Lingling Wei, "China Blocked Jack Ma's Ant IPO After Investigation Revealed Likely Beneficiaries," *The Wall Street Journal*, Feb. 16, 2021.

11. The Panopticon and Potemkin AI

For background on the Social Credit System, we relied heavily on an extended interview with Lin Junyue, data from the Chinese national planning agency's China Economic Information Network, and outside research: Martin Chorzempa, Paul Triolo, and Samm Sacks, "China's Social Credit System: A Mark of Progress or a Threat to Privacy?" Peterson Institute of International Economics, June 2018; Rogier Creemers, "China's Social Credit System: An Evolving Practice of Control," Institute for Area Studies, Leiden University, May 2018; "Understanding China's Social Credit System," Trivium China, Sept. 2019; Xin Dai, "Toward a Reputation State: The Social Credit System Project of China," Peking University Law School, June 2018; work by Samantha Hoffman at the Australian Strategic Policy Institute; and work by Yale University's Jeremy Daum.

215 **relied on deception:** Philip Steadman, "Samuel Bentham's Panopticon," *Journal of Bentham Studies* 14, no. 1 (2012): 1–30.

215 **six floors of prisoners:** Simon Werrett, "Potemkin and the Panopticon: Samuel Bentham and the Architecture of Absolutism in Eighteenth Century Russia," *Journal of Bentham Studies* 2, no. 1 (1999).

216 **"maintenance of social order":** The full quote reads: "Bentham laid down the principle that power should be visible and unverifiable. Visible: the inmate will constantly have before his eyes the tall outline of the central tower from which he is spied upon. Unverifiable: the inmate must never know whether he is being looked at at any one moment; but he must be sure that he may always be so." Michel Foucault, *Discipline and Punish: The Birth of the Prison*, trans. Alan Sheridan (New York: Vintage, 1977), 195.

218 **"Abracadabra! Alakazam!":** Jathan Sadowski, "Potemkin AI," *Real Life*, Aug. 6, 2018.

218 **behavior of friends:** Jay Stanley, "China's Nightmarish Citizen Scores Are a Warning for Americans," American Civil Liberties Union, Oct. 5, 2015.

219 **"engine of economic growth":** From "Zhongguo xinyong tixi jianshe diyi ren," Shenzhen Special Zone Daily, Sept. 9, 2012.

219 **privacy movement:** Malgorzata Wozniacka and Snigdha Sen, "Credit Scores— What You Should Know About Your Own," *Frontline*, PBS, Nov. 23, 2004.

220 **"entirety of society":** A full English translation of the meeting decision is available from "Central Committee of the Chinese Communist Party Decision Concerning Deepening Cultural Structural Reform," *China Copyright and Media* blog, Oct. 18, 2011, updated Feb. 26, 2014, https://chinacopyrightandmedia.wordpress.com/2011/10/18/central

-committee-of-the-chinese-communist-party-decision-concerning-deepening-cultural-structural-reform/.

220 **invisible monster stalking you:** Andrew Jacobs, "A Rare Look into One's Life on File in China," *The New York Times*, Mar. 15, 2015.

228 **"the required standard":** Jeremy Page and Eva Dou, "In Sign of Resistance, Chinese Balk at Using Apps to Snitch on Neighbors," *The Wall Street Journal*, Dec. 29, 2017.

228 **space of a year:** See, for example, Tong Jiangping, "Yuhang gong'an ronghe zhihui pingtai shixian shequ jingwu xin tupo," *Yuhang Chenbao*, Mar. 19, 2019.

229 **their legal obligations:** Liu Yuanyuan, "2682 wanrenci yin shixin bei xianzhi chengji," *Keji Ribao*, July 17, 2019.

230 **"prevented those events":** From *Tous Surveillés: 7 Milliards de Suspects*, directed by Ludovic Gaillard and Sylvain Louvet, CAPA Presse, 2020, https://www.youtube.com/watch?v=jPDoi6U4vwU&t=5s.

230 **"not the government system":** Genia Kostka, "China's Social Credit Systems and Public Opinion: Explaining High Levels of Approval." *New Media and Society* 21, no. 7 (2019): 1565–93.

12. Contagion

235 **country at any time:** Lu Keyan, "Fa duanxin kecha ziji de xingzong guiji, shi shenme jishu zai bangmang," Jiemian Xinwen, Feb. 19, 2020, https://tech.sina.cn/2020-02-19/detail-iimxyqvz4130813.d.html.

235 **their target lists:** Zhao Chao, "Gongxinbu: Dianxin dashuju ke tongji fenxi renyuan liudong qingkuang zhuli yiqing fangkong," Renminwang, Feb. 15, 2020, http://tc.people.com.cn/n1/2020/0215/c183008-31588491.html.

237 **"one of analysis":** Michel Foucault, *Discipline and Punish: The Birth of the Prison*, trans. Alan Sheridan (New York: Vintage, 1977), 197.

238 **February 2020:** Liza Lin, "How China Slowed Coronavirus: Lockdowns, Surveillance, Enforcers," *The Wall Street Journal*, Mar. 10, 2020.

239 **picture of stability:** Lingling Wei and Chao Deng, "China's Coronavirus Response Is Questioned: 'Everyone Was Blindly Optimistic,'" *The Wall Street Journal*, Jan. 24, 2020.

241 **turned to green:** "Lüma, zhuhe ni tongguo zhengzhi tijian," *The Paper*, May 2, 2020, https://mp.weixin.qq.com/s/cFnp_5cgYnQHfYyXeqG0cQ.

241 **overtime work culture:** Ye Ruolin, "City's Plan for Permanent 'Health Codes' Sparks Online Backlash," *Sixth Tone*, May 25, 2020.

243 **fall from grace:** See, for example, Abraham Denmark, "Will the Coronavirus Be Xi's Chernobyl?" *Asia Dispatches* (Wilson Center), Mar. 10, 2020.

243 **around the government:** Chuncheng Liu, "Chinese Public's Support for COVID-19 Surveillance," *Surveillance and Society* 19, no. 1 (2021), https://papers.ssrn.com/sol3/papers.cfm?abstract_id=3799322.

244 **"may be necessary":** Quoted in Kristen Grind, Robert McMillan, and Anna Wilde Mathews, "To Track Virus, Governments Weigh Surveillance Tools That Push Privacy Limits," *The Wall Street Journal*, Mar. 17, 2020.

245 **health was inevitable:** Bruno Maçães, "Only Surveillance Can Save Us from Coronavirus," *Foreign Policy*, Apr. 10, 2020.

247 **in August 2020:** Remarks delivered at the *Priv8: Digital Summit on the Future of Privacy*, March 25, 2021, https://www.youtube.com/watch?v=jxDoZ_Z4TwE.

248 **in June 2021:** Huang Yanzhong, "The Myth of Authoritarian Superiority: China's Response to Covid-19 Revisited," *China Leadership Monitor*, June 1, 2021.

13. New Order?

252 **and semiconductors:** See Liza Lin, "China's Trillion-Dollar Campaign Fuels a Tech Race with the U.S.," *The Wall Street Journal*, June 11, 2020.

252 **"bad grades":** Vidushi Marda and Shazeda Ahmed, "Emotional Entanglement: China's Emotion Recognition Market and Its Implications for Human Rights," *Article 19*, Jan. 2021.

252 **Yellow River:** Paul Mozur, "One Month, 500,000 Face Scans: How China Is Using A.I. to Profile a Minority," *The New York Times*, Apr. 14, 2019.

252 **around the world:** See "Dahua and Hikvision Co-author Racial and Ethnic PRC Police Standards," *IPVM*, Mar. 30, 2021.

253 **"West is declining":** Xuan Yan, "Women wei shenme nenggou chenggong," *People's Daily*, Sept. 27, 2021, http://paper.people.com.cn/rmrb/html/2021-09/27/nw.D110000renmrb_20210927_9-01.htm.

256 **of the United States:** Megha Rajagopalan and Alison Killing, "China Can Lock Up a Million Muslims in Xinjiang at Once," Buzzfeed News, July 21, 2021.

257 **"single nodal point":** Zeng Jingyan and Wang Lixiong, "Imagining the Digitalisation of Politics: A Conversation with Wang Lixiong," *Made in China Journal*, July–Sept. 2018.

257 **China's surveillance exports:** Sheena Chestnut Greitens, "Dealing with the Demand for China's Global Surveillance Exports," Global China: Assessing China's Growing Role in the World, Brookings Institution, Apr. 2020.

258 **"cannot tolerate complexity":** Anne Applebaum, *Twilight of Democracy: The Seductive Allure of Authoritarianism* (New York: Knopf Doubleday, 2020), 16.

259 **after the attack:** Kashmir Hill, "The Facial-Recognition App Clearview Sees a Spike in Use After Capitol Attack," *The New York Times*, live briefing, Jan. 9, 2021.

259 **"shows its promise":** Floyd Abrams and Lee Wolosky, "The Promise and Peril of Facial Recognition," *The Wall Street Journal*, Jan. 13, 2021.

260 **to preempt them:** Mark Andrejevic and Kelly Gates, "Big Data Surveillance: Introduction," *Surveillance and Society* 12, no. 2 (2014): 185–96.

261 **"could be protesting":** Testimony of Robert Williams, hearing on "Facial Recognition Technology: Examining its Use by Law Enforcement," July 13, 2020, https://docs.house.gov/meetings/JU/JU08/20210713/113906/HMTG-117-JU08-Wstate-WilliamsR-20210713.pdf.

Epilogue

265 **police basement:** See, for example, "China: Voice Biometric Collection Threatens Privacy," Human Rights Watch, Oct. 22, 2017.

266 **December 19, 2017:** Josh Chin and Clément Bürge, "Twelve Days in Xinjiang: How China's Surveillance State Overwhelms Daily Life," *The Wall Street Journal*, Dec. 19, 2017.

268 **members of society:** Eva Dou and Josh Chin, "China: Xinjiang Camps Are Actually Vocational Schools for Criminals," *The Wall Street Journal*, Aug. 13, 2018.

271 **questions in Mandarin:** Alexandra Ma, "This Man's Family Vanished in China's Most Oppressed Region. The Next Time He Saw His Son Was 2 Years Later, in a Chinese Propaganda Video," *Business Insider*, Feb. 6, 2019.

271 **"atmosphere at home":** "Quanguo tongchou xianyu nei chengxiang yiwu jiaoyu yitihua gaige fazhan xianchang tuijinhui: jiaoliu cailiao," *Jiaoyubu Jichu Jiaoyuci*, Dec. 2017, http://www.moe.gov.cn/jyb_xwfb/xw_zt/moe_357/jyzt_2016nztzl/ztzl_xyncs/ztzl_xy_dxjy/201801/W020180109353888301306.pdf.

272 **war on terror:** "China Issues White Paper on Anti-Terrorism, Human Rights Protection in Xinjiang," Xinhua, Mar. 18, 2019, http://www.xinhuanet.com/english/2019-03/18/c_137904167.htm.

272 **was going strong:** Some details of this gathering are altered to protect the relatives of participants.

273 **"come and go":** Ben Blanchard, "China Says Pace of Xinjiang 'Education' Will Slow, but Defends Camps," Reuters, Jan. 6, 2019.

275 **their menstrual cycles:** See, for example, Matthew Hill, David Campanale, and

Joel Gunter, "'Their Goal Is to Destroy Everyone': Uighur Camp Detainees Allege Systematic Rape," BBC News, Feb. 2, 2021.

275 **4.5 million by 2040:** Cate Cadell, "China Policies Could Cut Millions of Uyghur Births in Xinjiang," Reuters, June 7, 2021.

276 **more forcefully intervene:** The Uyghur Tribunal, "Uyghur Tribunal Judgment: Summary Form" (Dec. 9, 2021), 55, https://uyghurtribunal.com/wp-content/uploads /2021/12/UT-judgment-version-for-approval-by-GN-07.25–2.pdf.

277 **"a complete lie":** See "Uighurs: Chinese Foreign Minister Says Genocide Claims 'Absurd,'" BBC News, Mar. 7, 2021.

277 **"completely correct":** See Chun Han Wong, "Xi Says China Will Continue Efforts to Assimilate Muslims in Xinjiang," *The Wall Street Journal*, Sept. 26, 2020.

277 **"persons of interest":** Liza Lin, Eva Xiao, and Jonathan Cheng, "China Targets Another Region in Ethnic Assimilation Campaign: Tibet," *The Wall Street Journal*, July 16, 2021.

277 **loved ones behind:** Tahir Hamut Izgil, "One by One, My Friends Were Sent to the Camps," *The Atlantic*, July 14, 2021.

278 **"into the distance":** Tahir Hamut Izgil, "Somewhere Else," trans. Joshua L. Freeman, May 28, 2018, originally published in *Asymptote*.

279 **"can't escape it":** From "The Experiment Podcast: A Uyghur Teen's Life After Escaping Genocide," *The Atlantic*, Aug. 19, 2021.

INDEX